# THE FAMILY

# IN

# THE BIBLE

*

## By EDITH DEEN

1817

Published in San Francisco by

HARPER & ROW, PUBLISHERS

New York   Hagerstown   San Francisco   London

TO OUR FAMILY
Edgar
Lois——Ward
Edgar, Jr.——Betty
Esta Fay——Ken
George——Nancy
Janie——Don

FIRST HARPER & ROW PAPERBACK EDITION PUBLISHED IN 1978.

LIBRARY OF CONGRESS CATALOG CARD NUMBER: 63-7601

INTERNATIONAL STANDARD BOOK NUMBER: 0-06-061831-0

This book was originally published under the title FAMILY LIVING IN THE BIBLE.

The text of this book is printed on 100% recycled paper.

78  79  80  81  82  10  9  8  7  6  5  4  3  2  1

# General Contents

✳

# Contents by Sections

*

### SECTION III

## FAMILY BREAKDOWN

### SECTION IV

## FAMILY STRENGTH

SECTION V

FAMILY CONCERNS

# Preface

The idea for this book had its beginning in 1959 in our downstairs living room, next to which is our family sanctuary with its small altar. The religious books on the shelves there provided material for the first stage of research.

It was early spring. I noticed that the newly unfurled leaves of the old trees in our garden were beginning to cast shadows on the windows of our living room. My husband, Edgar Deen, and I were talking with our house guest, Dr. Pauline Beery Mack, dean and director of the College of Household Arts and Sciences of Texas Woman's University, Denton. My husband, ever eager for me to continue my quest for knowledge, was encouraging me to become a candidate for a master's degree.

"Family living would be an ideal subject for your advanced study at the university," said Dr. Mack, an eminent scholar and scientist. "It is a comparatively new field and a rapidly developing one."

After three years of enormous labor on my second book, *Great Women of the Christian Faith,* I was reluctant to rush into another project. But I listened with growing interest and enthusiasm to Dr. Mack, director of the first doctorates at Texas Woman's University, where I have served on the Board of Regents for twelve years.

Before long I had signed up at the university for courses in family living. I read everything I could find on the subject, participated in class discussions, visited divorce courts, and interviewed authorities on family life. Among those with whom I had personal conferences during their visits to my home city of Fort Worth, Texas, were Dr. Hazen G. Werner, chairman of family life for the Methodist Churches of America, and Dr. John Charles Wynn, director of the Family Education Research Office of the Presbyterian Board of Christian Education.

Dr. Mack and I later discussed the subject for a thesis. I first suggested studying the mother's role in Bible civilization. But one day as I sat in my study working on an outline, I turned to Hitchcock's *Topical Bible* and the page opened at The Family. The inspiration for another subject, Family Living in the Bible, seemed to write itself across the pages of this book. The first subject would have been easier, for I had done the major research in my first book, *All of the Women of the Bible*. Dr. Mack and I found Family Living in the Bible a more challenging subject, but neither of us dreamed that we were entering upon the pioneering stages for this book.

As I worked I discovered how rich and varied are the biblical references. In searching for information for my thesis, many aspects of the Bible's message came alive, for the subject of family living is intimately linked with biblical teaching.

Again I perceived how deep and real are the human experiences recorded in the Bible. The stories of the patriarchs are narrated against a background of family living basically understandable today. Much of Hebrew law concerns family relationships. In the records of Jesus' ministry and of the apostles' labors, families are prominent. In every one of the sixty-six books of the Bible I found some reference shedding light on family living.

I soon came to the conclusion that the Bible covers the subject of the family more thoroughly than any ancient book on record. This is easy to understand when it is recalled that the Bible was written by many authors over a period of more than one thousand years. Every facet of life has been covered, and much of the Bible deals with the basis of all life, the family.

After I had received my master's degree, I decided to expand my thesis into a book, because I had discovered that a comprehensive study had not been made on this subject, and my own studies inspired me with the knowledge of its importance.

While I worked, I carried on the normal duties of my own family. "Do you have children?" is usually the first question strangers ask me. I always answer, "I inherited my family." When Mr. Deen and I were married in 1945, I acquired his family of four children, two of whom already had homes of their own. They had lost their own mother. I came into her well-established, rambling hillside home, which has been my best laboratory for studying family life. Now, with eight fine young people (counting the in-laws), ten grandchildren and the members of my sister's family, who are very close to me, I am in intimate touch with the joys, perplexities, problems, and responsibilities of today's young families.

Without the encouragement and help of many people no book comes into being. In addition to my own family and to Dr. Mack I owe special thanks to a number of individuals. Dr. Michael Zunich of Texas Woman's University counseled me during my graduate program. Dr. T. B. Maston of the School of Theology, Southwestern Baptist Theological Seminary, made invaluable suggestions. My former University of Texas classmate, Dr. Bernice Milburn Moore, assistant to the Director of The Hogg Foundation for Mental Health and Consultant, Home and Family Education, Texas Education Agency, read several chapters and gave me wise advice, as did Rabbi Robert J. Schur.

Librarians are among an author's best helpers, and so I extend my thanks to Dr. William C. Greenlee, reference and research librarian at Southwestern Baptist Theological Seminary in Forth Worth; Mrs. Sarah Blum, head of the general reference department, and Mrs. Mabel Fischer, administrative assistant in charge of research, Fort Worth Public Library.

I am most fortunate in my home surroundings. Three doors to the south lives my neighbor, Ella Higginbotham, who typed this manuscript as well as the manuscripts for my two other books. I do not know what I would have done without her diligent help. Some blocks to the north lives our faithful housekeeper, Versie Roberts, who kept the routine of my home going while I worked many hours each day for almost three years in my downstairs study and library.

The Authorized or King James Version of the Bible, with its incomparable beauty, its vivid language, and its familiar rhythms, has been my basic text. In a few instances when, for the sake of clarity, I have quoted from Moffatt's Translation, the Revised Standard Version (RSV), or the New English Bible (NEB), I have indicated the fact. Occasionally I have followed later versions by rendering certain passages from the King James Version in verse form, and punctuation has sometimes been modernized.

Today's families, though more fortunate in most ways than biblical families, face bewildering sociological changes and complex problems unknown in ancient times. Yet, I believe, the Bible contains clues to the answers to the problems that beset us. I send this book forth with the fervent prayer that it will help its readers find the sources of family wholeness and happiness.

EDITH ALDERMAN DEEN

*Fort Worth, Texas*

# Family Beginnings

*

# CHAPTER I

# Marriage: A Union Ordained by God

---

Therefore shall a man leave his father and his mother, and shall cleave unto his wife; and they shall be one flesh.

Genesis 2:24

---

\*

## 1. THE CREATION OF MAN AND WOMAN

The first chapter of Genesis presents the creation of man and woman as the climax of those mighty acts by which God formed the universe in all its vast splendor. In the beginning when God said "Let there be light," Genesis tells us that light began to pierce the primal darkness. Next, God created heaven and earth, and made grass, plants, and trees to grow. In the sky He made the sun, moon, and stars to give light and to separate day from night. Upon earth He brought forth living creatures of every kind: fish, birds, cattle, creeping things, and beasts. On the sixth day of creation God declared:

"Let us make man in our image, after our likeness. And let them have dominion over the fish of the sea, and over the fowl of the air, and over the cattle, and over all the earth. . . ."

Genesis 1:26

Man, patterned after his Maker, has been described as the crown and culmination of God's creation. Man is the only being of whom it is written that he is made in God's image. Of all earthly creatures only man thinks, talks, and worships his Creator. Only man is endowed with freedom of choice and granted the gift of spiritual life. A reverent three-part chant celebrates man's creation:

So God created man in his own image, in the image of God created he him; male and female created he them.

Genesis 1:27

After their creation, God blessed man and woman and said to them, "Be fruitful, and multiply, and replenish the earth" (Genesis 1:28). Thus, according to the Bible, God's first command to them concerned their union and the birth of children from their union. When families came into being upon earth, men and women began to experience the joys of parenthood and to hear the happy voices of their children playing in the morning of the world.

At the end of each day of creation mentioned in Genesis, God surveyed what He had made and found it good. But on the final sixth day, when the glory and goodness, the beauty and harmony of all His work found their sublime culmination in the creation of man and woman, "God saw every thing that he had made, and behold, it was *very* good" (Genesis 1:31).


## 2. ONENESS IN MARRIAGE

In the story of Adam and Eve, the second chapter of Genesis adds vital insights to the concept of marriage. This chapter tells how the Lord God formed man from the dust of the earth and breathed into his nostrils the breath of life so that he became a living soul. Then the Lord God placed him in the beautiful Garden of Eden. Something, however, was lacking—the man was not complete, for he was alone in the garden. Then the Lord God said, "It is not good that the man should be alone. I will make him an help meet for him" (Genesis 2:18).

This early Bible story points to one of woman's important roles—that of helpmeet to her husband. Wives have rendered valuable help to their husbands in every field of human activity and in every period of the world's history from the time of Eve to the present. But woman was not created solely to be man's subordinate helper.

After the Lord God had decided to make woman, He caused a deep sleep to fall upon the man. Then God took one of Adam's ribs and made it into a woman. Created from the same substance as the man, woman was not inferior to him.

In a marriage "ceremony," with God Himself as the officiating minister, "the Lord God . . . brought her unto the man" (Genesis 2:22).

United with woman, man was now complete and whole. No longer were they two people but one. Adam expressed the closeness of their union when he declared, "This is now bone of my bones, and flesh of my flesh: she shall be called Woman . . ." (Genesis 2:23).

Oneness in marriage is further emphasized in the verse quoted at the beginning of this chapter. Besides outlining a husband's duties to his wife, the verse states that both become "one flesh," an idiom to express blood kinship. In biblical marriage "one flesh" seems to signify corporate personality, with the unit of relationship the family. This connotation appears again when Laban says to Jacob, "Surely thou art my bone and my flesh" (Genesis 29:14).

Husband and wife, depicted as one in mind, heart and soul, are joined in a physical and spiritual union, a covenant between two families, ordained by God to fulfill His holy purpose. The husband-wife relationship is intended to be at its best one of mutual love and respect, with neither one dominating the other. Their relationship is elevated above sheer instinct and given spiritual meaning. In divinely instituted marriage, which is the basis for a well-ordered family, there is reverence for the mystery, dignity, and sanctity of life. With the birth of children from such a union, a mysterious, creative relationship with the Creator can be discerned.

Robert Browning, one of the great poets of the Victorian period, in his inspired tribute to his beloved wife Elizabeth Barrett Browning, who was herself a famous poet, expressed the oneness of marriage in these lines from his poem entitled "By the Fireside":

> Oh, I must feel your brain prompt mine,
>     Your heart anticipate my heart,
> You must be just before; in fine,
>     See and make me see, for your part,
> New depths of the Divine!

In her turn, Elizabeth Barrett Browning commemorated her love
for her husband in *Sonnets from the Portuguese,* so named because
his pet name for her was "Little Portuguese." Because of his wife's
beautiful dark complexion, he used this nickname lovingly. In the
forty-third sonnet of her popular love cycle, she wrote with frankness
of her love for her husband. He had freed her from years of invalid-
ism spent in a dark, loveless home in London, and given her a life
of love and sunshine in their home in Florence, Italy:

> How do I love thee? Let me count the ways.
> I love thee to the depth and breadth and height
> My soul can reach, when feeling out of sight
> For the ends of Being and ideal Grace.
> I love thee to the level of every day's
> Most quiet need, by sun and candlelight.
> I love thee freely, as men strive for Right;
> I love thee purely, as they turn from Praise.
> I love thee with the passion put to use
> In my old griefs, and with my childhood's faith.
> I love thee with a love I seemed to lose
> With my lost saints,—I love thee with the breath,
> Smiles, tears, of all my life!—and, if God choose,
> I shall but love thee better after death.

A number of museums display a cast made from the clasped hands
of Elizabeth Barrett and Robert Browning, symbolizing the oneness
of romantic love between man and woman.


## 3. CHRISTIAN MARRIAGE

Jesus' great words about the sanctity and permanence of marriage
are regarded as the most comprehensive and penetrating statement on
the subject to be found in the Bible:

Jesus answered and said unto them . . . "But from the beginning of
the creation God made them male and female. For this cause shall a
man leave his father and mother and cleave to his wife, and they twain
shall be one flesh; so then they are no more twain, but one flesh. What
therefore God hath joined together, let not man put asunder."

Mark 10:5-9

Jesus spoke in reply to a question of the Pharisees. Hoping to trap
Him into a criticism of the Law of Moses, the Pharisees had asked

Him if it were lawful for a man to divorce his wife, for the Law permitted divorce for certain causes. Jesus, however, would not be drawn into legal argument.

On the authority of these verses from the first two chapters of Genesis, Jesus reaffirmed that marriage is divinely instituted, sacred, and in the purpose of God a lifelong union in which two people become one.

## 4. HONOR BESTOWED UPON MARRIAGE

In two parables, as well as in His teachings and acts, Jesus showed His high esteem for marriage. When He attended a wedding in Cana with His mother and some of His disciples, His very presence blessed marriage. Toward the end of the feast, His mother told Him that the wine had given out. Jesus then turned the water which filled great stone waterpots into wine. That His first miracle recorded in the Gospel of John (2:1-11) took place at a wedding gives special honor to marriage.

His parable of the Wise and Foolish Virgins (Matthew 25:1-13) is a story of ten bridesmaids at a wedding. Five of them were wise, for they brought enough oil to keep their lamps burning until the bridegroom arrived. But five of them were foolish, for their oil failed, their lights went out, and they missed the marriage ceremony.

In the parable of the Wedding of the King's Son (Matthew 22:1-14), as in the parable of the Wise and Foolish Virgins, the marriage feast itself is a symbol of the Kingdom of God, while both stories illustrate the need for spiritual preparedness. On the surface, however, these two parables are lively tales of weddings. When the invited guests refused to come to the marriage of the king's son, the king said to his servants, "Go ye therefore into the highways, and as many as ye shall find, bid to the marriage." One of these guests, having neglected the elementary courtesies in failing to put on the customary wedding garment, arrived in unsuitable clothes.

Jesus' high regard for marriage is further evident in His reply to the question why His disciples did not fast. "And Jesus said unto them, 'Can the children of the bridechamber fast, while the bridegroom is with them? As long as they have the bridegroom with them, they cannot fast' " (Mark 2:19). He found nothing unworthy in comparing Himself to the bridegroom and His disciples to the wedding guests, all rejoicing at a marriage feast.

## 5. MARRIAGE FOR THIS WORLD ONLY

One day some of the Sadducees told Jesus a hypothetical story about a woman who married seven brothers, one after another. They asked Him, ". . . . in the resurrection whose wife shall she be of the seven, for they all had her?" (Matthew 22:28). Their question was craftily designed to make the idea of the Resurrection, in which they did not believe, appear absurd. The Sadducees, a powerful political and religious party with conservative views, were, throughout Jesus' ministry, His most dangerous enemies. Their question was clearly an attempt to embarrass Jesus, but he was careful, as usual, to avoid fruitless legal discussions. "In the resurrection," He told them, "they neither marry, nor are given in marriage, but are as the angels of God in heaven" (Matthew 22:30). Marriage, as we know it, is for this world only, but human love, we believe, shall become truer and holier when it is transfigured in the resurrection.

## 6. "A GREAT MYSTERY"

Jesus' teachings on marriage, spread far and wide throughout the Greek-speaking world by the apostle Paul and other missionaries, became the basis for Christian living. The following statement in the Epistle to the Ephesians guided members of the early Church:

So ought men to love their wives as their own bodies. He that loveth his wife loveth himself. For no man ever yet hated his own flesh. . . .
For this cause shall a man leave his father and mother, and shall be joined unto his wife, and they two shall be one flesh. This is a great mystery.

Ephesians 5:28-29, 31-32

Dr. Derrick Sherwin Bailey, in the last chapter of his book *Sexual Relation in Christian Thought,* says that "the metaphysical significance of sexuality," which Paul calls "a great mystery," "is one of the profoundest and most baffling enigmas of human existence." He explains that, "First, in every sexual relation of integrity man and woman enter together into a new dimension of experience, entirely different from that of non-sexual meeting, in which they discover a fresh understanding of humanity and another way of being human. . . . Secondly, each actual relation between man and woman has a potential creativity quite different from any belonging to non-sexual relation" (pp. 269-270).

Dr. Bailey quotes the Swiss theologian, Emil Brunner, who insists that man is not an isolated, individual entity, but a twofold being; he has been made "not simply as two human beings, but as two beings who necessarily belong to one another, who have been created for this purpose, and whose whole nature is ordered in this direction, that is, as two beings who cannot be apart from each other" (pp. 268-269).

Such a union, described in Ephesians as "a great mystery," is used in that epistle as a symbol of the union of Christ with His Church. Thus human marriage, with its unfathomable mystery, becomes a parable of the Kingdom of God.

## 7. MARRIAGE AT ITS BEST

Marriage, as ordained by the Creator, upheld by Jesus, and taught by Christian leaders like Paul, is monogamous. It is the most personal and cherished of all human relationships. In such a union the noblest and best relationship between a man and a woman is formed. A family composed of a husband and wife who love each other and of children conceived in their love, is the first and oldest as well as the holiest and greatest human institution. It is the most enduring of civilization's bulwarks.

A devoted young married couple, tenderly gazing into the bassinet of their first-born baby, represent the oneness of marriage; their child becomes part of the mystery arising from their union. Motherhood and fatherhood are illuminated with divine meaning. In the sanctity of a new family, civilization takes another step forward.

# CHAPTER 2

# Marriage Customs

---

Live joyfully with the wife whom thou lovest all the days of the life of thy vanity, which he hath given thee under the sun.

Ecclesiastes 9:9

---

＊

## 1. IDEAL MARRIAGE

Though there are unhappy marriages and unfortunate family situations in the Bible, indications of happy families and references to ideal unions are not uncommon. The good wife and mother, so glowingly described in Proverbs 31:10-31, seems to have enjoyed one of the latter. Her love was so deep and true that "the heart of her husband doth safely trust in her." He was assured that she would "do him good and not evil all the days of her life." She was blessed by his praise and "her children rise up and call her blessed." This ideal wife and mother was an industrious, capable, intelligent woman presiding over the affairs of a large household and a growing family. To her credit it could be said that her "many daughters have done virtuously," though she "excellest them all." Finally, as if to account for the secret of this outstanding woman's happy marriage and family life, the writer said, "a woman that feareth the Lord, she shall be praised."

The husband depicted in Psalm 128, like the good wife of Proverbs, stood in awe of God and offered Him profound reverence, for he was "one that feareth the Lord; that walketh in his ways." The man's wife and children are described poetically: "Thy wife shall be as a fruitful vine by the sides of thine house; thy children like olive plants round about thy table."

Marriage that endures for a lifetime is briefly referred to in the verse from Ecclesiastes quoted above. It is also mentioned by three of the prophets. The great, eighth-century prophet Hosea spoke of God's relation to Israel in marriage terms and wrote:

And I will betroth thee unto me for ever; yea, I will betroth thee unto me in righteousness, and in judgment and in lovingkindness, and in mercies. I will even betroth thee unto me in faithfulness. And thou shalt know the Lord.

Hosea 2:19-20

Two centuries after Hosea, in the period of the Exile, the prophet Ezekiel compared God's espousal of Israel to a marriage covenant and indicated that marriage, like the covenant with God, was an enduring union not to be broken. "Yea, I sware unto thee, and entered into a covenant with thee, saith the Lord God, and thou becamest mine" (Ezekiel 16:8).

By the fifth century B.C. the prophet Malachi took monogamy for granted. He sternly rebuked those who, dealing faithlessly with their Jewish wives, divorced them in order to marry foreign women. He reminded these disloyal husbands that the Lord had been a witness at their first marriage, which was an unbreakable covenant relationship.

Because the Lord hath been witness between thee and the wife of thy youth, against whom thou hast dealt treacherously; yet is she thy companion and the wife of thy covenant.

Malachi 2:14

Malachi attributed the distressing state of the nation to general contempt for the solemn obligations of marriage. Far too many people regarded marriage lightly, as a matter of personal pleasure, rather than as a sacred covenant witnessed by the Lord.

## 2. POLYGAMY, CONCUBINAGE

By New Testament times monogamy had become the ideal. In this kind of marriage one man and one woman form an exclusive union that endures while they both live. During the many centuries recorded in the Old Testament, however, other forms of marriage, notably polygamy and levirate marriage, were practiced. In an early period when the patriarchs were surrounded by their enemies, large family groups were essential for protection as well as for survival. During this era men took secondary wives and often concubines in order to raise many sons and daughters. Marriage with several wives at a time is called polygamy.

A concubine was a woman who lived with a man without being legally married to him, as were his wife and his secondary wives. In biblical times a concubine was usually a slave captured during warfare or obtained by purchase from her family or owner. Having no kinsfolk to defend her, the concubine had few rights until the Hebrew laws in Exodus in 21:7-11 and Deuteronomy 21:10-14 gave her some protection.

The first polygamist recorded in the Bible is Lamech, a descendant of Cain. "And Lamech took unto him two wives; the name of the one was Adah, and the name of the other Zillah" (Genesis 4:19). The combination of Adah's name, meaning "pleasure and beauty," with Zillah's, meaning "shadow of darkness," gives a rather apt description of a polygamous household in which a shadow lurks in the background of beauty and pleasure.

Besides being a polygamist, Lamech was a quarrelsome, brutal fellow whose spirit of revenge finally led him to homicide. In a folk song of wild beauty sung to his two wives, he boasted of his blood feud:

> Adah and Zillah, hear my voice,
> Ye wives of Lamech, hearken unto my speech,
> For I have slain a man to [for] my wounding,
> And a young man to [for] my hurt.
> If Cain shall be avenged sevenfold,
> Truly Lamech seventy and sevenfold.
>
> Genesis 4:23-24

As the families of the patriarchs grew, the practice of polygamy increased. Though Abraham's chief wife and the mother of his heir was Sarah, he took Sarah's servant Hagar, and another woman named Keturah, as concubines. Abraham's grandson Jacob married two sisters, Leah and his beloved wife Rachel. They became the mothers of eight of his twelve sons, while Jacob's two concubines, Bilhah and Zilpah, bore him four sons.

In later centuries the evils arising from plural marriages spread like a mantle over the kingdom of Israel. Polygamy caused many of King David's family problems. Though he longed with all his heart to be a righteous man, he followed the kingly custom of the day in marrying many wives, the names of at least eight of whom are recorded in the Bible: Abigail, Abital, Ahinoam, Bath-sheba, Eglah, Haggith, Maacah, and Michal. In addition, he had many concubines (II Samuel 5:13-16) whose children added to the size and complexity of the royal family. David's family life was marred by discord which led to jealousy, hatred, rape, murder, and finally the armed rebellion of David's beloved son Absalom, who forced his father to flee from the royal city of Jerusalem.

Like his father David whom he succeeded, King Solomon practiced polygamy. His favorite queen was the daughter of an Egyptian pharaoh, but Solomon married many other wives from neighboring states with which he hoped to establish favorable political connections.

But King Solomon loved many strange women, together with the daughter of Pharaoh, women of the Moabites, Ammonites, Edomites, Zidonians, and Hittites. . . . Solomon clave unto these in love. And he had seven hundred wives, princesses, and three hundred concubines. . . . For . . . his wives turned away his heart after other gods. . . . Then did Solomon build an high place for Chemosh, the abomination of Moab, in the hill that is before Jerusalem. . . . And likewise did he for all his strange wives, which burnt incense and sacrificed unto their gods.

I Kings 11:1-4, 7-8

Thus did Solomon's wives engage in heathen worship in Israel and use money from the royal treasury to build temples to their many gods.

Solomon's wife Naamah, believed to have been an Ammonite princess, bore him a son, Rehoboam, who became his successor. Rehoboam was a weak king, proud, obtuse, self-sufficient, who lost half his father's kingdom. During his reign the kingdom, united under Saul, David, and Solomon, came to an end and the bitter enmity of the northern kingdom of Israel with the southern kingdom of Judah began. Like his father and grandfather, King Rehoboam practiced polygamy, "for he took eighteen wives, and threescore concubines, and begat twenty and eight sons, and threescore daughters" (II Chronicles 11:21). Pagan worship, introduced earlier into Israel, flourished during Rehoboam's reign (I Kings 14:23-24).

To avoid the evils caused by polygamy as practiced by King David, by his son King Solomon, and by the latter's son King Rehoboam, the Law laid this injunction upon kings:

> Neither shall he multiply wives to himself, that his heart turn not away: Neither shall he greatly multiply to himself silver and gold.
>
> Deuteronomy 17:17

Polygamy, as well as too many riches, distracted a king from important state problems and often turned his heart away from the Lord.

In many periods of history besides Israel's tribal era and the years of her kings, polygamy has flourished. Even in America, plural marriages were revived by the Mormons under the leadership of Brigham Young. As early as 1862, however, Congress legislated against the institution.

"Polygamy is to be condemned because it has always shown itself incompatible with that search for a continuous fellowship in the whole of life which is the characteristic of marriage," writes Ryder Smith in the *London Quarterly and Holborn Review*, April, 1941. In polygamy, the marriage union loses its spiritual relationship and becomes a purely physical union. Woman is reduced to the ministrant to man's unmodified sensuality, and this is opposed to the biblical ideal of marriage and to Christ's affirmation of monogamy as the ideal.

## 3. LEVIRATE MARRIAGE

Levirate marriage was another form of union practiced in early biblical times. If a man died childless, his brother or his next of kin married his widow in order to perpetuate the dead man's family and save his name from extinction. The son born of a levirate marriage was considered to be the dead man's son. Levirate comes from the Latin word *levir,* meaning husband's brother.

Derived from earlier customs of more primitive tribes, the levirate law stated:

> If brethren dwell together, and one of them die and have no child, the wife of the dead shall not marry without unto a stranger. Her husband's brother shall . . . take her to him to wife . . . And it shall be that the firstborn which she beareth shall succeed in the name of his brother which is dead, that his name be not put out of Israel.
>
> Deuteronomy 25:5-6

If the dead man's brother refused to take the widow as his wife, she was supposed to pull off his shoe in the presence of the elders. The Bedouin form of divorce, in which the husband says, "She was my slipper, and I have cast her off," stems from the same ancient custom. In his work entitled *Hebrew Marriage*, David R. Mace says of the shoe removal ceremony:

It is more probably a ritual expression of the fact that by renouncing his duty toward her he forfeits also his right to his dead brother's estate, which was conditional upon his taking her to wife: since the right to walk over an estate at will belonged only to the owner, and the shoe was the natural symbol of possession (pp. 97-98).

Tamar was the first woman in the Bible to demand her right to motherhood under the levirate law. After losing through death her first husband Er and her second husband Onan, who was Er's brother, she was still childless. Though Er and Onan had a younger brother named Shelah, their father Judah refused to give Tamar as wife to his youngest son, for he said, "Lest peradventure he die also, as his brethren did" (Genesis 38:11).

After living as a widow for a number of years in her father's home, Tamar one day took off her widow's garment, dressed as a harlot, covered her face with a veil, and sat beside the road in sheepshearing time. When Judah came along the road he did not recognize Tamar as his daughter-in-law. Thinking that she was a harlot, he made advances to her. Tamar entered into a union with him and twins were born. Though illicit in most societies, this was considered by the early Hebrews to be a lawful example of levirate marriage. Tamar's action brought no discredit upon her in the society in which she lived. Judah said of her, "She hath been more righteous than I, because that I gave her not to Shelah my son" (Genesis 38:26).

The story of Ruth contains another example of levirate marriage. When Naomi returned to Bethlehem with her daughter-in-law Ruth, they were both widows. Naomi's husband Elimelech as well as her two sons Chilion and Mahlon had all died in Moab. In order to support the older woman, Ruth gleaned in the fields of a wealthy land-owner, Boaz, who was a distant kinsman of her late husband's. Boaz loved Ruth and desired to marry her. But there was a nearer kinsman who, under the levirate law, had a prior claim to her and to a field of Elimelech's which Naomi wished to sell.

Boaz summoned the unnamed kinsman to meet him before the city elders. There the kinsman renounced his right to buy the land, saying, "I cannot redeem it for myself, lest I mar mine own inheritance" (Ruth 4:6). Had he bought the land, he would also have been required to marry Ruth. Their son would have been considered the son of Ruth's first husband and the field would have reverted to the boy as the true heir. The unnamed kinsman, in token of the renunciation of his rights, drew off his shoe and told Boaz to buy the field for himself. Thereupon Boaz announced:

"Ye are witnesses this day that I have bought all that was Elimelech's and all that was Chilion's and Mahlon's, of the hand of Naomi. Moreover Ruth the Moabitess, the wife of Mahlon, have I purchased to be my wife, to raise up the name of the dead upon his inheritance, that the name of the dead be not cut off from among his brethren. . . ."

Ruth 4:9-10

Ruth's story is an example of levirate marriage, though in this case it was permissive rather than obligatory. Boaz was actually a generous benefactor rather than a duty-bound relative. The story contains the following irregularities: the near kinsman was not a brother of Elimelech's; in renouncing the property he pulled off his own shoe; Naomi as a widow could not inherit her husband's land and had no right to sell it; moreover, it should have been Naomi who married the redeemer of the property. But Naomi was evidently past the child-bearing age and tactfully arranged for the marriage of Ruth. Naomi's neighbors later referred to the boy Obed, born to Ruth and Boaz, as "a son born to Naomi" (Ruth 4:17).

Another biblical instance of levirate marriage is the hypothetical story of the woman who married seven brothers, one after another (Matthew 22:24-30)—a story, as we have already seen, invented by the Sadducees in an effort to trap Jesus into denying the validity of the Law.

## 4. THE MARRIAGE CEREMONY

A fairly complete picture of weddings in biblical times can be pieced together from various references to brides, bridegrooms, marriage ceremonies, and the prolonged festivities accompanying the latter. Weddings were in some respects similar to ours today, for many of our customs derive from those of the ancient Hebrews.

The wedding of Rebekah and Isaac is the first one narrated in the Bible. When Rebekah's father and brother were satisfied that her marriage to Isaac would be suitable, they said to her, " 'Wilt thou go with this man?' And she said, 'I will go' " (Genesis 24:58).

At Rebekah's departure her family blessed her, using a traditional formula expressing hope for many descendants and for their victorious strength: "Thou art our sister, be thou the mother of thousands of millions, and let thy seed possess the gate of those which hate them" (Genesis 24:60).

Wearing, no doubt, the gold ring or earring and the two gold bracelets brought to her as betrothal gifts from Isaac, Rebekah set out with her maids for Isaac's home in Canaan. At the end of her long journey, when she saw Isaac walking through the fields to meet her caravan, she alighted from her camel and "took a veil and covered herself" (Genesis 24:65).

No religious ceremony is indicated at this early period, but in evidence of the fact that she was now his wife, Isaac took Rebekah into the tent which had been Sarah's. Today, whenever a marriage canopy is used in a Jewish wedding, Rebekah's nuptial tent is symbolically represented.

On her wedding day a bride in biblical times put on her best garments which, like those of a princess, were often richly embroidered (Psalm 45:14) and in some cases may have been white (Revelation 19:8). If, like Rebekah, the bride was fortunate enough to possess jewels, she wore them (Isaiah 61:10). After she had fastened her traditional bridal girdle about her waist (Isaiah 49:18), she, like Rebekah, covered herself with a veil. She would then be "prepared as a bride adorned for her husband" (Revelation 21:2).

The bridegroom was also dressed in his best attire with a garland or crown upon his head (Isaiah 61:10; Song of Solomon 3:11). Escorted by friends and companions (Judges 14:11), as well as by singers and musicians, he joyfully set out from his quarters for the home of the bride's parents, "as a bridegroom coming out of his chamber, and rejoiceth as a strong man to run a race" (Psalm 19:5).

The bride's attendants usually "took their lamps and went forth to meet the bridegroom" (Matthew 25:1), but if the bridegroom were delayed, the maidens might fall asleep while their lamps burned out, as occurred in the parable of the Wise and Foolish Virgins.

When the bridegroom arrived at the bride's home, he found her deeply veiled. After receiving his bride from her parents, he led the whole wedding party through the streets with song and dancing. There could be heard "the voice of mirth and the voice of gladness, the voice of the bridegroom and the voice of the bride" (Jeremiah 7:34).

The joyful procession finally reached the home of the bridegroom's father, or of a friend, where there had been prepared an elaborate feast (Matthew 22:2-4) that sometimes lasted seven days or more after the wedding night (Genesis 29:27). The well-known wedding feast at Cana (John 2:1-11) either lasted so long or included so many unexpected guests that the wine gave out.

## 5. BIBLICAL LOVE LYRICS

The kind of songs sung at wedding celebrations can be found in the Song of Solomon, which is believed to be a collection of love and marriage songs. Though some scholars attribute the entire anthology to King Solomon, others see it as the work of many poets and singers from the tenth to the third century B.C.

The songs, with their rapturous words about the loved one and their vivid description of nature, show real understanding of nuptial and romantic love. Among the most famous and beautiful of the poems is this one referring to love and to springtime:

> My beloved spake, and said unto me:
> Rise up, my love, my fair one,
>     and come away.
> For, lo, the winter is past,
>     the rain is over and gone,
> The flowers appear on the earth,
>     the time of the singing of birds is come;
> And the voice of the turtle [dove]
>     is heard in our land.
> The fig tree putteth forth her green figs,
>     and the vines with the tender grape
>     give a good smell.
> Arise, my love, my fair one,
>     and come away.
>
>                 Song of Solomon 2:10-13

## 6. MARRIAGE SYMBOLISM

As we have already seen, Hosea was the first great prophet to use married love as a symbol of God's enduring relations with His people Israel. A later prophet, Jeremiah, used the marriage metaphor to illustrate Israel's unfaithfulness to her God. Speaking for the Lord, Jeremiah denounced Israel, saying, "Thou hast played the harlot with many lovers; yet return again to me, saith the Lord" (Jeremiah 3:1).

After the exile in Babylon, when Israel was again faithful to her God, a fifth-century prophet wrote, "as the bridegroom rejoiceth over the bride, so shall thy God rejoice over thee" (Isaiah 62:5). With this frequent application of the marriage metaphor to the Lord and His people, it is not surprising that the real love lyrics of the Song of Solomon were interpreted as allegories revealing God's love for Israel.

New Testament writers transferred marriage symbolism from God and His people Israel to Christ and His Church, as in this sentence: "For the husband is the head of the wife, even as Christ is the head of the church" (Ephesians 5:23). In Christian symbolism Christ was the bridegroom, the Church was His bride, while the Kingdom of Heaven was portrayed as a marriage feast. All this is exultingly proclaimed in the marriage song of Revelation:

> Alleluia! For the Lord God omnipotent reigneth.
> Let us be glad and rejoice and give honour to him,
> for the marriage of the Lamb is come,
> and his wife [bride] hath made herself ready.
> And to her was granted that she should be arrayed in
>     fine linen, clean and white,
> For the fine linen is the righteousness of the saints.
> And he saith unto me, Write:
> Blessed are they which are called unto the marriage
>     supper of the Lamb.
>
> Revelation 19:6-9

# CHAPTER 3

# Family Solidarity

Oh that men would praise the Lord for his goodness
    and for his wonderful works to the children of men! . . .
Yet setteth he the poor on high from affliction,
    and maketh him families like a flock.

                                        Psalm 107:31, 41

※

In no other families in ancient world history was there such solidarity as was found in the early families of Israel. Each family was regarded as a community of persons and included father, mother, sons, daughters, brothers, sisters, grandparents and other kinsmen as well as servants. Included in the household also were "strangers within one's gates," sometimes concubines, as well as foster fathers and nursing mothers. All lived closely together, often in a tent settlement, probably like the small villagers of later civilizations.

The solidarity of the early Bible family had its source in religious and economic ties which bound its members together. This solidarity was maintained largely by the father, who was regarded as the head of the family. The mother, who had a higher status than that of any mother in other civilizations of antiquity, also helped to maintain family wholeness.

## 1. THE FIRST FAMILY (Genesis 3-5)

Adam and Eve began their life together in the Garden of Eden, where there grew a special tree whose fruit God forbade them to eat.

But, tempted by the serpent, Eve "took of the fruit thereof, and did eat and gave also unto her husband with her, and he did eat" (3:6). For their willful disobedience of God, Adam and Eve were driven from Eden.

The couple's transgression is looked upon, in the third chapter of Genesis, as the direct cause of the burdens and distress that often accompany family living. These burdens, some of which must have been especially oppressive in biblical times, included travail in childbirth; a distorted relationship between husband and wife in which one dominates the other: "he shall rule over thee" (3:16); the frustration of unremitting toil for a livelihood; and finally, the haunting fear of death: "dust thou art, and unto dust shalt thou return" (3:19).

Though the first family suffered for their disobedience, they enjoyed at least one hour of recorded happiness when Eve bore Cain, her first son, and joyfully exclaimed, "I have gotten a man from the Lord" (4:1). Tragedy, however, soon ended family solidarity. Cain, jealous of his younger brother's favor with God, murdered Abel. When the Lord asked Cain where his brother was, Cain replied in words that scorned family responsibility, "I know not. Am I my brother's keeper?" (4:9).

With one son dead and another lost to the family group, Eve bore Adam a third son, whom she named Seth. " 'For God,' said she, 'hath appointed me another seed instead of Abel, whom Cain slew' " (4:25). Seth became father of a noble line, for it is reported that when Seth's son Enos lived, "began men to call upon the name of the Lord" (4:26). In this sentence we can perhaps find an indication of the beginning of prayer life in ancient families.

In the fifth chapter of Genesis, one line of Adam's descendants is traced through eight generations of antediluvian patriarchs. Of the queer old names only two are well known: Enoch, who did not die as other men do but who "walked with God, and he was not, for God took him" (5:24); and Enoch's son Methuselah, whose reported age of nine hundred and sixty-nine years has made his name a byword for longevity. Only fathers' names are listed in the genealogy, a fact that underlines the authority, strength, and importance of the father in these early families through which Noah and his sons and ultimately Abraham and the people of Israel traced their ancestry back to Adam.

## 2. NOAH'S FAMILY (Genesis 7-9)

The first biblical account of a cohesive family group whose members worked together for their common good is the story of Noah. It was the Lord who, uniting them all in the face of a great peril, said to Noah, "Come thou and all thy house into the ark, for thee have I seen righteous before me in this generation" (7:1). Loyal to their father, Noah's three sons Shem, Ham, and Japheth, together with their wives entered the ark with Noah and his wife and all the animals. In the ensuing flood that engulfed the world, only Noah's family and the animals they had taken into the ark survived. When the waters receded and the ark came to rest upon the earth, Noah led forth his sons and his wife and his sons' wives. His first act was to build an altar where he, undoubtedly attended by his entire family group, sacrificed to the Lord.

An instance of family solidarity and the loyalty of two of Noah's sons occurs in a story reflecting no credit upon Noah himself. Noah became drunk and lay in his tent. Ham discovered his father, but merely spread the news of his disgrace. Shem and Japheth, however, entered their father's tent and covered him, lest anyone see his shameful state. Shem and Japheth were rewarded for their filial loyalty by the promise, "God shall enlarge Japheth and he shall dwell in the tents of Shem" (9:27).

## 3. ABRAHAM, FOUNDER OF THE GREAT HEBREW FAMILY (Genesis 12:17-18, 21)

Shem's outstanding descendant, after the eight generations listed in Genesis, was Abraham, who, as Paul was to declare centuries later, "is the father of us all" (Romans 4:16). At God's command Abraham departed from his native country, from his kindred, and from his father's house to journey to a land which the Lord promised to him.

While Abraham and his wife Sarah were still childless, the Lord said to him, "Thou shalt be a father of many nations. . . . As for . . . Sarah . . . I will bless her and give thee a son also of her . . . and she shall be a mother of nations; kings of people shall be of her" (17:4, 15-16). The significance of Abraham's family was expressed in the promise, "In thee shall all families of the earth be blessed" (12:3).

Narratives of Abraham and Sarah give many vivid pictures of nomadic family life in ancient times. Wherever he pitched his tents, whether near Shechem, under the sacred tree of Moreh, at Bethel, or at Hebron, he built an altar unto the Lord. During the midday heat he used to sit in the shade at the door of his tent from which he could see anyone approaching his encampment.

One day three strangers appeared to whom he offered the customary desert hospitality (18:1-10). While water was being brought to refresh their weary, dusty feet, Abraham hastened to Sarah's tent to tell her to make bread. She measured the meal, kneaded it, formed cakes and baked them. Abraham, meanwhile, ran to his pasture to select a calf which, when prepared for eating, he placed before his three guests with butter, milk, and the bread Sarah had baked. The guests ate alone while their host, Abraham, stood nearby in the shade of a tree. Sarah listened eagerly at her tent door to their conversation.

Abraham's guests on this occasion were not ordinary visitors, but three divine beings one of whom announced that Sarah would bear Abraham a son in their old age. Sarah laughed at this news, but in due time their son Isaac was born, as the heavenly strangers had promised.

## 4. JACOB, FATHER OF THE TWELVE TRIBES OF ISRAEL
   (Genesis 32, 35)

To Abraham's son Isaac and to his wife Rebekah were born two sons, the younger of whom was Jacob, a man of destiny and ancestor of the people of Israel. After his strange struggle at night with a supernatural being at the ford of the Jabbok river, Jacob's name was changed. "Thy name shall be called no more Jacob, but Israel, for as a prince hast thou power with God and with men, and hast prevailed" (32:28).

At Bethel a promise was made to Jacob-Israel similar to the one made to his grandfather Abraham years earlier:

"I am God Almighty. Be fruitful and multiply. A nation and a company of nations shall be of thee, and kings shall come out of thy loins. And the land which I gave Abraham and Isaac, to thee will I give it, and to thy seed after thee will I give the land."

Genesis 35:11-12

Jacob indeed became the father of "kings," for his sons were the heads of the twelve tribes of Israel. By his first wife Leah, Jacob had six sons: Reuben, Simeon, Levi, Judah, Issachar, Zebulun. Jacob's favorite wife Rachel bore him Joseph and Benjamin. By his concubine Zilpah, Jacob had Gad and Asher, and by his second concubine Bilhah, Dan and Naphtali. Joseph's two sons, Ephraim and Manasseh, became heads of tribes. These two tribes descended from Joseph would have increased to thirteen the whole number of clans to be given land, had not the sons of Levi been denied territory in the Promised Land.

## 5. FAMILY REGISTERS

From the genealogies of Noah and of Abraham, we have seen that family records were important to the Israelites. Because the land promised to the descendants of Abraham, Isaac, and Jacob was divided and occupied according to tribes, great care was exercised in recording family names. As the priesthood was hereditary, descending from father to eldest son, it, too, depended upon accurate family registers. These became essential to families trying to re-establish property rights after many years of exile in Babylon.

Though the genealogical lists in the books of Genesis, Exodus, Numbers, Joshua, Ruth, I and II Samuel, I Kings, I and II Chronicles, Ezra, and Nehemiah make tedious reading, their contents were of vital importance to many Jews. The preservation of these lists during many centuries shows the emphasis placed upon the continuity of family groups.

In the census records of Numbers alone, the words *family* and *families* appear more than one hundred and twenty-five times, an indication of this early people's interest in genealogy.

"They set forward, every one after their families" (Numbers 2:34) is the introductory statement to this record of the history of the Israelites from their stay at Sinai until their arrival at the borders of Moab.

The longest family register in the Bible is in the first nine chapters of I Chronicles. Giving as it does a drama of families from Adam to the destruction of the kingdom of Judah, it represents genealogy on an immense scale. Its one summarizing theme might be described as an effort on the part of the Chronicler to show that the Hebrew people, even after downfall, decay, and division, could trace their descent back to the same family which, in the time of Abraham, united in a sacred covenant with God.

This genealogy of the Chronicler, like other genealogies in the Bible, gives little chronological assistance, because of the uncertainty as to the actual length of a generation and the custom of frequently omitting links in the descent. Its interest is largely historical and biographical.

In New Testament times, when family lineage was still carefully noted, John the Baptist's ancestry on both his father's and his mother's side is given in Luke 1:5. Paul was proud of his membership in the tribe of Benjamin (Philippians 3:5). The most detailed genealogy in the New Testament is that of Jesus, two different versions of which are given (Matthew 1:1-17; Luke 3:23-38).

## 6. ISRAEL AS A GREAT HOUSEHOLD

Knowing themselves to be descendants of Abraham, the people of Israel believed that they constituted one great household with which the Lord had established His covenant. As Amos wrote:

Hear this word that the Lord hath spoken against you, O children of Israel, against the whole family which I brought up from the land of Egypt, saying,
"You only have I known of all the families of the earth: therefore I will punish you for all your iniquities."

Amos 3:1-2

The idea of Israel as the family of God began with the patriarchs and continued through the time of Moses and on into the period of the monarchy. Finally, as old ways of living were abandoned, the continuity of Israel as a great household could not be maintained in practice, yet the ideal itself remained, as is shown by the passage quoted above from Amos. David R. Mace makes the following statement in *Hebrew Marriage*:

The family unit itself withstood the shock, and the ideal itself was preserved. It survived the upheavals of monarchy. It survived the disruption of the exile. It survived the final disintegration of the Jewish race as a national community. And it has made possible the preservation of the separate identity of the Jew throughout all the vicissitudes of his tempestuous experience, which is one of the miracles of history (p. 75).

## 7. TODAY'S FAMILY HERITAGE

A family tradition, coming down through the ages, can be compared to the flow of a river fed by various tributaries. Clifford Kirkpatrick in his book *The Family* comments:

The first contribution to the family heritage of the present day can be thought of as coming from the Hebrew patriarchal family. . . . For many centuries the Bible was a guide to living, and hence provided a model affecting family relationships. If a sacred book reflects a patriarchal age, a patriarchal pattern tends to permeate the family living of those guided by the sacred book. Our Puritan forefathers read their Bibles and acted accordingly. In log cabins on the frontier biblical characters affected thinking about the family (pp. 97-98).

One of the best modern definitions of the family was formulated in 1955 in Canada by the Montreal Committee of Family Life and Parent Education. Biblical ideals as well as the needs of twentieth-century living are reflected in the following statement:

The family is a cell of love, created by the life-long friendship between a man and a woman, with complete sharing of body and mind, and with, normally, the procreation of children. The family is not sufficient unto itself; it is dependent upon and contributes to society, and while making possible the richest personality development of its individual members, it also prepares them to serve their fellow men and to live together with them in the wider family of humanity (p. 190).

# CHAPTER 4

# An Early Family

And Isaac brought her into his mother Sarah's tent, and took Rebekah, and she became his wife, and he loved her.

Genesis 24:67

✳

## 1. WHO THEY WERE

Isaac, Rebekah, and their twin sons Esau and Jacob comprised a family that illustrates and brings into focus many aspects of life in the time of the patriarchs nearly four thousand years ago. Though Isaac's family can hardly be called typical, for no typical families can be found in the Bible, the problems Isaac and his wife and children faced, their manner of living, and their ideas are recorded in sufficient detail to make them absorbing today.

The character of Isaac, the son of promise born to Abraham and Sarah in their old age, is not so sharply drawn as that of his wife Rebekah; nevertheless he emerges clearly from the patriarchal records as a son, husband, and father.

After Abraham's death, God blessed Isaac, saying:

"Sojourn in this land, and I will be with thee, and will bless thee; for unto thee, and unto thy seed, I will give all these countries, and I will perform the oath which I sware unto Abraham thy father. And I will make thy seed to multiply as the stars of heaven . . . and in thy seed shall all the nations of the earth be blessed; because that Abraham obeyed my voice, and kept my charge, my commandments, my statutes, and my laws."

Genesis 26:3-5

The significance of this blessing is pointed out by Walter Russell Bowie in *The Interpreter's Bible* (Vol. 1, p. 663). "Here again," he writes, "is the great Hebrew conviction of religion binding a family together." Religion was more than the relationship of a single individual with God. "The covenant which enfolded father and son bound the generations in a continuing benediction."

Sharing in this covenant was Rebekah, whose marriage is pictured in Chapter 2, while the story of how she was prayerfully chosen to be Isaac's wife is narrated in the next chapter. As the Bible mentions no secondary wife or concubine belonging to Isaac, it is supposed that Isaac and Rebekah were monogamous, the only such pair among the patriarchs.

Their twin sons, Esau and Jacob, grew up to be totally dissimilar individuals whose clashing temperaments embroiled the entire family in drama and heartbreak.

## 2. WHERE THEY LIVED

Isaac was living in the wilderness, near the well at Beer-lahai-roi, when Rebekah came to be his bride (Genesis 24:62). His encampment was about fifty miles southwest of Beer-sheba, in the "south country," now called the Negeb, meaning "the dry." It is a bleak region of shifting sands, inhospitable hills, with only an occasional spring bubbling up in the valleys. During their married life they continued to live in this general region, their headquarters usually being at Beer-sheba, midway between the Mediterranean and the Dead Sea.

Once Isaac moved about fifty miles northwest toward the coast, into the territory of the king of Gerar. He pitched his tents at Gerar, an ancient town probably situated about eight miles south of Gaza. Before long, however, he returned to Beer-sheba. At the end of his life we find him at Mamre near Hebron, where Abraham had lived and where he was buried.

## 3. HOW THEY LIVED

Isaac and Rebekah began their marriage as a well-favored pair with a rich inheritance. They were nomadic tent dwellers, moving from pasturage to pasturage with their flocks and herds. As Abraham's heir, Isaac had inherited not only his father's vast wealth in cattle, but his silver and gold, his manservants and maidservants, and his many tents, for Abraham had been a very wealthy tribal chief (Genesis 13:5-6; 14:14; 24:53).

As we have already noted, Isaac and Rebekah spent their wedding night in the tent which had belonged to Sarah and from which she had eavesdropped on the conversation of the heavenly visitors who announced Isaac's impending birth. This tent, constantly patched, frequently rolled up and taken from one encampment to another, doubtless remained Rebekah's home for many years.

Nomad tents such as Rebekah's are not uncomfortable even in the hottest weather, for breezes blowing through the open entrance flaps cool the interior during the night. Fashioned of woven goat's hair fabric, which shrinks taut in the rain, these tents weather to a dark brown color, but they are black when new, "black as the tents of Kedar" (Song of Solomon 1:5).

After goat-shearing time, Rebekah and her servants in all probability wove new cloth on homemade looms, using the same type of stone spindle whorls and stone or clay loom weights as those excavated from Early Bronze Age deposits of 3000 to 2000 B.C. The new fabric would be used to patch old tents or to make new ones for the growing family and their servants, all dwelling together in a tent colony. In stormy weather some of the animals would take shelter in the tents and live with the family, as they sometimes do in the "houses of hair" of desert families today.

## 4. THEIR CHILDREN (Genesis 25-27)

For some years Isaac and Rebekah remained childless, a fact which must have caused deep concern to them in view of God's covenant with Abraham and His promise to Isaac. Then "Isaac entreated the Lord for his wife, because she was barren; and the Lord was entreated of him, and Rebekah his wife conceived" (25:21).

When she began to feel strange movements within her which seemed to portend unusual events, "she went to inquire of the Lord" (25:22). He replied, "Two nations are in thy womb . . . the one people shall be stronger than the other people, and the elder shall serve the younger" (25:23).

In due time Rebekah bore twin sons. The first child, who "came out red, all over like an hairy garment" (25:25), they called Esau. The second son, born with his hand grasping Esau's heel, they named Jacob. Esau grew up to be rough and wild, an outdoor man who became a cunning hunter with a voracious appetite. Jacob, on the other hand, was quieter, gentler, and more spiritual minded. Instead of hunting with his brother, Jacob remained at home, no doubt learning from his father how to direct the affairs of the tent colony and manage large flocks and herds. There was a quality about Jacob that appealed to his mother. He became her favorite, for she saw that he was marked for future greatness.

Esau, however, was his father's favorite, for Isaac was pleased when his elder son brought him tasty venison. The aging father was proud of Esau's prowess and relied on his son's great strength.

Neither Isaac nor Rebekah was happy about Esau's two wives, for he did not take them from his own clan and people, but chose two Hittite girls, Judith and Bashemath. Because these wives were foreigners, Isaac and Rebekah undoubtedly believed that Esau could not inherit God's promise.

Her daughters-in-law troubled Rebekah more than they did her quiet and serene husband, and she said to him, "I am weary of my life because of the daughters of Heth [the two Hittite wives]. If Jacob take a wife of the daughters of Heth, such as these which are of the daughters of the land, what good shall my life do me?" (27:46).

Esau's two foreign wives, however, were not the only source of trouble in Isaac and Rebekah's home, where the favoritism of one parent toward one son and the other parent toward the other son had already laid the foundation for conflict between the brothers. Jacob bided his time until one day his brother came home from the hunt weary and ravenously hungry. Jacob cleverly agreed to give Esau the stew he was cooking in exchange for Esau's birthright. In his greediness for food the elder brother recklessly gave away his rights as Isaac's first-born, rights which entitled him to a double inheritance and honor as head of the family.

Astute Jacob, aided and abetted by his resourceful mother, who stopped at nothing to help her favorite, deceived his old, blind father into giving him the blessing rightfully belonging to Esau.

Furious at being tricked again, Esau vowed to kill his younger brother. His mother, however, commanded Jacob to flee from his brother's wrath and take refuge with her brother, Laban, far in the north. Another reason for Jacob's flight to northern Mesopotamia was his parents' hope that in his uncle's family he would find a wife.

Jacob remained with Laban, not for a "few days" until Esau's anger cooled, as his mother had planned, but for many years, during which Rebekah undoubtedly died. When Jacob eventually returned to his old home, he and his brother Esau were reconciled to each other.

## 5. ISAAC'S VOCATIONS

Isaac was a good, though sometimes unwise, husband and father, but he was almost too easygoing for his own and his family's welfare. He had a calmer disposition than Rebekah's, for where he is depicted as mild and pensive, she is shown as aggressive, scheming, and outspoken.

Though frequently troubled in his family relationships, Isaac prospered not only as a cattleman but as an agriculturist—an unusual combination for one of the patriarchs. His large flocks and herds inherited from his father Abraham increased under his management. In the rich farming country at Gerar, the fields he planted yielded abundant grain. Perhaps he had vineyards, too, and gardens in which his servants raised onions, garlic, lentils, peas, beans, lettuce, and squash. The Bible describes his years encamped near Gerar in the lands of King Abimelech:

Then Isaac sowed in that land, and received in the same year an hundredfold, and the Lord blessed him. And the man . . . grew until he became very great. For he had possession of flocks, and possession of herds, and great store of servants, and the Philistines envied him. . . . And Abimelech said unto Isaac, "Go from us, for thou art much mightier than we."

Genesis 26:12-14, 16

Isaac was also a digger of wells so necessary to the life of all his dependents and to his many animals in the semi-arid country where he lived. Sometimes he reopened old wells originally dug by his father, but later filled in by the Philistines. His new camping grounds were marked by the successive digging of more wells. One well in particular must have required considerable engineering skill in view of the primitive tools which Isaac and his servants had for digging.

And it came to pass the same day that Isaac's servants came and told him concerning the well which they had digged and said unto him, "We have found water." And he called it Shebah, therefore the name of the city is Beer-sheba unto this day.

Genesis 26:32-33

Today the largest of the seven wells at Beer-sheba is twelve feet in diameter, forty-five feet deep to the surface of the water, its lower sixteen feet being cut through a vein of solid rock. If this is the well dug by Isaac's servants, their sense of triumph in striking water was justified.

## 6. REBEKAH AS A HOMEMAKER

Outstanding in many ways, Rebekah was doubtless an excellent cook, one of whose dishes is actually mentioned in the Bible. She said to her son, "Go now to the flock and fetch me from thence two good kids of the goats, and I will make them savoury meat for thy father, such as he lovest" (Genesis 27:9). This "savoury meat" was probably made with garlic and onions to which lentils were added.

Rebekah must have taught Jacob her recipe for a thick vegetable soup, containing pieces of meat, which was the "red pottage" Esau received for his birthright.

For seasonings Rebekah may have used home-grown herbs. From the caravans of traders she could purchase such spices as coriander, black cummin, dill, and mint.

Like her mother-in-law Sarah, Rebekah cooked in her kitchen tent whose hearth glowed with red-hot stones or ashes. She may also have used a portable clay stove, for the potter's craft was well advanced in the time of the patriarchs.

From wells dug by Isaac, water was carried in the same type of pottery jugs which Rebekah had used as a girl in her old home at Nahor. In addition to the jugs, other pottery utensils were available, including cooking pots, handleless cups, ladles, dippers, bowls, and large storage jars for grain, wine, oil, and milk. Archaeologists have unearthed in the region where Rebekah lived babies' feeding bottles and clay rattles, such as she probably had for her twin sons.

Rebekah was evidently a good seamstress, for she cut and stitched the skins of goats to fit Jacob's smooth hands and neck so that they seemed to blind Isaac's touch to be the hands of hairy Esau.

The many manservants and maidservants belonging to Isaac assisted Rebekah with household tasks. Her servants also included her own nurse she had brought from her childhood home (Genesis 24:59) who probably cared for Esau and Jacob when they were babies, just as she had cared for their mother. The nurse may have served Jacob's family also, for she is believed to be the Deborah who was traveling with his caravan when she died. "But Deborah, Rebekah's nurse, died and she was buried beneath Beth-el under an oak" (Genesis 35:8). Though she is only a name and a shadowy presence in the Bible, she must have been greatly beloved by this patriarchal family, three generations of which she served.

## 7. THEIR WANDERINGS

As tent dwellers living in the Negeb, Isaac, Rebekah, and their sons were often on the move in search of pastures for their flocks and herds. After the abundant rains of winter, the Negeb became a pleasant place, with flowers blooming along the trails, birds singing in the warm sunshine, and a mantle of green spreading over the highlands. In this season there was ample grazing for Isaac's animals. But when the long, hot, dry summer turned the landscape brown, Isaac and his family would roll up their tents, pack their saddlebags, and drive their animals to green pastures.

In this largely waterless region, with its rocky plateaus, arid wastes, and sparse vegetation, a nomad family was always concerned about water and could move only from one well to another. Wherever a well sunk deep in the ground afforded a reliable water supply, a settlement usually sprang up. As we have noted above, Isaac was a famous well digger, thus opening up for his family areas that had formerly been uninhabitable.

It was in a famine year, probably due to the failure of the winter rains in the Negeb, that Isaac moved his family to fertile Gerar where, as we have seen, he prospered in the unaccustomed role of farmer.

## 8. THEIR NEIGHBORS (Genesis 26)

As nomads in the sparsely settled regions of the Negeb, Isaac's family had few neighbors, but in well-populated Gerar they encountered a difficult situation. When the inhabitants asked Isaac about Rebekah, he replied, " 'She is my sister,' for he feared to say 'She is my wife,' lest, said he, 'the men of the place should kill me for Rebekah, because she was fair to look upon' " (26:7).

His father Abraham had used the same subterfuge years before when he entered Gerar with Sarah. She was taken into King Abimelech's harem for a short period, for in those days a king might choose whomever he wanted. In Rebekah's case, when the king of Gerar learned that she was Isaac's wife, he charged his people not to touch her or her husband.

While Isaac's tents were pitched in the valley of Gerar he was in frequent conflict with neighbors over possession of wells. As soon as Isaac's servants opened a new well, "the herdmen of Gerar did strive with Isaac's herdmen, saying, 'The water is ours' " (26:20). Isaac would then move on and dig another well only to have it taken from him. One of these disputed wells he named Esek, meaning "contention," and the other Sitnah, meaning "enmity."

He finally moved to a campsite about eighteen miles southwest of Beer-sheba where the contentious herdsmen of Gerar did not follow him. There he dug another well which he named Rehoboth, meaning "open spaces," for he declared, "For now the Lord hath made room for us, and we shall be fruitful in the land" (26:22).

Isaac's determination to live at peace with his neighbors finds further expression in the story of his covenant with Abimelech, king of Gerar. The strained relations between these two men after Abimelech expelled Isaac from Gerar had not been improved by the frequent clashes of their herdsmen at the wells. Isaac was therefore amazed to see Abimelech coming to visit him at Beer-sheba.

"Wherefore come ye to me, seeing ye hate me, and have sent me away from you?" (26:27), Isaac asked.

Abimelech replied, "Let there be now an oath betwixt us . . . and let us make a covenant with thee, that thou wilt do us no hurt, as we have not touched thee and as we have done unto thee nothing but good, and have sent thee away in peace. Thou art now the blessed of the Lord" (26:28-29).

Powerful though he was, Isaac had no desire to wage war with Abimelech, for he wished to settle all their differences in a friendly, neighborly manner. Accordingly, he made a feast for the king of Gerar and in the morning they swore their peace oath and "Isaac sent them away and they departed from him in peace" (26:31).

## 9. THE BURIAL PLACE OF THREE GENERATIONS

Rebekah died before her favorite son Jacob married Rachel and Leah, daughters of her brother Laban, so that she did not live to enjoy her twelve famous grandsons. At her death she was laid to rest beside her parents-in-law, Abraham and Sarah, in the cave of the field of Machpelah near Mamre. There her two sons later buried her husband Isaac beside her (Genesis 35:27-29).

Years afterward, during his long sojourn in Egypt, Jacob remembered his family burial place in far-off Canaan. He charged his sons, "Bury me with my fathers in the cave that is in the field of Machpelah . . . which Abraham bought with the field of Ephron the Hittite for a possession of a burying place. There they buried Abraham and Sarah his wife; there they buried Isaac and Rebekah his wife; and there I buried Leah" (Genesis 49:29-31).

The cave of Machpelah is the first family burial place mentioned in the Bible and the only one where three generations of a biblical family are known to be buried. This small plot of ground, bought for four hundred shekels of silver, was the only land in Canaan legally owned by the patriarchs.

CHAPTER 5

# Chastity in Young Womanhood

And the damsel was very fair to look upon, a virgin. . . .
Genesis 24:16

*

## 1. VIRGIN DAUGHTERS OF ISRAEL

The virginity of their young maidens was of great importance to the people of Israel. Young girls were protected within the family and clan. If a maiden were seduced, her family might take revenge upon her seducer, as did Dinah's brothers upon Shechem in the story in Genesis 34.

When the Israelites settled in Canaan, they lived among people who had not reached the relatively high degree of moral development of the people of God. The Israelites were often tempted to adopt such degrading rites practiced by their neighbors as temple prostitution. But as Israel advanced toward the belief that licentiousness is an offense against the holiness of God, her people formulated specific laws against prostitution in the "high places" where the Canaanites worshipped their gods of fertility.

Do not prostitute thy daughter, to cause her to be a whore, lest the land fall to whoredom, and the land become full of wickedness.

Leviticus 19:29

There shall be no whore of the daughters of Israel. . . . Thou shalt not bring the hire of a whore . . . into the house of the Lord . . . for even both these are abomination unto the Lord thy God.

Deuteronomy 23:17-18

Priests of Israel were forbidden to engage in heathen practices. When they married, they were enjoined to "take a virgin of his own people to wife" (Leviticus 21:14).

The Leviticus law makes it clear that those who dishonor God dishonor themselves as well as their families. The Deuteronomy law above stresses that only that which is without blemish can form a worthy offering to God.

Laws were also enacted to guard a daughter's chastity, to protect from slander the reputation of a wife, and to punish a seducer.

Commenting on the laws dealing with sexual purity in Deuteronomy 22:13-30, Henry H. Shires and Pierson Parker in *The Interpreter's Bible* say:

Chastity is stressed more strongly than might have been expected at the time. The standards of physical purity were much higher in Israel than among the neighboring peoples. Canaanite worship, as we have seen, actually involved prostitution, and sensuality was considered no vice. In the Hebrew code more was expected of women than of men, and the penalties exacted of women were correspondingly more severe. . . . Women had nevertheless achieved certain rights, and the law reflects a measure of reverence for their dignity. There is a sense of the body's own sacredness. Man and woman are holy because they are children of God who is holy (Vol. 2, pp. 465-467).

The Israelites, proud of their descent from the patriarchs Abraham, Isaac, and Jacob, looked back with respect to the mothers of their race. There was Sarah, Abraham's loyal, faithful wife, whose very name indicated that she was a princess among women. There was Rebekah, the chaste bride of Isaac; and beautiful Rachel with her sister Leah, both nurtured in the same high ideals of the patriarchal family. These women's stories, which set a high standard of virtue, helped the people of Israel combat dark and ancient evils, and established a high ideal of womanhood worthy of their faith in a holy God. The Israelites believed that "a virtuous woman is a crown to her husband" (Proverbs 12:4). Of a princess they sang, "the king's daughter is all glorious within" (Psalm 45:13). And finally, they prayed that their daughters might attain spiritual beauty and "be as corner stones, polished after the similitude of a palace" (Psalm 144:12).

## 2. A BRIDE FOR ISAAC (Genesis 24)

Abraham was a very old man when he set himself the task of finding a chaste young maiden to be Isaac's wife and the mother of his children. The matter was not left to chance nor to the whim of the moment, but was prayerfully and deliberately planned. It would have been easy and convenient for Abraham to select a daughter from the neighboring Canaanites, but he was determined to separate his family from these people whose crude fertility cults and idol worship seemed immoral to one who believed, as he did, in the Lord, the God of heaven and earth. Abraham therefore charged his most trusted servant: ". . . thou shalt not take a wife unto my son of the daughters of the Canaanites, among whom I dwell, but thou shalt go unto my country, and to my kindred, and take a wife unto my son Isaac" (24:3-4).

The journey from Canaan to Abraham's homeland across the Euphrates in northern Mesopotamia was a costly one of nearly five hundred miles, over rough and sometimes dangerous caravan trails. When his servant hesitated about making the trip and found difficulties in the plan, Abraham replied in words that expressed his faith, "The Lord, before whom I walk, will send his angel with thee and prosper thy way . . ." (24:40).

After his long journey the servant arrived safely at his destination in the city of Nahor, where Abraham and Sarah had once paused on their way toward the land of Canaan. Beside a well of water at the outskirts of the city the servant made the ten camels of his caravan kneel down. It was the evening hour when women came to draw water. Wisely the servant devised a test to indicate to him which of the damsels coming to the well was the one appointed to be Isaac's bride. The test would demonstrate that the maiden was kind, friendly to a strange old man, quick to show mercy toward animals, and generously willing to undertake an arduous task for others.

As the maidens of the city approached, laughing and chattering among themselves, Abraham's servant prayed:

"O Lord God of my master Abraham . . . let it come to pass that the damsel to whom I shall say, 'Let down thy pitcher, I pray thee, that I may drink,' and she shall say, 'Drink, and I will give thy camels drink also,' let the same be she that thou hast appointed for thy servant Isaac. . . ."                                    Genesis 24:12, 14

## 3. A DAUGHTER WHO QUALIFIED (Genesis 24)

Abraham's servant had no sooner finished his prayer than a maiden arrived with an empty pitcher upon her shoulder. She was Rebekah, who is described as "a virgin, neither had any man known her . . ." (24:16). She was a girl of natural charm and loveliness, innocent and pure-hearted. Her chastity was not merely a personal matter, but of concern to her family. In order to safeguard the purity of their race as the people of God, the Hebrews required high standards of conduct from their maidens, all of whom looked forward to marriage and the joys of motherhood and desired to become praiseworthy wives and mothers.

Before the thankful, admiring eyes of Abraham's old servant, Rebekah drew water from the well and gave him a drink. But was she the girl destined to be Isaac's bride? Of her own accord she generously and warmheartedly offered to draw water for his thirsty camels also. It was a backbreaking task to haul up from a deep well pitcher after pitcher brimming with water and dump it into a trough, so that ten camels with their enormous capacity for water might drink. But Rebekah was strong, good natured, and cheerful.

While she worked, Abraham's servant watched her in silence, wondering if this girl were indeed the one ordained to be Isaac's bride. By the time she had finished her task, he was sure that Rebekah was no ordinary girl, but the one for whom he had come so many miles. Accordingly he unpacked his saddlebags containing the betrothal gifts: golden bracelets and earrings.

One question remained: "Whose daughter art thou?" (24:23). Learning that she was the daughter of Abraham's brother, the old servant bowed his head and thanked the Lord God for leading him to such a suitable maiden. Thereupon, he gave her the earrings and bracelets.

His next question was a practical one: "Is there room in thy father's house for us to lodge in?" (24:23).

Rebekah assured him that there was. Quick, perceptive and practical, she saw that more than room was needed for a ten-camel caravan just in from the desert, so she said, "We have both straw and provender enough and room to lodge in" (24:25).

In the scene that followed in Rebekah's home, family life at its best is depicted. The excited girl ran ahead of the slowly moving caravan to tell her family about her adventure at the well. Her brother Laban went out to meet the camel train and extend a courteous invitation, "Come in, thou blessed of the Lord, wherefore standest thou without? For I have prepared the house and room for the camels" (24:31).

Eastern hospitality was offered to Abraham's servant and the men with him, but before he ate he told the eager family circle how Abraham had sent him on his mission. He asked for the consent of Rebekah's father and brother to her marriage to Isaac. Both Laban and Bethuel, sensing the guidance of God in the entire affair, answered, "The thing proceedeth from the Lord" (24:50).

The final decision, surprisingly, was left to Rebekah who, throughout the story, is depicted as a person worthy of respect. As we have already noted in the second chapter, when her family asked her if she would go to the land of Canaan to be Isaac's bride, Rebekah gave her answer swiftly and decisively, "I will go" (24:58). One senses her amazement that Abraham's servant had been divinely led to her and her eagerness to follow the guidance of God.

Rebekah, who had shown by every word and deed that she measured up to the highest qualities in mind, heart and character, journeyed with her nurse and other servants into a marriage that implied material as well as spiritual blessings. And as she jogged along on a camel, it is easy to imagine she carried in her heart her family's departing wish that she might become "the mother of thousands of millions" (28:60), a blessing which fulfilled the dreams of the chosen family toward which she journeyed.

An inborn desire to live closely to God, the narrative seems to say, is the chief requirement for a well-favored betrothal. As his bride's caravan was seen approaching, Isaac went forth "to meditate in the field at the eventide." His marriage to this chaste young maiden from his father's homeland was carried out in this manner:

And Isaac brought her into his mother Sarah's tent, and took Rebekah, and she became his wife; and he loved her: and Isaac was comforted after his mother's death (24:67).

## 4. JACOB'S JOURNEY FOR A WIFE (Genesis 28)

The years of Isaac and Rebekah's marriage passed rapidly. Soon it was time for their son Jacob to choose a bride. Because of their disappointment and unhappiness over Esau's Hittite wives, Isaac and

Rebekah decided that Jacob, now the possessor of their family's birthright and chief blessing, must not marry a Canaanite girl. And Isaac called Jacob, and blessed him and charged him, and said unto him:

"Thou shalt not take a wife of the daughters of Canaan. Arise, go to Padan-aram . . . and take thee a wife from thence of the daughters of Laban, thy mother's brother. And God Almighty bless thee, and make thee fruitful, and multiply thee, that thou mayest be a multitude of people; and give thee the blessing of Abraham. . . ."

Genesis 28:1-4

The verbs *charge, arise,* and *go* impart an urgent tone to Isaac's command. He did not delegate a faithful old servant to secure a wife for his son, as had his father Abraham. But Isaac commanded his son Jacob to go himself. The urgency of Jacob's journey to Mesopotamia, the home of his mother's brother Laban, seems to echo directions given earlier by Abraham to his servant.

On his long journey from Beer-sheba to northern Mesopotamia, Jacob stopped one night to rest at Bethel. He was fearful, for he was alone and far from home. For all he knew he was journeying beyond the protection of his fathers' God toward a land in which the great promise of land to Abraham might be of no value. That night at Bethel he dreamed of a ladder stretching between earth and heaven, and on the ladder the angels of God were ascending and descending. Then Jacob heard God's voice renewing the promise made to Abraham and Isaac that their family would become great and inherit the land. Awaking from sleep, Jacob exclaimed in awe, "Surely the Lord is in this place and I knew it not" (28:16). As he proceeded toward his destination he was sustained by a rekindled faith and by renewed strength and purpose.

## 5. LOVE AT FIRST SIGHT (Genesis 29)

Once again a romantic scene took place beside a well. This time there was no intermediary; Jacob himself waited at the well-head. Unlike Rebekah's well, which had been a city's water supply, this one was dug in the midst of fields to serve the flocks of several neighboring shepherds. They guarded its precious water by closing the well's mouth with a massive stone, so heavy as to require several men to move it. Thus the scarce water could be rationed in the presence of all to whom the well belonged.

From the shepherds waiting for their whole group to arrive so that they could water their sheep, Jacob learned that his journey was at an end, for he was at Haran near his uncle Laban's home. Moreover, the shepherds told him that Laban's daughter was already approaching with a flock. "And while he yet spake with them, Rachel came with her father's sheep, for she kept them" (29:9).

Devoted as Jacob was to his mother, he probably rejoiced that this was her niece, in whom he may have seen a family resemblance to his beloved mother. He also saw in her a competent young woman, entrusted with the care of a flock representing a large part of her father's wealth. He watched her as she self-confidently took her place at the well with the other shepherds.

Then it happened—Jacob fell in love with this fair young shepherdess. For her he singlehandedly and quite easily "rolled the stone from the well's mouth, and watered the flock of Laban, his mother's brother" (29:10). Then "Jacob kissed Rachel" as a kinswoman, though he already loved her, and in the emotional manner of the East he "lifted up his voice and wept" (29:11).

There was joy in Laban's household when Rachel ran home to tell her family of Jacob's arrival. Laban went out to meet his nephew, the son of his sister Rebekah, whom he had not seen since she left home, years before, to become Isaac's bride. When Laban met Jacob he "embraced him, and kissed him, and brought him to his house. . . . And Laban said to him, 'Surely thou art my bone and my flesh' " (29:13-14).

Because Jacob loved Rachel, his "beautiful and well favoured" (29:17) cousin, he agreed that, instead of paying the customary bride price, he would serve her father seven years for her, "and they seemed unto him but a few days, for the love he had to her" (29:20).

Jacob received a bride who was heavily veiled. Because of this manner of dress, Laban was able to trick Jacob into taking as his first bride Rachel's older sister Leah, who was less lovely than herself. But Jacob's heart was set on Rachel, so he served seven more years for her and he loved her more than Leah.

Rachel, like Rebekah, incarnated much of the moral excellence of Hebrew life. Both were examples for chaste maidens of later generations.

CHAPTER 6

# Nobility in Young Manhood

---

How can a young man keep his way pure?
  By guarding it according to thy word . . .
I will meditate on thy precepts,
  and fix my eyes on thy ways.
I will delight in thy statutes;
  I will not forget thy word.

Psalm 119:9, 15-16, RSV

---

\*

## 1. YOUTH'S RESPONSIBILITIES

Israel required the same high standards for its young men as it did for its young women. In the years of one's youth, according to the Old Testament, one should lead a clean, moral life, as indicated in verse above, respect one's father as a guide (Jeremiah 22:21), rejoice and walk in the paths of right, put away evil from the flesh (Ecclesiastes 11:9-10), and bear a yoke (Lamentations 3:27).

In outlining other responsibilities for young men, the New Testament states that in youth one should be "an example of the believers, in word, in conversation, in charity, in spirit, in faith, in purity" (I Timothy 4:12); "flee also youthful lusts . . . follow righteousness, faith, charity, peace, with them that call on the Lord out of a pure heart"; be "gentle, patient, meek" (II Timothy 2:22-25); "sober-minded, a pattern of good works" (Titus 2:6); and "resist temptation" (I John 2:13).

In Proverbs, a prime source of moral teaching, "My son, Oh my son" rings forth more than a dozen times, like a refrain in a song. The mother of the unidentified King Lemuel tells her son to consent not, if sinners entice him (1:10); to trust in the Lord (3:5); to despise not the chastening of the Lord (3:11); to ponder the path of his feet (4:26); to bow his ear to understanding (5:1); to lust not after the evil woman's beauty (6:25); to remember that wine biteth like a serpent (23:31-32); to be not envious of evil men, nor desire to be with them (24:1); and to be wise and make her heart glad (27:11).

This mother of Proverbs seems to speak the language of all good mothers of sons. She might be Sarah speaking to Isaac, or Jochebed to Moses, or Hannah to Samuel, or Eunice to Timothy. She might also typify the great Christian mothers of later centuries, such as Monica, mother of Augustine; Nonna, mother of Gregory the Divine; Anthusa, mother of John Chrysostom; Susannah, mother of John and Charles Wesley.

## 2. RACHEL'S SON JOSEPH

Joseph, the son of Jacob and his favorite wife Rachel, typifies some of these noblest qualities of young men in biblical times. In both good fortune and bad, Joseph remained faithful to his ideals. He fought valiantly against evil in many forms and resisted temptations to act ignobly. By his perseverance, loyalty, and wisdom, he finally became the savior of his family.

Joseph was still a child when his father Jacob moved his family of eleven sons, four wives, and many servants, together with all his flocks and herds southward from Mesopotamia, where Joseph had been born, into the land of Canaan. On this long journey when the caravan was in danger of attack, Jacob placed his wife Rachel and her son Joseph in the rear of the whole company where they would enjoy the position of greatest safety. In another peril Jacob was powerless to save his beloved Rachel, for at Bethlehem she died giving birth to Joseph's younger brother Benjamin.

## 3. HIS FATHER'S FAVORITE (Genesis 37)

Grieving over the loss of Rachel, Jacob turned to his little son Joseph who, like his mother, was both beautiful and lovable. The words "well-favoured" were used to describe both mother and son (Genesis 29:17; 39:6). The lad's unusual promise gave his father another reason for showering special favors on him. (Apparently Jacob had forgotten that long ago the enmity between him and his brother had been increased by his mother's favoritism for him and his father's for Esau.) Jacob spoiled Joseph. He gave the lad a flowing long-sleeved robe made of many-colored fabrics all carefully stitched together. This princely garment set young Joseph apart from his older brothers, who wore the common, short, sleeveless tunics of hard-working Canaanite shepherds.

His ten half-brothers naturally became jealous of Joseph. They "hated him and could not speak peaceably unto him" (37:4). When they discovered that he was a talebearer who "brought unto his father their evil report" (37:2), they resented him even more. Too sure of himself even to notice their indignation, Joseph continued to antagonize his brothers. He arrogantly boasted of two dreams, in the first of which he saw his sheaf of grain stand upright while his brothers' sheaves bowed down to his. Angrily his brothers asked him, "Shalt thou indeed reign over us?" (37:8).

In his second dream Joseph saw the sun, the moon, and eleven stars bowing down to him. Even Joseph's doting father, disturbed by this evidence of his favorite son's overweening pride, rebuked Joseph for revealing his conceited dream.

## 4. WHEN MISFORTUNE STRUCK (Genesis 37)

The relationship between Joseph and his half-brothers had become tense and dangerous when the ten older men drove their father's flock to pasture in the valley of Shechem. When the brothers failed to return home at the expected time, Jacob sent young Joseph to search for them.

At Dothan the ten men saw their hated young brother Joseph approaching. They knew him by his confident stride, his light, springing step, and his long coat billowing out behind him, its many colors brilliant in the sunshine.

"Behold, this dreamer cometh" (37:19), they exclaimed in scorn and anger. Now was their opportunity to plot against their self-assertive brother. The more envious and evil-minded of them planned to slay him, but Reuben counseled moderation, saying, "Shed no blood, but cast him into this pit that is in the wilderness . . ." (37:22).

Judah, agreeing with this idea, proposed, "Come, and let us sell him to the Ishmeelites and let not our hand be upon him, for he is our brother and our flesh" (37:27).

So they seized young Joseph, stripped him of his princely coat of many colors, and threw him into an empty pit. They themselves callously sat down to eat. Soon a caravan of spice merchants came by from Gilead bound for Egypt with their wares of balm and myrrh. To these traders the brothers sold young Joseph for twenty pieces of silver. Later the brothers were to remember "the anguish of his soul when he besought us, and we would not hear" (42:21). Now as they eagerly counted their silver, they turned deaf ears to Joseph's entreaties.

Fearful of their father's rage when he should discover their treachery to Joseph, they dipped his princely garment of many colors in the blood of a goat and brought it to Jacob, saying, "This we have found. Know now whether it be thy son's coat or no" (37:32).

Recognizing the blood-stained robe as the one he had given Joseph, the father sorrowfully declared, "It is my son's coat. An evil beast hath devoured him; Joseph is without doubt rent in pieces" (37:33). For many days Jacob mourned for his beloved Joseph while ten sons and all his daughters tried to comfort the grieving father. But their efforts were in vain, for they withheld from him the truth which would have given him hope.

## 5. STRONG IN ADVERSITY (Genesis 39)

In anguish of soul Joseph began his tedious journey in a strange caravan toward an unknown country. From a spoiled young prince, he had become a miserable slave. His fortunes seemed to have reached bottom, though he was later to experience even greater disaster. How he conquered heartbreak and despair and kept alive his faith and hope through his early years in Egypt is not told in the record of his life. During the hardships of those years his character was forged, and "God was with him" (Acts 7:9).

The spice merchants who had purchased him from his brothers offered Joseph for sale in the Egyptian slave market. As he was a sturdy and well-favored lad with a keen, intelligent air, he was immediately bought by Potiphar, captain of the pharaoh's bodyguard. When Potiphar discovered that his new slave was both capable and trustworthy and that everything he undertook succeeded, this wealthy Egyptian made Joseph overseer of his estate. Joseph was now manager not only of his master's house and slaves but of his stables, gardens, and fields. Whenever Potiphar went abroad in the pharaoh's service, he left Joseph in authority over his entire household. "And . . . the Lord blessed the Egyptian's house for Joseph's sake; and the blessing of the Lord was upon all that he had in the house, and in the field" (39:5). Thus Joseph became familiar with Egyptian ways of life and began to exercise his talent for administration.

## 6. HIS MORAL INTEGRITY (Genesis 39)

Potiphar's wife began to notice that the young Hebrew overseer was handsome in his fine new garments. While her husband was absent, she made overtures to Joseph and tried to entice him, but Joseph, though he was surely greatly tempted, refused her and said, ". . . because thou art his wife, how then can I do this great wickedness, and sin against God?" (39:9). Nothing could shake Joseph's loyalty to his master and, more importantly, to his God. He acted as a good man, because he had become a godly man.

Joseph was pursued relentlessly by Potiphar's wife, but he steadfastly refused her and tried to avoid her presence. One day, stung by his repeated refusals, she grabbed off his coat. Upon her husband's return she showed him Joseph's garment and declared that, after boldly forcing his way into her room, Joseph had become frightened by her cries for help and had fled, leaving his coat behind. Thus falsely accused by Potiphar's revengeful wife, Joseph was cast into prison.

## 7. RESOURCEFUL IN PRISON (Genesis 39-41)

As a slave imprisoned on so unjust a charge, Joseph seemed to have reached the depths of misfortune. Who would rescue him? What hope remained for him? "But the Lord was with Joseph, and showed him mercy and gave him favour in the sight of the keeper of the prison" (39:21).

Joseph's fellow prisoners were the pharaoh's chief butler and his chief baker, both of whom had incurred royal displeasure. After Joseph correctly intepreted the dreams of these prisoners, the chief butler was hanged, as Joseph had predicted, but the chief baker was restored to his high position in the palace. Joseph asked no recompense from the baker, except that he would mention him to the pharaoh. The fortunate baker, however, forgot Joseph for two long years.

When the pharaoh had two disturbing dreams, which none of the magicians nor wise men of Egypt could interpret, the chief butler suddenly remembered Joseph and had him brought from prison to stand before the ruler of Egypt. Joseph interpreted the strange dreams and said that they portended seven years of abundance followed by seven years of grievous famine. Lest the people perish during the famine, he advised that an official be appointed to store up grain during the years of plenty.

Joseph never returned to prison, for to all who saw him standing in the midst of the court interpreting the pharaoh's dream, he seemed "a man in whom the spirit of God is" (41:38). His good judgment and wisdom so impressed the pharaoh that, with the advice of his counselors, he immediately appointed Joseph superintendent of the Egyptian granaries and chief minister of state, saying, "Thou shalt be over my house, and according unto thy word shall all my people be ruled. Only in the throne will I be greater than thou. . . . See, I have set thee over all the land of Egypt" (41:40-41).

The onetime Hebrew slave and prisoner, though still relatively young and with experience only in the management of Potiphar's estate, was now raised to a position of enormous power and responsibility. But he showed wisdom and good judgment in dealing with the problems of his high office, and began to store grain during Egypt's seven years of abundance. When famine finally arrived, "Joseph opened all the storehouses and sold unto the Egyptians. And the famine waxed sore in the land of Egypt. And all countries came into Egypt to Joseph for to buy corn, because that the famine was so sore in all lands" (41:56-57).

## 8. EVIL TURNED TO GOOD (Genesis 45-47)

To old Jacob in far-off Canaan came news that there was corn in Egypt. Without delay he sent his ten older sons there to buy food for his entire family, which was on the verge of starvation. Joseph's half-brothers did not recognize in the powerful ruler of Egypt the lad they had once sold into slavery. He finally revealed himself to them in very simple words: "I am Joseph. Doth my father yet live?" (45:3).

The brothers, trembling with fear, were unable to reply, but seeing their consternation Joseph spoke kindly to them:

"I am Joseph your brother, whom ye sold into Egypt. Now therefore be not grieved, nor angry with yourselves, that ye sold me hither, for God did send me before you to preserve life. . . . And . . . to preserve you a posterity in the earth, and to save your lives by a great deliverance. So now it was not you that sent me hither, but God."

Genesis 45:4-8

At Joseph's direction, his brothers hastened back to their father and brought him and all their families together with their flocks and herds to Egypt. "And Joseph placed his father and his brethren . . . in the land of Egypt, in the best of the land of Rameses. . . . And Joseph nourished his father, and his brethren, and all his father's household with bread according to their families" (47:11-12).

## 9. IN THEIR FATHER'S SERVICE

Joseph was but the first of many young men to perform outstanding service to Israel. As we have seen, Joseph was in Dothan acting on his father's orders when his brothers, all unwittingly, started him toward greatness. Interestingly enough, many of the youths whose stories are narrated in the Old Testament were likewise engaged as loyal, helpful sons in tasks for their fathers when they were called to higher service for the whole people of Israel. The three following incidents, typical of a pastoral and agricultural society, underline the close relationship between fathers and sons and the strength of family loyalty in biblical times.

While the "judges" ruled Israel in the twelfth or thirteenth century B.C., hordes of Midianites swarmed over the country, plundering goods and destroying crops. In this time of danger, when the wheat crop of a certain obscure man named Joash was harvested, "his son Gideon threshed wheat by the winepress, to hide it from the Midianites" (Judges 6:11). In the partly concealed winepress, where

Gideon was helping his father save his crop from the enemy, an angel of the Lord appeared to the young man and said, "The Lord is with thee, thou mighty man of valour. . . . Go, in this thy might, and thou shalt save Israel from the hand of the Midianites" (Judges 6:12, 14).

Gideon was deeply concerned for his harried fellow countrymen, yet he felt powerless to free them: "Oh my Lord, wherewith shall I save Israel? Behold, my family is poor in Manasseh and I am the least in my father's house" (Judges 6:15). But Gideon, called by God to be a savior of the people, came out of hiding, and led three hundred intrepid men to a decisive victory over the Midianites.

Two or three hundred years later, young Saul was likewise working for his father when his opportunity came for wider service. "And the asses of Kish, Saul's father, were lost. And Kish said to Saul his son, 'Take now one of the servants with thee, and arise, go seek the asses' " (I Samuel 9:3). While searching for the strayed beasts, Saul met the prophet Samuel, who anointed him for his task of leading Israel. Later he became Israel's first king.

David, too, was on an errand for his father when his opportunity came to confront Goliath. In so doing, he won undying fame which started him on his triumphant road toward the kingship of Israel.

And Jesse said unto David his son, "Take now for thy brethren an ephah of this parched corn, and these ten loaves, and run to the camp to thy brethren; and carry these ten cheeses unto the captain of their thousand, and look how thy brethren fare, and take their pledge."

I Samuel 17:17, 18

Finally, there was young Elisha whom the fiery prophet Elijah found one day plowing on his father's large farm. "Elisha the son of Shaphat . . . was plowing with twelve yoke of oxen before him and he with the twelfth. And Elijah passed by him and cast his mantle on him" (I Kings 19:19).

At this, young Elisha ceased plowing, for he understood the meaning of Elijah's act of ordination in which he invested the young man with the prophetic mantle. But remembering his family loyalties, Elisha said to the old prophet, "Let me, I pray thee, kiss my father and my mother, and then I will follow thee" (I Kings 19:20). After bidding farewell to his family, Elisha followed the older prophet Elijah and ministered to him to the end of his life.

A close father-son relationship was customary in Old Testament times, when the effort of an entire family group was necessary to gain a living for them all. The social pattern underlying these stories reappears in the New Testament in the case of Zebedee's sons, James and John, who were with their father in the fishing boat when Jesus called them to be His disciples (Mark 1:19-20).

Jesus Himself evidently worked with His father Joseph in his carpenter's shop, for not only is He called "the carpenter's son" (Matthew 13:55), but "the carpenter" (Mark 6:3). As a boy, Jesus learned from stories of Israel's heroes, from social customs around Him, and from His own experience that a working relationship between a father and his son can be a fruitful one, full of love, trust, and shared responsibility.

Sonship, however, has far deeper aspects than those discussed above. Even at the age of twelve, when Mary and Joseph found Him in the Temple questioning the teachers, Jesus was already pondering the meaning of a son's relationship to the heavenly Father, for He said to His parents, "Wist ye not that I must be about my father's business?" (Luke 2:49).

## 10. LOYAL TO THEIR RELIGION (Daniel 1, 3, 6)

Another aspect of ideal young manhood emerges in the story of Daniel and his three companions, Shadrach, Meshach, and Abednego. They were four young Hebrew captives transported to Babylon and selected for special education at the royal court. King Nebuchadnezzar specified that the youths chosen for his training program were to be those

.... in whom was no blemish, but well favoured, and skilful in all wisdom, and cunning in knowledge, and understanding science, and such as had ability in them to stand in the king's palace and whom they might teach the learning and the tongue of the Chaldeans.

Daniel 1:4

It was no small honor to be chosen and the rewards were high, for, during the three years of their instruction, the youths were daily to be given meat, wine, and delicacies from the king's own table. But Daniel, true to the faith of his fathers, "purposed in his heart that he would not defile himself with the portion of the king's meat, nor with the wine which he drank" (1:8). Lest they eat any food prohibited by their religion, Daniel and his three companions ate a monotonous diet of beans and peas. So well did these nourish them that at the end of ten days "their countenances appeared fairer and fatter in flesh" (1:15) than those of the other youths. Moreover, "God gave them knowledge and skill in all learning and wisdom. And Daniel had understanding in all visions and dreams" (1:17).

Two other stories are told of the steadfast loyalty of Daniel and his three friends to the faith of their fathers. When his three companions refused to worship Nebuchadnezzar's golden image, they were thrown into a burning, fiery furnace from which, by divine help, they emerged unharmed. Daniel continued to practice his religion, which had been declared illegal. One day when he was found praying to God, his enemies threw him into a den of lions; but he escaped uninjured.

Such sons as these—Daniel and his companions, Elisha, David, Saul, Gideon, Joseph, and many others, both known and unknown—all contributed to the picture of nobility in Israel's young manhood.

# Family Relationships

*

# CHAPTER 7

# Stories of Husband-Wife Relationships

---

Nevertheless, let every one of you in particular so love his wife even as himself; and the wife see that she reverence her husband.

Ephesians 5:33

---

Beginning with Adam, the Bible's rich and lifelike portrait gallery of men and women includes various husbands and wives whose relationships were affected by their traits of character. Some of the distinguishing qualities of the men and women in the following stories ennobled their marriages and contributed to ideal relationships, such as that described in the above quotation from Ephesians. Other characteristics marred the marriage relationship. All of the traits selected for study, however, are human, recognizable, and as timely as today's newspaper.

## 1. A HUSBAND WHO BLAMED HIS WIFE (Genesis 3:8-13)

Shifting blame to one's spouse is as old as the first couple. Though it was Adam's misfortune to be the first person in the Bible to display this quality, it is by no means confined to husbands—or to adults, for that matter. Children are wonderfully ingenious in shifting blame to something or someone else. Adam himself seems to have behaved in a childish manner when he tried to shift his own responsibility for eating the forbidden fruit onto his wife.

When the Lord God walked in the Garden of Eden in the cool of the day, He perceived that all was not well, so He called Adam and asked, "Hast thou eaten of the tree whereof I commanded thee that thou shouldest not eat?" (3:11).

Adam excused himself adroitly: "The woman whom thou gavest to be with me, she gave me of the tree and I did eat" (3:12).

He was sure it was Eve's fault, not his. Moreover, he darkly hinted that by creating Eve, in the first place, it was really the Lord God who was responsible for the whole unfortunate episode.

When Eve was questioned about the matter, she, too, attempted to shift the blame onto another: "The serpent beguiled me and I did eat" (3:13).

## 2. THE LIFELONG DEVOTION OF A HUSBAND

The story of Abraham's lifelong devotion to his wife began when he departed from his old home in northern Mesopotamia to journey to the Promised Land. He and his wife Sarah, not knowing where they might be led, set out together at the Lord's command. Sarah responded to her husband's devotion by loyally following him into all the strange lands where he journeyed. Twice Abraham pretended that Sarah was his sister, to spare them both, so we are told, from harm, but these are the only times the Bible records that the pair was separated.

Abraham's devotion survived the many years of Sarah's barrenness. According to the belief of ancient Hebrew times, a woman who bore her husband no son had failed in her chief duty as a wife. Yet Abraham did not send his wife home and, though he took her maid Hagar as his concubine, Sarah remained his chief wife.

At her death "Abraham came to mourn for Sarah and to weep for her" (Genesis 23:2) and was later buried beside her.

## 3. COURTESY IN A HUSBAND (Ruth 2-4)

Boaz is one of the most courteous and honorable husbands in the Bible. From the beginning of their romance he was graciously polite to Ruth, the young widow from Moab who was trying to earn a living for herself and her mother-in-law Naomi. As a foreigner, Ruth might well have met with hostility, yet Boaz, moved by her loyalty to Naomi, kindly offered to protect the young woman. He ordered his reapers not to molest her when she gleaned in his fields and he told her to drink all the water she wanted from his jars. His openhearted welcome to the young foreigner was crowned by his beautiful blessing: •

The Lord recompense thy work, and a full reward be given thee of the Lord God of Israel, under whose wings thou art come to trust.

Ruth 2:12

At mealtime Boaz graciously invited Ruth to eat bread and parched grain with him and to dip her morsel in his wine. To make her task of gleaning easier and more productive, he instructed his men to leave some of the grainstalks for her to gather.

During their courtship he showed a strong sense of honor in protecting her reputation from malicious gossip. When, as we have already seen in the section on levirate marriage, he undertook the duty of a near relative, Boaz arranged their marriage in the presence of the elders at the city gate. The Book of Ruth, in which their story is told, depicts a courteous husband who was a man of fine feelings and, above all, honorable.

## 4. AN ANCIENT COUPLE'S LOVING RELATIONSHIP
   (I Samuel 1-2)

The story of Samuel's parents, Hannah and Elkanah, provides a rare glimpse of the intimacies of family life in ancient Israel. Samuel's early home, despite certain problems, was one marked by pure happiness and a heartwarming relationship between a husband and wife who were devout worshipers of the Lord.

Elkanah loved his wife Hannah, listened patiently to her problems, and tried to comfort her. In respecting her wishes and allowing her to decide what was best for their son, he treated her as an equal. Theirs was, with a few exceptions, an idyllic husband-wife relationship. Yet, at the time the story opens, Hannah was miserable, for she was childless.

According to the custom of those remote days, Elkanah, being a man of substance and able to support a large family, had taken a second wife, Peninnah, to bear him sons and daughters. Every year as the whole household, including all of Peninnah's children, journeyed to the sanctuary at Shiloh to make their sacrifice at the altar, they appeared to be a contented family.

One year Hannah's childlessness seemed a heavier affliction than she could endure, for her rival, Peninnah, had been taunting her. "And her adversary also provoked her sore, for to make her fret, because the Lord had shut up her womb. . . . therefore she wept and did not eat" (1:6-7).

Disturbed by his wife's grief, Elkanah gently asked, "Hannah why weepest thou? And why eatest thou not? And why is thy heart grieved?" (1:8).

No sooner had he asked these questions than he perceived the real cause of his wife's sorrow. He tried to comfort her by reminding her of his love: "Am not I better to thee than ten sons?" (1:8).

Consoled by his loving attention and understanding, Hannah ate, drank, and went to pray to the Lord, saying, "O Lord of hosts, if thou wilt indeed look on the affliction of thine handmaid, and . . . wilt give unto thine handmaid a man child, then I will give him unto the Lord all the days of his life . . ." (1:11).

Hannah's prayer was answered, for "she bare a son and called his name Samuel, saying, 'Because I have asked him of the Lord' " (1:20).

Until Samuel was weaned, Hannah decided not to accompany her husband on his yearly visit to the sanctuary at Shiloh. Elkanah gladly complied with his wife's wishes, saying, "Do what seemeth thee good. Tarry until thou have weaned him" (1:23).

When Samuel was old enough, his parents, bearing gifts for the sanctuary, "brought him unto the house of the Lord in Shiloh" (1:24). Pride was mingled with sorrow in Hannah's heart as she presented Samuel to the old priest Eli. "For this child I prayed," she said, "and the Lord hath given me my petition. . . . Therefore also I have lent him to the Lord" (1:27). In making her decision to leave her son at Shiloh to be educated in the Lord's service, Hannah had acted for Samuel's good, but she returned from Shiloh heavyhearted, knowing that her child would never be at home with her again.

Hannah did not forget her growing son while he was in "the house of the Lord." With loving stitches she "made him a little coat, and brought it to him from year to year when she came up with her husband to offer the yearly sacrifice. And Eli blessed Elkanah and his wife" (2:19-20).

## 5. A CHURLISH, DRINKING HUSBAND (I Samuel 25)

Abigail needed all the tact, charm, and resourcefulness a woman can possess, for her husband Nabal, though a wealthy sheep owner, was "churlish and evil in his doings" (25:3). A mean man, given to heavy drinking, and a fool, Nabal afforded his wife little protection during the perilous days of Saul's reign when bandits roaming the countryside exacted tribute from herdsmen and cattle raisers.

In the highlands of southern Judah, Nabal's three thousand sheep and a thousand goats grazed in peace, for in that region David and his band of shepherds were acting as a volunteer police force. Nabal's shepherds later testified, "They were a wall unto us both night and day, all the while we were with them keeping the sheep" (25:16).

At sheepshearing time Nabal gave a feast to which David sent ten of his men with his greetings and a request: "Give, I pray thee, whatsoever cometh to thine hand unto thy servants, and to thy son David" (25:8).

David's men had good reason to expect food and a rich gift from Nabal in return for the protection they had given his sheep. But Nabal answered them roughly, railing at them and giving them nothing.

Angered by Nabal's ingratitude and insolence, David and his four hundred men girded on their swords, vowing to take revenge on him. One of Nabal's servants, learning of this threat to the household, was afraid to speak to his irascible master but warned his wife of the impending danger, saying, "Now therefore know and consider what thou wilt do, for evil is determined against our master and against all his household; for he is such a son of Belial that a man cannot speak to him" (25:17).

Fortunately, Abigail was "a woman of good understanding and of beautiful countenance" (25:3), who knew how to handle her sullen, drinking husband, and how to make gracious amends to a man who had been friendly to her household but who now threatened to destroy it. Without revealing her plan to her husband, she hastily loaded their asses with bountiful provisions of bread, wine, meat, grain, raisins, and figs. Having done this, she set out to find David.

When Abigail met him, she fell at his feet and begged him to forgive her husband for his churlishness. His blame she took entirely upon herself. She admitted that "as his name is, so is he; Nabal is his name and folly is with him" (25:25). She was also shrewd enough to foresee that because David was fighting the battles of the Lord he would one day become ruler of Israel.

David was charmed by Abigail's speech, accepted her gifts, and granted her petition. He blessed her and her household, saying, "Go up in peace to thine house. See, I have hearkened to thy voice . . ." (25:35).

As Nabal was very drunk when his wife returned, Abigail did not tell him how she had averted ruin from their home. But the next morning "when the wine was gone out of Nabal, and his wife had told him these things, that his heart died within him and he became as a stone" (25:37). Possibly his anger, combined with his heavy drinking, caused apoplexy. Ten days later, following another stroke, he died.

When David heard that Nabal was dead, he wooed and won Abigail.


## 6. A WIFE WHO MOCKED HER HUSBAND
   (II Samuel 6:14-23)

Theirs had been a love match in the beginning, for "Michal, Saul's daughter, loved David" (I Samuel 18:20). It was a romantic marriage, too, for she was a princess and he, the idolized hero who had vanquished Goliath. But Saul's plot to use his daughter as a snare to entrap David introduced a sinister note.

Soon after their marriage, David's life was threatened by his royal father-in-law, who sent men to kill David. Learning of her father's plot in time, Michal let her husband down from a palace window (I Samuel 19:12). Thus escaping from Saul, David fled and became an outlaw, but during his absence from court the king gave his daughter Michal in marriage to a man named Phalti or Phaltiel. It was during this period that David married Abigail, as narrated in the previous section.

After Saul's death and David's accession to the throne of Israel, the young king demanded that his former wife Michal be restored to him. She must have inspired real love in her second husband Phaltiel, for he was heartbroken at their forced separation and wept as he followed behind her until he was curtly ordered to go home (II Samuel 3:15-16). The Bible says nothing of Michal's feelings, though they may have influenced her behavior when the Ark of the Covenant was brought into Jerusalem.

Amid great rejoicing this golden chest, above which the presence of God was believed to dwell, was brought triumphantly into the royal city of Jerusalem. David himself, clad in a short linen garment, led the joyful procession, dancing and whirling in a frenzy of zeal as people shouted and trumpets blared. But Michal, looking from a window, "saw king David leaping and dancing before the Lord and she despised him in her heart" (6:16). Not sharing his religious exaltation, she thought his dancing was not only unbecoming to his kingly dignity, but even shameless, for he had taken off his royal robes and was wearing only the linen ephod of a priest when he made his appearance before his people.

Filled with elation and with the shouts of the people still ringing in his ears, David returned home to be greeted by Michal's mocking sarcasm, "How glorious was the king of Israel today!" (6:20). She poured out her bitter scorn of him, calling his linen ephod an indecent garment and himself a shameless fellow.

Stung by her bitter tongue, David defended his dancing. "It was before the Lord" (6:21), he explained, though he must have known that his resentful, proud, worldly wife could not understand his profound but joyous devotion to the Lord.

From that hour David and Michal became estranged and "Michal the daughter of Saul had no child unto the day of her death" (6:23).

## 7. A KING DOMINATED BY HIS WIFE (I Kings 21)

Ahab, ruler of the northern kingdom of Israel between 869 and 850 B.C., was dominated by his baneful queen, Jezebel. In some ways he was a statesmanlike ruler, fighting his enemies, strengthening his foreign alliances, and building new cities, notably Samaria. Here his energetic father Omri had established and fortified a new capital from which he could control Israel's growing trade. Ahab beautified Samaria with a splendid palace. But in the Bible, Ahab's accomplishments are overshadowed by the evil machinations of his wife, for whose overbearing ways he was no match.

Jezebel was a Phoenician princess, daughter of the king of Tyre and Sidon, and a worshiper of Baal. Her ambition seemed to have been to impose her crude nature cult with its fertility rites and its licentious practices, together with her ideas of kingly absolutism, upon her husband's kingdom of Israel. Ahab offered no opposition to his domineering wife, and had it not been for the formidable prophet Elijah, Jezebel might have succeeded in planting Baal worship in Israel and in transforming the God-centered kingdom into a tyrannical Oriental despotism.

The decisive defeat of Jezebel's four hundred and fifty prophets of Baal by the valiant prophet Elijah and the Lord God of Israel in a fiery contest on Mount Carmel is dramatically narrated in I Kings 18. Jezebel's plans to stamp out the worship of God in Israel failed.

Jezebel, however, was not a woman to admit defeat. One day Ahab's self-willed, imperious wife had an opportunity to try out her political ideas.

Beside Ahab's palace at Jezreel was a vineyard which the king greatly desired for a herb garden. But Naboth, the vineyard's owner, refused to sell his ancestral property to the king. To Ahab's credit, king though he was, he accepted Naboth's refusal. Hebrew law guaranteed to a man the possession of his family lands. The king was so bitterly disappointed at this turn of events that he moped like a spoiled child. "And he laid him down upon his bed and turned away his face and would eat no bread" (21:4).

Jezebel saw her chance to force her weak, irresolute husband to act as the absolute ruler she wanted him to be. It was impossible for her to understand, as did Ahab and the people of Israel, that even a king is subject to the laws of God. With withering sarcasm she asked her sulky husband, "Dost thou now govern the kingdom of Israel?" (21:7).

If he declined to rule as befitted a king, she would show him how it should be done. Without her husband's knowledge, Jezebel wrote letters in the king's name and sealed them with his royal seal, an act equivalent to forging a signature on a state document. With diabolical cleverness, her letters directed that two false witnesses be found to accuse Naboth of blasphemy against God and the king. The legal penalty for blasphemy was death by stoning. At Jezebel's direction this punishment was carried out not only against Naboth but against his sons also, for at their father's death they would normally have inherited the property (II Kings 9:26). At the death of Naboth and his sons the vineyard became ownerless and could be possessed by Ahab.

The king meekly, but no doubt quite happily, accepted the fruits of his wife's crime, but his satisfaction in owning the vineyard was brief. On his going to take possession of it, the fiery, old prophet Elijah confronted him.

"Hast thou found me, O mine enemy?" (21:20) cried Ahab in guilty dismay.

Elijah replied, "I have found thee, because thou hast sold thyself to work evil in the sight of the Lord" (21:20).

Though Jezebel had committed the crime, Elijah held the king responsible for royal acts done in his name. The Bible judged him thus: "But there was none like unto Ahab, which did sell himself to work wickedness in the sight of the Lord, whom Jezebel his wife stirred up" (21:25).

The conclusion of this story is well known. Ahab, wounded in battle by a stray arrow, died in his chariot. Jezebel's horrible death occurred eight years later when Ahab's kingdom was wrested from his murdered son Jehoram, and the royal line of Omri and Ahab came to an end.

## 8. A WIFE WHO WAS DISCARDED (Esther 1:9-22; 2:17)

"All the wives shall give to their husbands honour, both to great and small (1:20)." This was the decree sent out over the more than one hundred and twenty-seven provinces by King Ahasuerus of Persia, after his wife Vashti refused to make a public appearance before his drinking guests, among whom were his nobles and princes from all of his provinces in Persia and Media.

They had been entertained at his magnificent palace at Shusan for one hundred and eighty days, during which he showed them "the riches of his glorious kingdom and the honour of his excellent majesty" (1:4). When these feasting days drew to an end, the king invited into his court garden all of the people, "both great and small," to drink of the royal wine in abundance. This revelry continued for seven more days. At the same time his wife Vashti gave a feast in the royal house for women guests.

On the seventh day, "when the heart of the king was merry with wine" (1:10), he commanded his seven chamberlains to bring Vashti "to shew the people and the princes her beauty: for she was fair to look on" (1:11). But she defied her husband's commands, king though he was. He had placed her in a very embarrassing position in demanding that she come before his drinking guests, for Persian wives did not make public appearances.

The Bible account seems to indicate that Vashti felt the king had dishonored himself as a husband. An honorable, loving husband seeks to protect his wife's modesty.

The king was so angered at Queen Vashti's refusal to some before his banqueting guests that he called his council to inquire if legal means should be taken against her. Memucan, a council member, declared that Vashti had not only insulted her husband but that she had set the wrong example for all the princes and others in provinces of the king. Her refusal to obey would become known among all the women of the provinces, and wives of lesser rank would cite Queen Vashti to their husbands as an example of a wife who did not obey. Husbands in the kingdom were in danger of losing their places as heads of their households.

It was therefore recommended by the council that the king send forth a royal command, which should be written into the laws of the Medes and Persians, that Queen Vashti come no more before her husband and that her royal estate be given to another wife. Letters also were sent into every royal province "that every man should bear rule in his own house" (1:22).

Though Vashti was dethroned when the king was sober again, "he remembered Vashti, and what she had done, and what was decreed against her (2:1). . . . And the king loved Esther above all the women. . . . and made her queen instead of Vashti" (2:17).

## 9. A WIFE WHO SUCCUMBED TO ADVERSITY (Job 2:7-10)

Job and his wife lost everything. Bandits stole his asses and oxen, carried off his camels, and killed his servants. His sheep were struck by lightning and died. Most grievous of all, his sons and daughters were crushed to death when their house collapsed in a high wind. Job himself was afflicted with boils which caused him extreme discomfort.

He had no money with which to pay a physician or buy healing ointments, no servants to minister to him, no sons and daughters to comfort him. Only his wife remained to him, but her courage and faith sagged beneath the weight of adversity. She was so lacking in sympathy and understanding that the bitterly cynical advice she gave her husband merely added to his already great tribulations.

Her ten recorded words reveal her character in all its ignoble cowardice. "Dost thou still retain thine integrity?" (2:9), she asked. It was a bitterly mocking question that implied he was a fool for remaining loyal to God. The last thing Job needed at this time was a nagging wife who imputed ignorance and naïveté to him. Her final words must have struck him like a whiplash: "Curse God and die!" (2:9). Perhaps she could no longer endure to see his sufferings. It was better, she thought, to invite death, for in those days blasphemy was believed to be followed by immediate death.

Job reproved his wife. "Thou speakest as one of the foolish women speaketh" (2:10). Her words sounded to him like those of an impious fool. "Shall we receive good at the hand of God, and shall we not receive evil?" (2:10), he asked her, in a vain effort to explain his unshakable love and loyalty to God.

For all time Job's wife remains as an example of a woman who, because she lacked understanding, courage, and faith, could not help her husband in his deepest trouble.

## 10. A HUSBAND'S LOVING FORGIVENESS

The prophet Hosea preached to the people of the northern kingdom of Israel a message concerning God's unfailing love. If the story of Hosea's love for Gomer is the record of an actual husband-wife relationship rather than an allegory, his prophetic message was forged out of his own heartbreak and suffering.

Gomer may have been a harlot before she became Hosea's wife, but it seems more likely that only after her marriage and the birth of their first son did she take other lovers. Hosea continued to love his unfaithful wife, and amid the personal anguish of his tragic experience, he began to understand God's unchanging love for the people of Israel.

Like Gomer who had taken other lovers, Israel had been unfaithful to the Lord in her worship of other gods. But the Lord remained steadfast in His love for His wicked people.

In the light of his own forgiveness of Gomer and of his rare loving kindness to her, Hosea wrote of the Lord's relation to Israel: "I will have mercy upon her that had not obtained mercy, and I will say to them which were not my people, 'Thou art my people.' And they shall say, 'Thou art my God' " (Hosea 2:23).

# CHAPTER 8

# The Father's Role

For I know him, that he will command his children and his household after him, and they shall keep the way of the Lord, to do justice and judgment; that the Lord may bring upon Abraham that which he hath spoken of him.

Genesis 18:19

*

## 1. THE CENTRAL AND DOMINANT MEMBER OF THE FAMILY

The earliest records of Hebrew families show them to be of the patriarchal type with the father as the founder and ruler. Eight generations of antediluvian patriarchs listed in Genesis 5, as we have already noted, establish Noah's descent from Adam and underline the dominant position of the father in early Hebrew society. Genesis 10 and 11 record the names of Noah's sons and grandsons through many generations to the birth of Abraham. The period in which he and his descendants, Isaac, Jacob, and Jacob's twelve sons, lived is often called the Patriarchal Age. Thereafter the whole people of Israel thought of themselves as the children of Abraham and the land of Canaan as "the land of the fathers."

In a patriarchal society, with the father as the central figure in the family, his authority was never questioned. He was the master ruling his wife, his children, his servants, and his property. But if all family authority was vested in him, he, as the center of family strength, safety, and survival, ideally served not for himself alone, but for the protection and welfare of all members of the family. Together they formed a close-knit group in which no single person acted without the father's direction. To him they owed honor, obedience, and love.

## 2. TEACHER AND GUARDIAN OF SPIRITUAL RICHES

When it was revealed to Abraham that he was to be the father of a great nation and that all families of the earth would be blessed in him, his duties as a father were outlined in the quotation at the head of this chapter. Abraham knew that he must faithfully teach his descendants to follow "the way of the Lord" and to do what is right and good, for by transmitting the laws of God to his sons and grandsons, Abraham would become worthy of the Lord's promise to him.

Since the real strength of a family is derived from its spiritual values, it was the Hebrew father's duty to remember and pass on to his sons the stories which showed how God had loved and led His people throughout their history.

Only take heed to thyself, and keep thy soul diligently, lest thou forget the things which thine eyes have seen, and lest they depart from thy heart all the days of thy life; but teach them thy sons, and thy sons' sons. . . . And I will make them hear my words, that they may learn to fear me all the days that they shall live upon the earth, and that they may teach their children.

Deuteronomy 4:9-10

From beginning to end, the Bible depicts fathers as teachers of their children and guardians of the family's spiritual riches. The father was one who loved his children (Genesis 37:4), but sometimes had to rebuke them (Genesis 34:30). He also instructed them (Proverbs 1:8), guided them (Jeremiah 3:4), exhorted and comforted them (I Thessalonians 2:11), and tried to give them a proper upbringing (Ephesians 6:4).

A father might also be tenderly familiar with his children, as in Jesus' Parable of the Importunate Friend. The father says to the friend: "Trouble me not: the door is now shut, and my children are with me in bed; I cannot rise . . ." (Luke 11:7).

Hebrew fathers, like fathers everywhere, delighted in their sons, but also disciplined them (Proverbs 3:12) and controlled them (I Timothy 3:12). Fathers pitied their children's sufferings (Psalm 103:13) and grieved over their children's folly (Proverbs 17:25).

A father was one who could be depended upon to deal honorably with his children, and never cheat them, but always give them the best gifts in his possession (Matthew 7:11) and provide for them (II Corinthians 12:14).

Paul likened himself to a good father, "for you know how, like a father with his children, we exhorted each one of you and encouraged you and charged you to lead a life worthy of God, who calls you into his own kingdom and glory" (I Thessalonians 2:11-12, RSV).

## 3. THE TESTING OF A FATHER'S FAITH (Genesis 22)

No father of a beloved son ever felt called upon to make a greater sacrifice than that of Abraham. He believed that Isaac, his son of promise, must be offered up as a burnt offering to God. This was the utmost price Abraham could pay for his faith. If Abraham questioned why such a sacrifice was required of him, no word of his doubt is recorded, but heartbreaking heaviness and a mood of sorrowful reluctance mark his preparations.

And Abraham rose up early in the morning, and saddled his ass, and took two of his young men with him, and Isaac his son, and clave the wood for the burnt offering, and rose up, and went unto the place of which God had told him.

Genesis 22:3

After a three-day journey the sad little caravan approached its destination. Desiring to be alone with his son, Abraham took Isaac and trudged on ahead with him. The aged father carried the knife and a vessel containing live coals to kindle a fire, while on Isaac's young shoulders was placed the heaviest burden—wood for the fire.

Isaac was troubled by their preparations, for he thought his father had forgotten the chief part of the sacrifice. "My father!" he cried.

"Here am I, my son" (22:7), replied Abraham, though the encouraging words of a father must have torn his heart.

Pointing to the wood and the live coals, Isaac said, "Behold the fire and the wood, but where is the lamb for a burnt offering?" (22:7).

"My son," declared Abraham in a comforting manner which belied his true feelings, "God will provide himself a lamb for a burnt offering" (22:8). Having said the words, Abraham's own faith in God's providence strengthened.

Yet no word came from God, so in utter obedience to what he believed to be God's will, Abraham prepared to sacrifice his son. Just as he raised his knife, an angel called his name and said, "Lay not thine hand upon the lad, neither do thou anything unto him, for now I know that thou fearest God, seeing thou hast not withheld thy son, thine only son from me" (22:12).

In that moment God revealed a new aspect of His nature to Abraham. Though his obedience was pleasing to God, in this instance his concept of God's will was false. Primitive men placated their gods with such human sacrifices as Abraham was prepared to make, but the Lord God revealed his abhorrence of these sacrifices and forbade the father to lay violent hands on his son.

At the angel's words Abraham looked up. Behind him in the thicket he saw a ram caught by its horns. Here was a fitting sacrifice for him to offer upon the altar.

For sheer beauty of expression and for a perfect example of a father's love for God and a son's love for his father, there is a no more inspiring incident of faith in all literature. As James put it so well in his epistle:

Was not Abraham our father justified by works, when he had offered Isaac his son upon the altar? Seest thou how faith wrought with his works, and by works was faith made perfect? And the scripture was fulfilled which saith, Abraham believed God, and it was imputed unto him for righteousness; and he was called the Friend of God.

James 2:21-23

## 4. PRAYER FOR GOD'S GUIDANCE IN THE TRAINING OF A CHILD (Judges 13)

Manoah and his wife were a godly couple living in Israel during the period of the "judges." One day an angel of the Lord appeared to Manoah's childless wife with the good news that she would bear a son and "he shall begin to deliver Israel out of the hands of the Philistines" (13:5).

Both as prospective parents and as loyal members of Israel, Manoah and his wife rejoiced at the angel's message. Awed by the role of a father that would soon be his and resolved to carry out his responsibility of training his son of promise, Manoah prayed: "O my Lord, let the man of God which thou didst send come again unto us and teach us what we shall do unto the child that shall be born" (13:8).

When the angel appeared again to Manoah's wife she was sitting alone in the field, but she ran to fetch her husband. Earnestly desiring to know what was to be their son's manner of life and how he was to be trained for it, Manoah asked the angel, "How shall we order the child and how shall we do unto him?" (13:12).

The angel instructed them to bring up their son in the austere ways of a consecrated Nazarite set apart and dedicated to the Lord's service. "And the woman bare a son and called his name Samson. And the child grew and the Lord blessed him" (13:24).

Though Samson's later career failed to match the bright promise of his youthful training by his godly parents, he became one of Israel's favorite heroes in the struggle against the Philistines.


## 5. "HE RESTRAINED THEM NOT" (I Samuel 2-4)

During Samuel's childhood training in the sanctuary at Shiloh, where the Ark of the Covenant was kept, the chief priest was venerable Eli. Though Eli was wise and consecrated as a teacher of young Samuel, as a father he was a failure. His two sons, Hophni and Phinehas, were also priests, but they were unworthy of their holy calling, using it to get special favors for themselves. When animals were sacrificed at the altar, they seized more than their priestly share of the meat and they put their greed ahead of God's service, for they demanded the choicest cuts before the whole sacrifice had been offered to God.

A messenger from God rebuked old Eli, saying, "[Thou] honourest thy sons above me, to make yourselves fat with the chiefest of all the offerings of Israel my people" (2:29).

Eli tried to reprimand his evil sons, but to no avail. Long ago he had failed in his duty as a father, and it was now too late to undo the harm caused by his weak indulgence and lack of discipline.

Now Eli was very old, and heard all that his sons did unto all Israel, and how they lay with the women that assembled at the door of the tabernacle of the congregation. And he said unto them, "Why do ye such things? . . . Nay, my sons, for it is no good report that I hear. Ye make the Lord's people to transgress. . . ." Notwithstanding they hearkened not unto the voice of their father. . . .

I Samuel 2:22-25

One night the Lord, calling to the child Samuel, warned of the punishment that would overtake Eli and his sons: "I will judge his house for ever for the iniquity which he knoweth, because his sons made themselves vile [blasphemed God], and he restrained them not" (3:13).

Eli's irresponsible sons were guardians of the Ark of the Covenant at Shiloh. During the war against the Philistines, Hophni and Phinehas took the sacred chest into combat in a desperate attempt to turn the tide of battle in their favor. Their blind old father, remaining behind at Shiloh, sat beside the road at the city gate where he anxiously awaited news, "for his heart trembled for the ark of God" (4:13). Soon a disheveled messenger arrived to announce a staggering defeat: "Israel is fled before the Philistines, and there hath been also a great slaughter among the people; and thy two sons also, Hophni and Phinehas, are dead; and the ark of God is taken" (4:17).

Hearing this catalogue of disasters, blind Eli "fell from off the seat backward by the side of the gate, and his neck brake, and he died, for he was an old man and heavy" (4:18).

## 6. ANOTHER FATHER WHO FAILED (I Samuel 8:1-3)

It would not have been easy for anyone to succeed Samuel as a judge and prophet in Israel, for this courageous and dedicated man of God inspired and led the people during many years. But Samuel's sons Joel and Abiah were clearly unfit to take his place. Perhaps, because of the many demands upon his attention, Samuel had neglected his sons' training. Had he given them adequate instruction in the demands of high office? Or did Joel and Abiah, as Eli's sons a generation earlier, look upon public office merely as an opportunity for selfish gain?

It seems clear that Samuel, who had been objective in his appraisal of other people, became so blinded by fatherly pride that he failed to perceive what manner of men his two sons really were. Without questioning their honesty, justice, and unselfishness, Samuel very unwisely made them "judges over Israel." But Joel and Abiah "walked not in his ways, but turned aside after lucre, and took bribes, and perverted judgment" (I Samuel 8:3).

## 7. "O ABSALOM, MY SON, MY SON!" (II Samuel 13-19)

King David's heartbroken cry ended the tragic episode of a father's ruined relationship with a beloved but rebellious son. Retiring to his chamber to weep, the sorrowing king cried bitterly, "O my son Absalom, my son, my son Absalom! Would God I had died for thee, O Absalom, my son, my son!" (18:33).

A tragic chain of events, leading to the breakup of David's family, had been set in motion when David's eldest son Amnon wronged his beautiful half-sister Tamar. Her own brother Absalom was first to learn of the outrage, and his hatred of his half-brother Amnon soon turned to a burning desire for revenge.

If, at this point, David had punished Amnon, the royal family might not have been split asunder so disastrously. But David, though "very wroth" with Amnon, did nothing. He was as tragically unable to discipline his own children as Eli and Samuel had been before him.

Because David failed to act, his son took justice into his own hands. Absalom ordered his servants to murder his half-brother Amnon while he himself fled to his grandfather, the king of Geshur, with whom he remained in exile for three years. David was as unable to punish Absalom as he had been to punish Amnon, and finally allowed his son to return from exile. He refused, however, to forgive him or restore him to his position as a royal prince.

Angered at this treatment, Absalom began to plot rebellion against his own father. The ambitious son "stole the hearts of the men of Israel" (15:6), sent spies through the kingdom, raised a revolutionary army, and occupied Jerusalem, thus forcing David to flee from his royal city. The final showdown took place in a battle in the forest of Ephraim.

Before the battle David, with tragic pathos, charged his generals: "Deal gently for my sake with the young man, even with Absalom" (18:5). But David's commanders knew that a rebellion could not be successfully crushed if its leaders were not destroyed. Accordingly, when Absalom, riding upon his mule, caught his head in the thick branches of an oak tree, one of David's generals thrust three darts through the rebellious son's heart.

A messenger from the battlefield announced that David's army had won a great victory, but David's only concern was for his son.

"Is the young man Absalom safe?" (18:32), he asked. On learning of his death, David uttered his heartbroken cry of mourning in which grief was mixed with self-reproach for his tragic failure as a father.

## 8. A FATHER'S INIQUITY OR HIS SON'S RESPONSIBILITY
### (Ezekiel 18)

The truth, so clearly apparent in the stories of Eli, Samuel, and David, that a father's sins and failures damage his son's life, was recognized in early times by the people of Israel. It was proclaimed that "the iniquity of the fathers" shall be visited "upon the children, and upon the children's children, unto the third and to the fourth generation" (Exodus 34:7).

Weeping at the downfall of Jerusalem, a prophet exclaimed, "Our fathers have sinned, and are not; and we have borne their iniquities" (Lamentations 5:7). The decisive effects of heredity, environment, and early training upon the life of a child can hardly be overstressed.

Yet Ezekiel, the visionary prophet of the Exile, thought that men were failing to shoulder responsibility for their own acts. He declared that Israel placed too much stress on the old adage, "The fathers have eaten sour grapes, and the children's teeth are set on edge" (18:2).

Ezekiel asked why God should punish a son for his father's iniquities. Unless the son followed in his father's evil footsteps, Ezekiel was sure that God would not punish him. On the other hand, a good father cannot pile up merit for his son. God rewards each man according to his individual merits. "The soul that sinneth, it shall die," said Ezekiel, but the man who "hath walked in my statutes, and hath kept my judgments, to deal truly, he is just, he shall surely live. . . . Therefore I will judge you, O house of Israel, every one according to his ways, saith the Lord God. Repent, and turn yourselves from all your transgressions, so iniquity shall not be your ruin" (18:4, 9, 30).

Ezekiel's message contained comforting words for the individual men and women of Israel:

"Behold, all souls are mine. . . . Cast away from you all your transgressions . . . and make you a new heart and a new spirit, for why will ye die, O house of Israel? For I have no pleasure in the death of him that dieth," saith the Lord God. "Wherefore turn yourselves and live ye."
                                                            Ezekiel 18:4, 31-32

## 9. GOD THE FATHER

Countless Hebrew fathers used their dominant position in the family for the good of their children. Of many a father it could be said, "The just man walketh in his integrity; his children are blessed after him" (Proverbs 20:7). Though, as we have seen, a few fathers were conspicuous failures, many, many others must have been wise, kind, and loving toward their sons and daughters, for the idea of fatherhood became, at its best, a concept worthy of being used for God Himself.

One of the outstanding Hebrew prophets spoke these words for God: "When Israel was a child, then I loved him, and called my son out of Egypt" (Hosea 11:1). In the Law it was written, "O foolish people and unwise, is not he thy father that hath bought [created] thee? Hath he not made thee and established thee?" (Deuteronomy 32:6).

The faith that God was the Father of Israel applied, at first, only to the whole people, rather than to individuals. But Ezekiel and other prophets began to reveal God's fatherlike relation to individuals. Finally, in later Hebrew literature God is addressed as the Father of a person: "O Lord, Father and Ruler of my life" (Sirach [Ecclesiasticus] 23:1, RSV).

From His great heritage of Hebrew faith, Jesus chose the profound idea of God's Fatherhood in which to anchor His teachings. The prayer He taught the disciples begins with the familiar address, "Our Father, who art in heaven." In Gethsemane Jesus used the intimate term for father, "Abba," in His anguished prayer to God (Mark 14:36).

Jesus Himself bridged the great gulf between the littleness of men and the awful holiness and majesty of God, so that the apostles could proclaim, "But as many as received him, to them gave he power to become the sons of God" (John 1:12).

Finally, Paul in one of his letters voiced the ancient faith inherited by Christians when he proclaimed, " 'I will receive you, and will be a Father unto you, and ye shall be my sons and daughters,' saith the Lord Almighty" (II Corinthians 6:17-18). Again Paul spoke of "God, even our Father, which hath loved us, and hath given us everlasting consolation and good hope through grace" (II Thessalonians 2:16).

CHAPTER 9

# The Mother's Role

---

Her children shall rise up and call her blessed.
Proverbs 31:28

---

\*

## 1. HONOR FOR MOTHERHOOD

The mother of sons was Israel's most honored woman, as the stories of the pariarchs amply demonstrate. God's promise to Sarah, "Yea, I will bless her and she shall be a mother of nations . . ." (Genesis 17:16), gave Abraham's wife hope during the years of her barrenness. The promise focused attention on a wife's chief duty—that of giving her husband children.

In Hebrew homes there was rejoicing at the birth of the first child, especially a son, for childlessness was looked upon as an affliction. Jacob's wife Leah happily exclaimed at the birth of her eldest son, Reuben, "Surely the Lord hath looked upon my affliction; now therefore my husband will love me" (Genesis 29:32). A husband's respect and affection for his wife increased when she bore him the son every Israelite so greatly desired.

Leah's lovely sister Rachel grieved at her barrenness and in her despair uttered the pathetic plea, "Give me children, or else I die" (Genesis 30:1). What seemed to her a disgrace was removed when her prayer was answered.

And God remembered Rachel, and God hearkened to her, and opened her womb. And she conceived and bare a son, and said, "God hath taken away my reproach." And she called his name Joseph.

Genesis 30:22-24

## 2. MOTHERHOOD IN ITS SENSE OF WONDER

From earliest times a sense of wonder filled the heart of a mother when she looked into the face of her new-born child. Every mother, says Bishop Fulton J. Sheen in his book *The First Love,* is "the bearer of life that comes from God." She is "to humanity the bearer of the Divine . . . when she gives birth to a child, for the soul of every child is infused by God. She thus becomes a co-worker with Divinity; she bears what God alone can give" (p. 80).

The sense of wonder deepened for many a Hebrew maiden as she meditated on the prophecy, "Behold, a virgin shall conceive and bear a son, and shall call his name Immanuel" (Isaiah 7:14). Would her son be the one destined to bear this name meaning "God is with us"? When the prophecy was interpreted as a reference to the coming Savior who would deliver his people (Matthew 1:22-23), motherhood became a holier calling, for every maiden might then look forward to being the mother of the Messiah.

## 3. MOTHERS AND FATHERS EQUALLY ESTEEMED

Beginning with the Ten Commandments, the Law clearly required children to pay the same respect and honor to both parents. "Honor thy father and thy mother, that thy days may be long upon the land which the Lord thy God giveth thee" (Exodus 20:12).

A mother's status in this commandment is higher than in any other legal system of antiquity. In one sentence of the Law the mother is actually mentioned before the father, "Ye shall fear [revere] every man his mother and his father" (Leviticus 19:3).

As the years went by, the old laws enjoining equal honor for mothers and fathers continued in force. Gathering up the wisdom of the past in regard to filial respect, the Book of Proverbs, compiled in the fifth century B.C. or later, offered advice to young people. The teachings of mothers and fathers were to be equally heeded, "My son, hear the instruction of thy father, and forsake not the law [teaching] of thy mother" (Proverbs 1:8).

Violence offered to either parent was condemned, "He that wasteth [does violence] to his father, and chaseth away his mother, is a son that causeth shame, and bringeth reproach" (Proverbs 19:26).

Proverbs added a note of gruesome warning to its teaching concerning filial respect:

> The eye that mocketh at his father,
>   and despiseth [scorns] to obey his mother,
> the ravens of the valley shall pick it out,
>   and the young eagles shall eat it.
>
> Proverbs 30:17

Neither the Law nor any dire warning, but deep human love and tender regard for a mother in her old age inspired this verse, "Hearken unto thy father that begat thee, and despise not thy mother when she is old" (Proverbs 23:22).

Finally, in an apocryphal book of wisdom, written about 180 B.C., mothers are joyfully and lovingly extolled:

> Whoever honors his father atones for sins,
>   and whoever glorifies his mother
>     is like one who lays up treasure.
>
> Sirach [Ecclesiasticus] 3:3-4,RSV

Commenting on the high position of mothers within Judaism, Frank Kobler in his book, *Her Children Call Her Blessed,* says:

Judaism is as unique in its provision for the honoring of the mother as it is in investing her with superior qualities. By including the honoring of the mother in the fifth commandment . . . and by placing the latter behind the hallowing of the Sabbath and the preceding most sacred imperatives, Judaism has raised the mother to high rank as has no other religion (p. 2).

4. "AND HIS MOTHER WAS" (I and II Kings; I and II
   Chronicles)

In naming the rulers of Judah, southern kingdom of the divided monarchy (922-587 B.C.), the phrase above appears again and again. In tracing the lives of its many rulers, including the one ruling queen Athaliah, the Chronicler places much stress upon the character of the mothers of these rulers.

Of seven, it is written that they did "good or right in the sight of the Lord." These kings and their mothers are: Azubah, mother of King Asa; Zibiah, mother of king Jehoash; Jehoaddan, mother of King Amaziah, who started well but ended badly; Jecoliah, mother of King Uzziah (Azariah) ; Jerusha, mother of King Jotham; Abi, mother of King Hezekiah, and Jedidah, mother of King Josiah.

Of eight, it is written they did "evil in the sight of the Lord." These eight kings and their queen mothers as listed in juxtaposition to their sons are: Naamah, mother of King Rehoboam; Maachah (Miciah), mother of King Abijah; Athaliah, also a queen and mother of King Ahaziah; Heph-zibah, mother of King Manasseh; Hamutal, mother of two kings, Jehoahaz II and Zedekiah; Zebudah, mother of King Jehoiakim; and Nehusta, mother of King Jehoiachin, who with his mother became a captive in Babylon when King Nebuchadnezzar of Babylon took over Jerusalem. It is significant that before the kingdom of Judah fell to Babylonia these last three queen mothers and their reigning king-sons are listed as being "evil in the sight of the Lord."

Some decades before the fall of the monarchy, two mothers, Jezebel, wife of King Ahab in the northern kingdom, and her daughter, Queen Athaliah in the southern kingdom, helped to set in motion the destruction of the monarchy. Jezebel, though not the ruling head, was a domineering, self-willed, determined, immensely energetic woman, who ruled through her husband Ahab. She was a worshiper of the false gods Melkart and Asherah of her native Sidonia, and promoted the worship of these gods in her husband's kingdom. She cut off the prophets of Yahweh, attacked Yahweh's places of worship, and had His altar thrown down. Her evil influence as a mother was felt first through her eldest son Ahaziah in the northern kingdom and her daughter Athaliah in the southern kingdom.

Athaliah was married to Jehoram, son of the pious Jehoshaphat, but as the ruling head she carried on in the domineering, wicked influences of her mother. Her evil influence as a mother and as a queen spread far and wide. Of her son, another Ahaziah, it is recorded that he "walked in the ways of the house of Ahab: for his mother was his counsellor to do wickedly" (II Chronicles 22:3). Finally, of her it is said:

For the sons of Athaliah, that wicked woman, had broken up the house of God: and also all the dedicated things of the house of the Lord did they bestow upon Baalim.

II Chronicles 24:7

Of Jerusha, one of the good mothers, it is recorded that her son Jotham built "the high gate at the house of the Lord" and became mighty, because she had "prepared his ways before the Lord his God" (II Chronicles 27:6).

Greater stress is laid upon the character of the mothers of men, especially the men in power, in Kings and Chronicles than in any other part of the Bible. Was the Chronicler, as he analyzed so well the character of the mothers of the kings of Judah, trying to stress that a nation's rise or fall may be determined by its mothers? Does the Chronicler seem to say to us that if you would sway the world in the direction of good, you must begin with its mothers?

## 5. TRIBUTES TO MOTHERHOOD

Literature's unequaled portrait of a mother and her service to her household appears in the last chapter of Proverbs. This mother typifies the God-loving mothers of Israel, whose godliness, chastity, charity, diligence, efficiency, and earnestness have influenced all God-loving mothers in later history.

> She seeketh wool, and flax,
>     and worketh willingly with her hands.
> She is like the merchants' ships;
>     she bringth her food from afar.
> She riseth also while it is yet night,
>     and giveth meat to her household,
>     and a portion to her maidens.
> She considereth a field, and buyeth it;
>     with the fruit of her hands she planteth a vineyard.
> She girdeth her loins with strength,
>     and strengtheneth her arms.
> She perceiveth that her merchandise is good:
>     her candle goeth not out by night.
> She layeth her hands to the spindle,
>     and her hands hold the distaff.
> She stretcheth out her hand to the poor;
>     yea, she reacheth forth her hands to the needy.
> She is not afraid of the snow for her household:
>     for all her *household* are clothed with scarlet. . . .
> She looketh well to the ways of her *household*,
>     and eateth not the bread of idleness.
>
>                         Proverbs 31:13-21, 27

The Bible's eulogy to a mother goes far beyond her service of bearing, preserving, and educating her children. She comforts them with her love all the years of her life.

Isaiah gives another eulogy to a mother's spiritual role when he draws the analogy of one "whom his mother comforteth, so will I comfort you" (66:13).

Here the prophet, in conveying the unfailing certainty and infinite degree of divine love, compares it with the highest manifestation of love in the realm of the finite, a mother's love for her child.

The Psalmist pays beautiful tribute to motherhood when he depicts deepest grief as that of "one that mourneth for his mother" (35:14). This is best illustrated in Isaac's poignant grief at the death of his mother Sarah. It appears that he might have delayed his marriage to Rebekah because of this grief. When he finally took Rebekah into his mother's tent on their wedding night, "Isaac was comforted after his mother's death" (Genesis 24:67).

## 6. OLD TESTAMENT MOTHERS

As the story of family living in the Bible has unfolded, references have already been made to some of the most notable mothers, but we shall refer to several of these again here, as well as others who will be mentioned later, in order to point out the varied roles played by Bible mothers.

Rebekah, the wife of the second patriarch, Isaac, promoted the flight of her son Jacob from Canaan back to her homeland of Mesopotamia. Where else could she send her son for safety but back to her own people? As a mother she seemed to perceive that her other son Esau was weak and vacillating but that Jacob had qualities of greatness that would enable him to carry on the family blessing and birthright. She did not always exhibit admirable qualities as a mother, especially when she promoted Jacob's deceit of his blind and ailing father Isaac, but she made possible Jacob's preparation for his role as one of the great patriarchs of Israel.

A beloved mother often inspired the people of Israel for centuries. So it was with Jacob's wife Rachel, mother of Joseph and Benjamin, who died and was buried at Bethlehem after the birth of Benjamin. As Jeremiah contemplated the desperate plight of the Northern exiles in Babylonia centuries later, he wrote:

A voice was heard in Ramah, lamentation; and bitter weeping; Rachel
weeping for her children refused to be comforted for her children,
because they were not.

Jeremiah 31:15

Deborah's highest title was "a mother in Israel" (Judges 5:7).
Her motherly function transcended the limits of her own home, so
that in her love for her people, which was akin to her love for her
children, she protected Israel and trained its people in the direction
of greatness.

When the Canaanite general Sisera rode off in his chariot to battle,
his devoted mother suffered keen anxiety on his behalf. She was
doomed to grieve for the death of her warrior son (Judges 5:28-30).

Throughout his long, turbulent career as a judge and prophet,
Samuel must always have remembered with gratitude and tender
affection his mother Hannah, who had prayed so earnestly for his
birth. The little coat she brought to him each year while he was a lad
serving in the sanctuary at Shiloh was to him a symbol of her motherly love (I Samuel 2:19). Hannah, so often called the prayerful
mother, influenced Samuel's whole life. Fleming James, in his *Personalities of the Old Testament*, says: "It is indeed likely that he
[Samuel] brought to Shiloh from his early home a deep sense of
God's being and character which would be fostered by his mother's
yearly visits. He was thus prepared to take his part in the ministry of
the temple and to be educated as one of its priests" (p. 82).

Rizpah, the sorrowing mother who guarded the dead bodies of
her sons during a long summer, is a tragic example of a mother's
enduring love. Her terrifying vigil showed the depth of her devotion to her children as well as the greatness of her indomitable character. Even her enemy King David, moved to compassion because of
her heroic endurance, finally gave her sons decent burial in their
family grave (II Samuel 21:8-14).

Solomon owed his throne to his mother Bath-sheba, who successfully pleaded with her dying husband David to make Solomon his
heir. After Solomon succeeded his father, he acknowledged his indebtedness to his mother by treating her with unusual honor, giving
her the seat of authority at his right hand (I Kings 1:15-21; 2:19).

When the prophet Elijah met the starving widow of Zarephath,
she was preparing to cook her last meal. Though she had only a
handful of grain left in her jar and a few drops of oil in her cruse,

like any mother, she planned to share even this tiny remaining portion of food with her son. Thanks, however, to Elijah, the jar of meal and the cruse of oil belonging to the widow of Zarephath never failed while the famine lasted (I Kings 17:10-16).

The mother from Tekoah (II Samuel 14:1-20) possessed three distinctive qualities: eloquence, tact, wisdom. At the request of Joab, commander of David's army, she came from her home in Tekoah to Jerusalem to see David. David had banished his son Absalom three years earlier when he murdered his brother Amnon for violating the honor of his sister, Tamar, full sister of Absalom and half-sister of Amnon, a tragedy mentioned earlier. And yet "the soul of David longed to go forth unto Absalom" (II Samuel 13:39).

This mother from Tekoah, feigning a story of her two sons, made one of the most dramatic appeals in the Bible:

"Help, O king." And the king said to her, "What is your trouble?" She answered, "Alas, I am a widow; my husband is dead. And your handmaid had two sons, and they quarreled with one another in the field; there was no one to part them, and one struck the other and killed him. And now the whole family has risen against your handmaid, and they say, 'Give up the man who struck his brother, that we may kill him for the life of his brother whom he slew'; and so they would destroy the heir also."

II Samuel 14:4-7, RSV

Though King David pardoned her son, this mother from Tekoah continued her eloquent plea for David to bring his son Absalom back to Jerusalem again:

"Pray let your handmaid speak a word to my lord the king. . . . Why then have you planned such a thing against the people of God? For in giving this decision the king convicts himself, inasmuch as the king does not bring his banished one home again. We must all die, we are like water spilt on the ground, which cannot be gathered up again; but God will not take away the life of him who devises means not to keep his banished one an outcast."

II Samuel 14:12-14, RSV

The plea of this unnamed, humble mother from the obscure little village of Tekoah so warmed David's heart that he immediately commanded Joab to bring Absalom back from Geshur to Jerusalem.

This mother had no doubt suffered grievously herself over her sons, and she knew how to appeal to a lonely king, who had tenderly yearned to see his beloved son again.

The unnamed mother of Jabez, whose son was the head of a family of Judah noted for his "honorable character," is honored in the Bible record because she gave to Judah "a son more honourable than his brethren" (I Chronicles 4:9). What more magnificent tribute could be paid to a mother in only a few words?

Summing up Israel's highest experiences of motherhood, the Talmud declared, "The home is the temple of the woman, the education of children her divine service, and the family her congregation."

## 7. NEW TESTAMENT MOTHERS

The wonder and glory of motherhood reach a climax in two stories found in the first chapter of the Gospel of Luke. The first narrates the birth of John the Baptist to Elisabeth and Zacharias. "And thou shalt have joy and gladness, and many shall rejoice at his birth . . . and he shall be filled with the Holy Ghost, even from his mother's womb" (Luke 1:14-15), said the angel to his marvelling father. All the beauty of heaven shines in the second story, which tells the ageless miracle of the coming of Christ, and which is related in detail in a later chapter on the Holy Family.

Salome, mother of James and John, is probably the Bible's most ambitious mother. Although she was not wise in her zealousness when she said to Jesus, "Grant that these my two sons may sit, the one on thy right hand, and the other on the left, in thy kingdom" (Matthew 20:21), at least she had high goals for her sons. Early she must have recognized outstanding qualities in her sons, who later became Jesus' disciples. No other mother furnished two sons to that distinguished group of twelve.

Illuminated with all the glories of motherhood are Mary, wife of Cleophas and mother of the other James and Joses, and another Mary, the mother of John Mark. Both they and their sons labored with and for Jesus. Though their Bible biographies are short, their motherhood is sharply etched by the gospel writers.

The role of faith is best typified by Timothy's mother Eunice, of whom Paul spoke so glowingly (II Timothy 1:5). Spiritual sensitivity is etched in the character of the unnamed mother of Rufus, because

Paul includes her as well as her son in his salutations to the church at Rome (Romans 16:13).

Although there are more than one hundred mothers listed in the Old Testament and only eighteen listed in the New Testament, it was through Mary alone, the mother of Christ, that Christianity shed a new radiance upon a mother's role. And with Christianity came new ideas of moral and religious responsibility for women, and new womanly perfection.

# Children in the Home

Lo, children are an heritage of the Lord,
  and the fruit of the womb is his reward.
As arrows are in the hand of a mighty man,
  so are children of the youth.
Happy is the man that hath
  his quiver full of them.

Psalm 127:3-5

＊

## 1. THE UNBORN CHILD

From the time of his conception, a Hebrew child was rightly regarded as one of God's most wonderful creations. No one knew exactly how the tiny embryo grew. One writer declared, "As thou knowest not . . . how the bones do grow in the womb of her that is with child, even so thou knowest not the works of God who maketh all" (Ecclesiastes 11:5).

The marvelous development of the child in his mother's womb seemed to be an extraordinary manifestation of God's goodness, for which the Psalmist offered his praise:

Thou hast covered me [knit me together] in my mother's womb.
I will praise thee, for I am fearfully and wonderfully made.

Psalm 139:13-14

In a superb dramatic passage an oustanding Hebrew poet expressed his wonder at the miracle of gestation as follows:

Thine hands have made me
    and fashioned me together round about. . . .
Remember, I beseech thee, that thou hast made me as the clay,
    and wilt thou bring me into dust again?
Hast thou not poured me out as milk,
    and curdled me like cheese?
Thou hast clothed me with skin and flesh,
    and hast fenced me with bones and sinews.
Thou hast granted me life and favour,
    and thy visitation hath preserved my spirit.

                                        Job 10:8-12

How or when an unborn child became endowed with the central element of his being, with his soul, no one could say. Some of the transcendent mystery and grandeur is expressed in the old story of Adam's creation when God "breathed into his nostrils the breath of life, and man became a living soul" (Genesis 2:7). The people of Israel firmly believed that the unborn child's body and soul were fused together by the Lord, who "stretcheth forth the heavens, and layeth the foundation of the earth, and formeth the spirit of man within him" (Zechariah 12:1).

Some of the prophets declared that the Lord had ordained them as early as their prenatal period. During this time He prepared them to be His spokesmen. Isaiah explained his call to be a prophet in these words:

The Lord called me from the womb,
    from the body of my mother he named my name.
He made my mouth like a sharp sword,
    in the shadow of his hand he hid me;
he made me a polished arrow,
    in his quiver he hid me away.

                                        Isaiah 49:1-2, RSV

In a similar way Jeremiah expressed his prenatal call and preparation in poetic terms, as follows:

Now the word of the Lord came to me saying,
"Before I formed you in the womb I knew you,
and before you were born I consecrated you;
I appointed you a prophet to the nations."

                                        Jeremiah 1:4-5, RSV

Centuries later Paul voiced a conviction comparable to those of

Jeremiah and Isaiah when he said, ". . . it pleased God, who separated me from my mother's womb, and called me by his grace, to reveal his Son in me, that I might preach him among the heathen . . ." (Galatians 1:15-16).

The unborn child and its mother were afforded special care and protection by a law which stated:

> If men strive, and hurt a woman with child, so that her fruit depart from her, and yet no mischief [no further harm] follow, he shall be surely punished, according as the woman's husband will lay upon him, and he shall pay as the judges determine.

> Exodus 21:22

The need of mothers for tender consideration was present in Jesus' mind when He spoke of a coming cataclysm attended by disorders. Compassionately He sighed, saying, "And alas for those who are with child and for those who give suck in those days!" (Matthew 24:19, RSV).

## 2. CHILDBIRTH

Though Israelite women in Egypt were said to have given birth easily (Exodus 1:19), as do many Bedouin women in Palestine today, the pains of childbirth were a common experience. "Pain, as of a woman in travail" (Psalm 48:6) is mentioned often by the prophets: Isaiah (13:8; 21:3; 26:17), Jeremiah (4:31; 6:24; 13:21; 22:23; 50:43), and Hosea (13:13).

Jesus expressed the feelings of mothers when He said, "A woman when she is in travail hath sorrow, because her hour is come, but as soon as she is delivered of the child, she remembereth no more the anguish, for joy that a man is born into the world" (John 16:21).

Midwives customarily assisted women in childbirth. These are so named in Genesis 35:17; 38:28 and Exodus 1:15-22. Such attendants, as in the story of Ichabod's mother (I Samuel 4:20), were usually the older relatives and friends of the mother.

After a baby was born he was washed, rubbed with salt which was believed to harden him, and wrapped in swaddling clothes, because of a false notion that movement would harm his arms and legs (Ezekiel 16:4). Almost immediately his mother gave him a name expressive of his personality, though sometimes the father named his children (Genesis 35:18).

Seven children seem to have been the average number in the Hebrew family, as in these specified cases: "the barren hath born seven" (I Samuel 2:5) and "she that hath borne seven languisheth" (Jeremiah 15:9). Seven daughters are once mentioned (Exodus 2:16) and seven sons are twice mentioned (Job 1:2 and Job 42:13).

Mothers generally suckled their babies (I Samuel 1:21-23), but a wet nurse was occasionally employed (Exodus 2:7; II Kings 11:2). Isaiah speaks of the tender love of a mother for her nursling: "Can a woman forget her sucking child, that she should not have compassion on the son of her womb?" (Isaiah 49:15).

Birth was sometimes dangerous for mother and child. The Bible records two difficult deliveries in which the mothers died though their babies lived: Rachel (Genesis 35:16-20) and the unnamed mother of Ichabod, already cited. Premature births are mentioned (Job 3:16, Psalm 58:8, Ecclesiastes 6:3). The death of an infant from accidental suffocation occurred during Solomon's reign (I Kings 3:19).

For forty days after a son's birth and fifty days after a daughter's, a mother was considered ceremonially unclean. Before taking up her normal life again, she offered a sacrifice in the ritual of purification (Leviticus 12:2-8). Faithful to the old laws, Mary went up to Jerusalem forty days after the birth of Jesus to offer her sacrifice (Luke 2:22-24).

## 3. INFANCY

Sons were circumcised on the eighth day after birth (Leviticus 12:3), the day on which, in New Testament times, a boy was given his name (Luke 1:59-63; 2:21).

A touching sentence indicates that Hebrew children, like children everywhere, were helped and encouraged by their parents to take their first steps: "I taught Ephraim also to go [walk], taking them by their arms" (Hosea 11:3).

When a child was weaned at the age of two or three, the family often celebrated the event with a feast, as did Abraham when Isaac was weaned (Genesis 21:8).

Though most children were brought up by their parents, royal children were placed in the care of nurses and tutors. Jonathan's five-year-old son, Mephibosheth, was in his nurse's care when news came of the deaths of his grandfather King Saul and his father

Jonathan. Fearful for the little prince's safety, his nurse grabbed him up and fled. But in her haste to escape with her royal charge, she let Mephibosheth fall, thus making him lame for life (II Samuel 4:4).

Ahab's "seventy sons," a number which included the king's own children as well as those belonging to the royal family, were in the care of the "bringers up of the children" (II Kings 10:5). The youngest children had nurses (II Kings 11:2).

## 4. TENDERNESS TOWARD CHILDREN

Children were spoken of with warmth and feeling. The tender relationship between mother and nursing child is mentioned in the Psalmist's phrase, "like a child quieted at its mother's breast" (Psalm 131:2, RSV).

The following verse gives an intimate glimpse of a mother lovingly playing with her child: ". . . ye shall be borne upon her sides [carried upon her hip] and be dandled upon her knees" (Isaiah 66:12).

Looking forward to the birth of an ideal king, the Messiah, Isaiah exulted, "For unto us a child is born, unto us a son is given, and the government shall be upon his shoulder . . ." (Isaiah 9:6). The prophet described the reign of the ideal king as a time when even a defenseless child would be safe:

> The wolf also shall dwell with the lamb,
>   and the leopard shall lie down with the kid;
> and the calf and the young lion and the fatling together,
>   and a little child shall lead them. . . .
> And the sucking child shall play on the hole of the asp,
>   and the weaned child shall put his hand on the
>     cockatrice's den.
> They shall not hurt nor destroy
>   in all my holy mountain;
> for the earth shall be full of the knowledge of the Lord,
>   as the waters cover the sea.
>
>                                   Isaiah 11:6-9

No one in the Bible treated children with such tenderness as Jesus, nor drew such profound meaning from childhood. On one occasion "he took a child and set him in the midst of them, and when he had taken him in his arms, he said unto them, 'Whosoever shall receive one of such children in my name, receiveth me' " (Mark 9:36-37).

Later, when His disciples tried to prevent some parents from bringing their children to Jesus for His blessing, He said, " 'Suffer the little children to come unto me, and forbid them not, for of such is the kingdom of God. Verily, I say unto you, Whosoever shall not receive the kingdom of God as a little child, he shall not enter therein.' And he took them up in his arms, put his hands upon them, and blessed them" (Mark 10:14-16).

## 5. CHILDHOOD TRAINING

Parents heeded the admonition, "Train up a child in the way he should go, and when he is old, he will not depart from it" (Proverbs 22:6). As we shall see later in the chapter on family discipline, home training was firm though loving.

Teaching children the faith of their fathers was one of the parents' chief obligations. A command enshrined in one of their oldest traditions stated that each year at the feast of the Passover children were to hear the story of Israel's deliverance from Egypt—a custom still observed by Jews today (Exodus 12:14, 26-27).

The Law also enjoined parents to teach their children the basic principles of their faith, so that each generation would know, obey, and love the Lord their God.

Hear, O Israel: The Lord our God is one Lord. And thou shalt love the Lord thy God with all thine heart, and with all thy soul, and with all thy might. And these words . . . thou shalt teach them diligently unto thy children, and shalt talk of them when thou sittest in thine house, and when thou walkest by the way, and when thou liest down, and when thou risest up. . . . And thou shalt write them upon the posts of thy house and thy gates.

Deuteronomy 6:4-7, 9

Then, as now, children possessed inquiring minds and were eager to know the reasons for their faith.

And when thy son asketh thee in time to come, saying, "What mean the testimonies, and the statutes, and the judgments, which the Lord our God hath commanded you?" Then thou shalt say unto thy son, "We were Pharaoh's bondmen in Egypt, and the Lord brought us out of Egypt with a mighty hand."

Deuteronomy 6:20-21

## 6. WORK AND PLAY

Childhood was short in Israel, for boys and girls at an early age were given tasks and soon shouldered family responsibilities. From childhood, boys helped their fathers with the flocks and herds or worked in fields and vineyards. We have already noted in the chapter on nobility in young manhood that Joseph, Gideon, Saul, David, Elisha, as well as Jesus all worked for their fathers.

The girls were taught the household arts of spinning, weaving, sewing, grinding corn, and baking bread. They were expected to care for younger brothers and sisters and to help with outside chores as well, such as drawing water, watching over the father's flock, and filling the trough for their father's sheep.

The seventh-century prophet Jeremiah pictured children gathering wood while the father lit the fire and the mother kneaded the dough (Jeremiah 7:18). When he wrote of a father plaintively lamenting, "my children are gone forth of me, and they are not: there is none to stretch forth my tent any more, and to set up my curtains" (Jeremiah 10:20), he indicated that children were expected to help set up the tents of nomad families.

Despite the work placed so early upon their young shoulders, little Israelites enjoyed some fun with other boys and girls, for the Bible affords brief glimpses of children at play. In the sixth century B.C. the prophet Zechariah may have heard the narrow streets of Jerusalem ring with shouts of happy children, for he wrote, "And the streets of the city shall be full of boys and girls playing in the streets thereof" (Zechariah 8:5).

In the rubble of biblical cities, archaeologists have found such durable children's toys as whistles, balls, dolls, animals, and models of furniture used perhaps in ancient dollhouses. Such playthings must have gladdened the hearts of children adept at inventing all sorts of games.

With effervescent spirits, undaunted by life's burdens, children abandoned themselves to the joys of dancing and singing, as is seen in this vignette of childhood happiness and high spirits:

> They send forth their little ones like a flock,
> and their children dance.

They take the timbrel and harp,
> and rejoice at the sound of the organ.
>> Job 21:11-12

Children then as now played at being grown-up. In the first century of the Christian era games of weddings and funerals were popular. Jesus must have observed one group of children proposing a game which a second group refused to join, for He referred to this common childhood behavior in the following:

"But whereunto shall I liken this generation? It is like unto children sitting in the markets, and calling unto their fellows, and saying,

> 'We have piped unto you,
>> and ye have not danced;
> we have mourned unto you,
>> and ye have not lamented.' "
>>> Matthew 11:16-17

## 7. REJOICING IN ONE'S CHILDREN

From the time of Eve's exultant cry at the birth of her first son, "I have gotten a man from the Lord" (Genesis 4:1), mothers and fathers have rejoiced in their children. In an outpouring of joy the psalm quoted at the beginning of this chapter declares, "Children are an heritage of the Lord."

The same theme is repeated in a psalm apparently written by a happy man surrounded by his loved ones. Looking around his family circle, he saw his beloved wife and healthy, growing children and in deep contentment he wrote:

> Blessed is every one that feareth the Lord,
>> that walketh in his ways.
> For thou shalt eat the labour of thine hands;
>> happy shalt thou be, and it shall be well with thee.
> Thy wife shall be as a fruitful vine
>> by the sides of thine house;
> thy children like olive plants
>> round about thy table. . . .
> Yea, thou shalt see thy children's children,
>> and peace upon Israel.
>>> Psalm 128:1-3, 6

# CHAPTER II

# The Son of Two Environments

And the name of Amram's wife was Jochebed, the daughter of Levi, . . . and she bare unto Amram Aaron and Moses, and Miriam their sister.

Numbers 26:59

And the child grew, and she brought him unto Pharaoh's daughter, and he became her son. And she called his name Moses: and she said, "Because I drew him out of water."

Exodus 2:10

\*

## 1. MOSES: HIS WORLD AND HIS PLACE IN HISTORY

Moses, who founded the religion and nation of Israel, was the product of two cultures: the Hebrew culture of his mother Jochebed and the Egyptian culture of his foster mother, the pharaoh's daughter. God seemed to have been preparing Moses early for his many responsibilities.

For he was to lead the Israelites out of oppression in Egypt. He was to give them their first laws. He was to assist his brother Aaron in the establishment of the first tabernacle. He was to become an orator, poet, prophet, statesman, and general. He would stand out for centuries as the man of ancient history who most influenced history, law, and religion.

Moses was born in a period which represents the greatest oppression in Hebrew history. There is much legend connected with the period, but there is no discounting the fact that Moses' people suffered greatly.

Therefore they did set over them taskmasters to afflict them with their burdens. And they built for Pharaoh treasure cities, Pithom and Raamses. But the more they afflicted them, the more they multiplied and grew. And they were grieved because of the children of Israel. And the Egyptians made the children of Israel to serve with rigour: And they made their lives bitter with hard bondage, in mortar, and in brick, and in all manner of service in the field: all their service, wherein they made them serve, was with rigour.

Exodus 1:11-14

## 2. HIS HEBREW FAMILY

Although the Bible gives only short hints about the months before and after the birth of Moses, the very reliable historian of Jewish antiquities, Josephus, relates that, about the time of Moses' birth, one of the Egyptian seers informed the king that a child was about to arise among the Israelites, one who would crush the power of Egypt and exalt his own nation to great eminence and splendor, if he lived to the years of maturity. This seer's prediction, Josephus tells us, was the reason for the pharaoh's edict to destroy all boy babies.

Josephus also describes Moses' father Amram as one of the nobler Hebrews. When Amram knew that his wife was with child, and the child would be destroyed if it were a boy, he went before God and entreated Him to deliver his people from the misery and oppression they endured. Much of this is substantiated in Hebrews 11:23: "By faith Moses, when he was born, was hid three months of his parents, because they saw he was a proper child; and they were not afraid of the king's commandment."

Josephus relates that Moses was wonderfully tall when only three years old, and was so handsome that even the common people stopped to look at him as they went by.

Both Amram and Jochebed handed down to their children, Aaron, Miriam, and Moses, the priestly tradition of the Levites. Aaron was founder of the Hebrew priesthood, which he served for almost forty years. Miriam led the Israelite women when their faith came alive as they crossed the Sea of Reeds on their departure from Egypt to Canaan.

## 3. HIS BIRTH AND EARLY YEARS

From the moment of his birth Moses, the youngest of Jochebed's and Amram's children, seemed destined to be the greatest of all three. Moses must have inherited his unyielding determination and brilliant resourcefulness from his mother, for Jochebed did not meekly submit to the pharaoh's cruel decree that all boy babies of the Israelites be killed. She seemed to sense that she had given birth to an exceptional child and she was determined to save him from being thrown into the river. How she managed to hush his cries and conceal him from the Egyptian authorities for three months is not told.

At the end of that time, when she could no longer hide him, she boldly resolved to find some way to preserve his life, never dreaming what great consequences hung upon her success. Her expedient was a watertight basket woven from reeds and coated with pitch. To this little ark she entrusted her baby, hiding him among the papyrus stalks growing at the river's edge.

And the daughter of Pharaoh came down to wash herself at the river; and her maidens walked along by the river's side; and when she saw the ark among the flags, she sent her maid to fetch it. And when she had opened it, she saw the child: and, behold, the babe wept. And she had compassion on him, and said, This is one of the Hebrews' children. Then said his sister to Pharaoh's daughter, Shall I go and call to thee a nurse of the Hebrew women, that she may nurse the child for thee? And Pharaoh's daughter said to her, Go. And the maid went and called the child's mother. And Pharaoh's daughter said unto her, Take this child away, and nurse it for me, and I will give thee thy wages. And the woman took the child, and nursed it.

Exodus 2:5-9

The light of God seemed to shine across the child's face. He is called a "goodly child" (Exodus 2:2), an "exceedingly fair child" (Acts 7:20), and a "proper child" (Hebrews 11:23).

Actually Moses was saved from the decree of a powerful monarch by a group of unorganized women. These included, in addition to his mother, sister, and the pharaoh's daughter, a corps of midwives, directed by Shiphrah and Puah (Exodus 1:15).

And he [the king of Egypt] said, When ye do the office of a midwife to the Hebrew women, and see them upon the stools; if it be a son, then ye shall kill him: but if it be a daughter, then she shall live. But the midwives feared God, and did not as the king of Egypt commanded them, but saved the men children alive.

Exodus 1:16-17

The boy grew, and possibly when he was seven, Jochebed "brought him unto Pharaoh's daughter, and he became her son. And she called his name Moses, and she said 'Because I drew him out of the water' " (Exodus 2:10), as explained in the verse at the head of this chapter. Thus Moses' life was spared; his earliest, formative years were spent learning the spiritual heritage of his people from his own brave and resourceful mother. Jochebed indeed accomplished much for her son. But his education and training for leadership came later through the family of his foster mother, the pharaoh's daughter.

## 4. HIS EGYPTIAN FAMILY AND HOME

Who was this pharaoh? Most scholars identify him as Rameses II, the Pharaoh of the Oppression. A few view him as the Pharaoh of the Exodus.

Ramesses II (1301-1234 B.C.) was the most famous of twelve Egyptian pharaohs of that name. He developed the Nile Delta, and he erected some of Egypt's most colossal structures with slave labor. Among some of these buildings were the colonnade at Luxor and its giant pylon, the hypostyle hall at Karnak, and the "Ramesseum," the memorial temple west of Thebes. This same Ramesses II erased the names of his predecessors on older structures and inserted his own. There is evidence of this at the crumbling statue at Memphis. He also probably erected the town Raamses, mentioned in Exodus 1:11.

The pharaoh's daughter would have been a lineal heir to the crown but was debarred by her sex. However, she would retain the right to the crown for her adopted son Moses. He could not supplant the reigning pharaoh, but he would have superseded his sons.

Moses spent his youth in the pharaoh's palace, where he was educated as a prince. This gave him the advantages of the highest civilization of this period.

The Old Testament gives no details of his education, but Acts 7:22 confirms that "Moses was learned in all the wisdom of the Egyptians, and was mighty in his words and in deeds."

Much of this phase of his life is legendary. But descriptions, based upon inscriptions on ancient walls and ruins uncovered by excavations, give us more than conjecture upon which to picture this palace. It was located in a cosmopolitan capital on the fringes of the desert, where lived a great many seminomads, quite possibly Moses' own people. Their slave labor might have helped to build the palace quarters where Moses resided as a youth.

It may be conjectured that Moses was educated with children from his royal Egyptian foster family and that he probably obtained a glimpse into the beliefs of his own people through Canaanites employed in the palace.

"Tradition assigns the great Temple of the Sun at On, the chief university of Egypt, as the scene of his education, and if so his experience of Egyptian life in many striking aspects must have been wide, for the population of the temple and its dependencies was well-nigh that of a small town," says Dr. Cunningham Geike in his *Hours of Study with the Bible*.

Shady cloisters opened into lecture-rooms for the students, and quiet houses for the professors and priests, in their many grades and offices. . . . Outside these, but still within the precincts, were the cottages of the temple servants, keepers of the beasts, gate-keepers, litter-bearers, water-carriers, washermen, washer-women, cooks; and the rooms of the pastophoroi who prepared the incense and perfumes. The library and writing chambers had their host of scribes, who all lived in the temple buildings, and there were besides, also as members of this huge population, the officials of the countinghouse, troops of singers, and, last of all, the noisy multitude of the great temple school—the Eton or Harrow of the time —from which Moses would pass upwards to the lectures of the various faculties of the university (Vol. 2, pp. 129, 130).

The library to which Moses could have had access is often mentioned in Egyptian book rolls, and the graves of two of its librarians under Ramesses II are still pointed out at Thebes. These libraries became so famous in the ancient world that Ramesses II bore a special title, that of "Chief of Books."

In his youth, Moses must have witnessed the low morals of the Egyptian court. Ramesses II, it is thought, built a temple to Astarte, goddess of sex and war. In this and other temples of the gods, Ramesses sanctioned sexual excesses of every kind, human sacrifice, and a repulsive cult of serpents.

## 5. HIS RETURN TO HIS OWN PEOPLE

The lowly life of Moses' parents came to have greater attraction for him than the palace of his foster mother, splendid though it was. As he witnessed, too, at first hand the oppression of his own people by the Egyptians, he must have desired at a young age to go forth and lift their burdens. In the palace he no doubt heard his people's groans as they were being beaten, and listened to their murmurs as they toiled for endless hours in the hot sun. As he pondered these sights, something must have flamed in his heart. And so the Bible tells us:

By faith Moses, when he was come to years, refused to be called the son of Pharaoh's daughter; Choosing rather to suffer affliction with the people of God, than to enjoy the pleasures of sin for a season.

Hebrews 11:24-25

Moses, the product of these two widely divergent families from two widely divergent cultures, inherited from his own Hebrew family a love for God, a strong character, a passion for the oppressed, and religious patriotism. From the family of the pharaoh he acquired knowledge and wisdom and the opportunity to train in military skills. God had prepared Moses as the leader of the Exodus, both by birth and by education.

# CHAPTER 12

# Problems Between Parents and Children

And, ye fathers, provoke not your children to wrath, but bring them up in the nurture and admonition of the Lord.

Ephesians 6:4

*

## 1. THEN AS NOW

Sons who disgraced their parents, fathers who failed to train their children wisely, daughters-in-law who made life bitter for their husbands' families, a headstrong daughter who ran into trouble, a son who boldly married a girl against his parents' wishes—all caused problems between parents and children in biblical times. Many of the perplexing situations and broken relationships in the Bible parallel family life today.

The essential difference between the two ages is that the former sought a continuing experience of God. He was their Lord, and the source of their hope and strength. The Israelites were always conscious of their covenant with God. Because He had chosen them to be His people, certain demands were laid upon them. The fulfillment of His promises depended upon the people's obedience. One member of a family might fall from grace, problems such as those common to any family might arise, but the people of Israel constantly turned to God for help.

## 2. SONS WHO DISGRACED THEIR PARENTS

In previous chapters we have already encountered sons who disgraced their parents: Ham, the son of Noah; Jacob, the son of Isaac; Hophni and Phinehas, the sons of Eli; and Joel and Abiah, the sons of Samuel.

Cain, whose story requires no retelling, was the first erring son (Genesis 4:1-5), and probably the worst. The Bible does not reveal his parents' emotions when they learned that their eldest son had murdered his brother and repudiated all family responsibility with the callous remark, "Am I my brother's keeper?"

Undoubtedly Adam and Eve had been proud of their two boys, Abel with his thriving flocks of sheep and Cain with his abundant crops. The progress of their sons helped to blot out bitter remorse for their own early transgression in the Garden of Eden. After failure and punishment Adam and Eve had doggedly gone on to a measure of success. Then came the murder, after which Cain turned into a fugitive and Adam and Eve experienced sorrow and loneliness. Their deepest suffering, however, came from the knowledge that they had trained and reared Cain.

## 3. FRICTION BETWEEN A STEPMOTHER AND A STEPSON
   (Genesis 16, 21:1-21)

As there is no exact word for the relationship between Sarah and Ishmael, they may be roughly described as stepmother and stepson. During the years of Sarah's childlessness she gave her slave woman Hagar to Abraham as his concubine. In that remote period it was customary for a wife to adopt as her own a child born to her maid and her husband, thus providing the family with a legitimate heir.

The arrangement produced intolerable tensions in Abraham's family, for when Hagar knew "that she had conceived, her mistress was despised in her eyes" (16:4).

Family discord, arising from the presence of two rival wives and two sets of children in a single family, reached a crisis after the birth of Isaac to Abraham and Sarah, probably about fourteen years later. When Isaac, Abraham's true heir and son of promise, was about three years old, a family feast was held to celebrate his weaning. Ishmael, who until Isaac's birth had been Abraham's only heir, was now supplanted by his half-brother. The situation was fraught with potential trouble.

At the feast, "Sarah saw the son of Hagar the Egyptian, which she had born unto Abraham, mocking" (21:9). As several modern translations, including the Revised Standard Version and Moffatt, substitute "playing with her son Isaac" for "mocking," it is hard to say whether Ishmael was ridiculing his half-brother or merely having fun with the child. A tradition preserved in Galatians 4:28-29 indicates that Ishmael "persecuted " Isaac. The elder boy's scorn and continual annoyance might well have proved to be an evil influence in the family.

One thing is certain. At the feast Sarah, seeing the two boys together, became fearful lest Hagar's son, as the elder of the two, usurp her son's rightful position as Abraham's heir. Sarah determined to fight for Isaac's rights and demanded of her husband that he "Cast out this bondwoman and her son, for the son of this bondwoman shall not be heir with my son, even with Isaac" (21:10).

There were undoubtedly good reasons for her concern for Isaac's rights, for Abraham clearly loved his elder son, Ishmael, and might well have accorded him a high position in the family. The Bible says that Sarah's demand "was very grievous in Abraham's sight because of his son" (21:11).

Continuing friction caused by basic jealousy and hatred between his two wives bid fair to bring Sarah and her son into a bitter struggle against Hagar and Ishmael, to the complete disruption of Abraham's home. In his unhappy predicament, Abraham received divine guidance:

"Let it not be grievous in thy sight because of the lad [Ishmael], and because of thy bondwoman. In all that Sarah hath said unto thee, hearken unto her voice, for in Isaac shall thy seed be called. And also of the son of the bondwoman will I make a nation, because he is thy seed."

                                                Genesis 21:12-13

The pathetic story of Hagar and Ishmael's expulsion from Abraham's home ends on a happy note, for the slave woman and her son learned to trust in God in their extremity. "And God was with the lad, and he grew, and dwelt in the wilderness, and became an archer" (21:20). Family divisions evidently were later healed, for it is reported that "his sons Isaac and Ishmael buried him [their father] in the cave of Machpelah" (Genesis 25:9).

## 4. ALIEN DAUGHTERS-IN-LAW A BITTER
## DISAPPOINTMENT

During the patriarchal era, nomadic families lived in such tightly knit tribal groups that the strength and solidarity of the clan were of paramount importance. Young men, following the example of Isaac and Jacob, were encouraged to choose their brides from within the clan, in order to preserve the purity of its blood, the strength of its ideals, and its power to prevail over enemies.

Esau, however, had other ideas. As the story of the selling of his birthright makes clear, he was reckless, impulsive, and pleasure loving. When he met two attractive girls named Judith and Bashemath he decided to marry them both. His own desire was his sole consideration, for he did not consult his parents, nor stop to consider whether or not the girls would make suitable wives for him. Actually, they were a poor choice, for both were Hittite girls with alien ideals and an alien religion, and they were closely connected with the rival group of Hittites living in the neighborhood.

By marrying these Hittite girls, Judith and Bashemath, Esau had disqualified himself. They could not be depended upon to uphold the high ideals of Abraham and Isaac, nor to teach their children to worship Abraham's God. These daughters-in-law became a "grief of mind," or in the words of another translation, "they made life bitter for Isaac and Rebekah" (Genesis 26:35, RSV).

Undoubtedly in her day-to-day contacts with Esau's wives, Rebekah found much to criticize in the unfamiliar customs and strange manners introduced into her household by the Hittite girls. Rebekah's ways, on the other hand, must have seemed equally queer and vexing to Judith and Bashemath. Irritated by the constant friction, Rebekah exclaimed, "These Hittite women tire me to death!" (Genesis 27:46, Moffatt).

Even Esau was troubled by the disharmony in his home, so he decided to marry another wife, of whom his parents would approve. He chose Mahalath, a daughter of Ishmael and hence a granddaughter of Abraham, though not in the legitimate line.

## 5. A HEADSTRONG DAUGHTER (Genesis 34)

Jacob and Leah reared their daughter Dinah very carefully and gave her a sheltered life in the midst of their large clan. Undoubtedly they warned her of the dangers awaiting a young girl who left the protection of her father's encampment to go alone among strangers. But Dinah, curious about the world outside her home and irked by restraint, wanted to venture out alone on an expedition to the neighboring village. She was evidently eager to make new friends, for it is said she "went out to see the daughters of the land" (34:1).

Dinah had eleven brothers, but she did not ask one of them to escort her, nor did she tell her parents where or why she was going, for she must have known they would prevent her had they known her plan. She was a headstrong girl and very unwise.

As Dinah arrived unescorted in a neighboring village, the inhabitants assumed that she was a common harlot, for women of good reputation never went abroad unaccompanied. When Shechem, a young prince of the country, saw her he loved her and seduced her, though, according to the confused and turbulent story, he planned to marry her honorably.

Dinah's brothers, Simeon and Levi, were incensed when they learned how their sister had been treated. They "were grieved and they were very wroth, because he [Shechem] had wrought folly in Israel in lying with Jacob's daughter, which thing ought not to be done" (34:7).

Simeon and Levi took brutal revenge not only against Shechem but against all his people, thus compounding the original wrong and bringing disgrace upon their father. The brothers justified their violent deeds by asking, "Should he deal with our sister as with an harlot?" (34:31). But it was Dinah, who, in leaving home unescorted and thinking only of an exciting day of pleasure in the nearby village, precipitated the evil that brought suffering to innocent people and dishonor to her family.

## 6. A RUDE, RECKLESS SON (Judges 15 and 16)

Samson was born into a God-loving family. The character of his father, Manoah, and his mother, are delineated in Chapter 8. With such a family background, it is hard to believe that Samson could have become so impulsive and wild in his romances. But immediately following the account of his wondrous birth is this story of his first romance:

And Samson went down to Timnath, and saw a woman in Timnath

of the daughters of the Philistines. And he came up, and told his father and his mother, and said, "I have seen a woman in Timnath of the daughters of the Philistines: now therefore get her for me to wife." Then his father and his mother said unto him, "Is there never a woman among the daughters of thy brethren, or among all my people, that thou goest to take a wife of the uncircumcised Philistines?" And Samson said unto his father, "Get her for me; for she pleaseth me well."

Judges 14:1-3

Samson's defiant words, "Get her for me; for she pleaseth me well," ring out as naturally as if he were today's youth talking back to dissenting parents. Against his parents' wishes, Samson, who lived some three thousand years ago, negotiated for his marriage to this Philistine woman. During the feast, at which he and not his parents was the host, Samson proposed a riddle to his guests. He offered a rich reward to whoever could answer the riddle. Unable to solve his puzzle, the guests coaxed and even threatened Samson's betrothed wife, saying, "Entice thy husband, that he may declare unto us the riddle, lest we burn thee and thy father's house" (14:15).

During all seven days of the feast the betrothed bride begged Samson to give her the clue to the riddle. She declared that if he did not tell her his secret, it was proof that he did not love her. Throughout the week she wept continually. Finally, weary of her importunity and irritated beyond measure by her weeping, Samson gave her the answer to his riddle. She thereupon promptly revealed it to their wedding guests, thus enabling them to win the promised reward.

Samson became so angry with his disloyal bride that he left her and returned to his father's house. To save their daughter from disgrace, her parents gave her in marriage to Samson's companion and best man.

Later Samson went to Gaza, the stronghold of the Philistines, "and saw there an harlot and went in unto her" (Judges 16:1). Afterward he went to the Valley of Sorek and fell in love with another Philistine woman, Delilah, and the lords of the Philistines came in unto her and said, "Entice him, and see wherein his great strength lieth" (Judges 16:5).

Samson's romances were his undoing. Had he first listened to his God-loving parents, his life might have taken a different course.

No mention is made of Samson's family following the wedding feast for his Timnath bride, but at Samson's death it is said that "his brethren and all the house of his father came down, and brought him up, and buried him . . . in the burying place of Manoah his father" (Judges 16:31).

## 7. IDEOLOGIES THAT DIVIDED PARENTS AND CHILDREN

In ancient Israel, no less than in today's convulsive world, families were sometimes torn apart by new ideas and new ways of thinking. Usually young people, with their fresh viewpoint and vibrant enthusiasm, adopted new ideologies, while their parents clung to old habits of thought.

Sometimes the new ideologies disrupted the established order of society, as in King Manasseh's notorious reign, about 687 to 642 B.C. (II Kings 21:16). This unhappy period, during which those suspected of treason were spied upon and denounced, even by their own families, may be reflected in the following lament:

> For the son dishonoureth the father,
> the daughter riseth up against her mother,
> the daughter-in-law against her mother-in-law;
> a man's enemies are the men of his own house.
> Micah 7:6

Two centuries later, in the time of the prophet Malachi, many Jewish parents feared that their children would be swept away from the moorings of their ancient faith by the attraction of a new philosophy, perhaps that of the Greeks. In this clash of rival religions and philosophies Malachi looked forward with confidence to a happy time when the prophet Elijah would reappear to "turn the heart of the fathers to the children, and the heart of the children to their fathers . . ." (Malachi 4:6). With this hopeful prophecy of family reconciliation the Old Testament ends.

## 8. A PRODIGAL SON, HIS ELDER BROTHER, AND THEIR FATHER (Luke 15:11-32)

Jesus' beautiful parable of the Prodigal Son is a family story of parent-child relationships, told so tenderly and with such vivid human touches that it has become one of the favorite stories in the Bible. It concerns a loving father of two sons, the younger of whom was self-willed, while the elder was self-righteous.

Irked by the restraints of family living, and longing for freedom to live his own life, the younger son asked his father to give him immediate possession of the one-third of the family estate to which he was entitled. Having received his legal inheritance, the self-confident young man set forth for a distant country in order to get as far from parental direction as he could.

Away from home he spent his patrimony recklessly. "And when he had spent all, there arose a mightly famine in that land, and he began to be in want" (15:14). He was finally reduced to hiring himself out as a swineherd, the most degrading of occupations for a Jew, who considered swine ritually unclean. Lonely, homesick, hungry, deserted by the companions of his spendthrift days of pleasure, and harshly treated by an unsympathetic master, the young man experienced utter despair.

Then "he came to himself" and, facing his life honestly, he realized how foolish he had been to leave his happy home and loving father for the questionable pleasures of "riotous living." He knew what he must do.

I will arise and go to my father, and will say unto him, "Father, I have sinned against heaven and before thee, and am no more worthy to be called thy son. Make me as one of thy hired servants."

Luke 15:18-19

Far in the distance the waiting father saw his son coming home. He had compassion on his boy "and ran, and fell on his neck, and kissed him" (15:20). The repentant youth blurted out his confession. Immediately the forgiving father hastened to restore his contrite son to his rightful place in the family. As the father looked at his boy, he did not see his past sins, but, instead, he noticed the ragged clothes covering his thin body, the weary droop of his shoulders, and the deep lines etched by dissipation and sorrow on his young face.

The father honored his prodigal son by placing around his shoulders the best robe kept for distinguished guests. He put on the young man's finger a family ring and gave him shoes to signify that he was a son, not a barefoot slave. When he ordered the fatted calf, kept for a special celebration, to be served up at the feast, the father explained, "For this my son was dead, and is alive again. He was lost and is found" (15:24).

While the feasting and merrymaking were at their height, the elder brother came in from the fields where he had worked long and diligently since his younger brother's departure. Learning that the music and dancing were in honor of the prodigal's safe return, the elder brother angrily refused to join the party, for he was consumed with jealousy and self-pity.

When his father went out to beg him to enter, he complained bitterly of the way he had been treated. With a self-righteousness as blind as that of the Pharisees of Jesus' day, he declared that *he* had never transgressed, yet his father had never rewarded *him*. Only for a returned profligate son did the father celebrate.

Gently the father reminded his elder son that the whole family estate belonged to him and that the restoration of the prodigal, who was "thy brother," provided sufficient reason for family-wide rejoicing. "It was meet that we should make merry and be glad, for this thy brother was dead, and is alive again, and was lost, and is found" (15:32).

The deepest impression left by this warmly human tale is not so much of a prodigal who finally "came to himself," nor of a self-righteous elder brother who refused to rejoice over his brother and share his family's joy, as it is of a loving, forgiving, patient father who did not wait for his erring son to say "I am sorry," but ran out to meet him.

Did the elder son continue to shut himself out of his father's love, or did he finally join the festivities and thus restore himself to his family circle? The parable ends before every question is answered, but it leaves us with an unforgettable picture of father-son relationships and vivid insight into Jesus' concept of our loving Heavenly Father.

# CHAPTER 13

# Various Other Family Relationships

And Abram said unto Lot, "Let there be no strife, I pray thee, between me and thee, and between my herdmen and thy herdmen, for we be brethren."

Genesis 13:8

*

## 1. BROTHERS AND SISTERS

Children of the same parents are normally bound together by close ties of affection and loyalty and by common memories of happy childhood days when they were surrounded by their parents' love. It is, therefore, with a sense of shock that we read such stories of fratricide as Cain's or Absalom's. We are dismayed to learn that Jacob cheated his brother Esau and that Joseph was sold by his brothers into slavery. These stark tragedies and other biblical stories of friction and bad feeling between brothers, as in the parable of the Prodigal Son, indicate that brotherliness does not automatically accompany blood ties, but is fostered by wise parents and achieved by mutual love and by acts of helpful consideration of brothers and sisters themselves.

Despite a few examples of conflict between brothers and sisters, brotherly love, loyalty, and helpfulness abound in the Bible, for the whole people of Israel were knit together in their families, their tribes, and their nation by a deep sense of unity. The Bible contains unforgettable pictures of the closeness and mutual helpfulness of family ties: Rebekah leaving home on her marriage journey with the blessing of her brother Laban ringing in her ears; Joseph weeping as he revealed his identity to the brothers who had wronged him; Moses' little sister hiding among the reeds near her baby brother's ark to guard him from harm; Aaron "glad in his heart" (Exodus 4:14) to meet his brother and use his eloquence in Moses' cause.

In the New Testament we meet the most famous pairs of brothers whose support of each other added strength to the company of Jesus' disciples. Peter and Andrew were business partners in the fishing industry in Galilee before they were called to become "fishers of men" (Mark 1:17). Zebedee's sons, James and John, were also brother fishermen before they, too, became important followers of Jesus.

The well-known pair, Mary and Martha, were united in their sisterly love for their brother Lazarus and in their common devotion to Jesus. Although their dissimilar temperaments caused some friction between them (Luke 10:38-42), these two sisters jointly welcomed Jesus to their home in Bethany and offered Him much-needed rest and gracious hospitality.

In the kinship of brothers, Jesus found a parallel to the close relationship of His followers. They were all children of the Heavenly Father, for Christ gave them "power to become the sons of God" (John 1:12). Bound closely together in God, they became brothers; as Jesus stated, "all ye are brethren" (Matthew 23:8). Immediately after Jesus' ascension, when His followers numbered only about one hundred and twenty persons, Peter addressed them as "brethren" (Acts 1:15-16), a name often used for Christians in the Acts of the Apostles and in many letters to the early churches. Love like that binding brothers and sisters together became a potent force in the early Church. Paul, counseling the Christians of Thessalonica, wrote:

> But as touching brotherly love ye need not that I write unto you, for ye yourselves are taught of God to love one another.
>
> I Thessalonians 4:9

## 2. ADOPTED CHILDREN

Adoptions within a family were not uncommon in biblical times. Both Rachel and Leah adopted the sons born to their maids and regarded these boys as their own (Genesis 30:3-13).

Jacob adopted his grandsons, Ephraim and Manasseh, sons of Joseph and his Egyptian wife Asenath, giving these two half-Egyptian boys the same status as that of Jacob's own sons (Genesis 48:5).

In a rite of adoption, Naomi placed the child of Ruth and Boaz on her bosom while the neighbors said, "There is a son born to Naomi" (Ruth 4:16-17).

Moses, whose adoption by Pharaoh's daughter is described in Chapter 11, was the most famous adopted child in the Bible.

Finally, there was Mordecai's orphan niece Esther, "whom Mordecai, when her father and mother were dead, took for his own daughter" (Esther 2:7).

## 3. WIDOWS

Unhappy was the lot of a widow in ancient times who, as Ruth and Naomi, had to struggle for a bare livelihood. With young children to support, their difficulties became greater. But the Israelites took pity upon widows as well as upon the fatherless and strangers living in their midst, for they believed that

> The Lord preserveth the strangers,
> he relieveth the fatherless and widow,
> but the way of the wicked he turneth upside down.
> Psalm 146:9

Humane laws in Deuteronomy offered strangers, orphans, and widows some protection and a measure of help, while the prophets exhorted men to "plead for the widow" (Isaiah 1:17) and "oppress not the widow, nor the fatherless, the stranger, nor the poor, and let none of you imagine evil against his brother in your heart" (Zechariah 7:10).

Among the widows in the Bible, besides Naomi, Ruth, and Orpah, are: Tamar who wore mourning (Genesis 38:14); the widow of Zarephath with whom the prophet Elijah stayed during a famine (I Kings 17:10-24); the prophetess Anna who beheld the child Jesus in the Temple (Luke 2:36-38); the widow of Nain whose son Jesus restored to life (Luke 7:11-15); the importunate widow (Luke 18:3, 5), who is mentioned in one of Jesus' parables; and the poor widow whom Jesus saw contributing two small coins to the Temple treasury (Mark 12:41-44).

In the early Church, Christian widows too old and poor to support themselves were given regular assistance (Acts 6:1), while widows in easier circumstances belonged to a group ministering to people in need (Acts 9:39).

## 4. GRANDPARENTS

The promise, "Yea, thou shalt see thy children's children" (Psalm 128:6), gave assurance of a long life, far less common in ancient times than it is today. A father's heart was gladdened by the expectation of seeing his grandchildren in the ongoing march of the generations under the merciful care of the Lord.

Blind old Jacob, though he was dying, "strengthened himself and sat upon the bed" (Genesis 48:2), when his two grandsons, Manasseh and Ephraim, were brought to his bedside for his final blessing. As we have noted above, he adopted as his own these two sons of his beloved Joseph. Jacob was not too old and blind to know to which boy he gave the greater blessing with his right hand, for he "stretched out his right hand, and laid it upon Ephraim's head, who was the younger, and his left hand upon Manasseh's head, guiding his hands wittingly, for Manasseh was the firstborn" (Genesis 48:14). Tenderly Jacob blessed Joseph and his sons with the solemn words:

"God, before whom my fathers Abraham and Isaac did walk, the God which fed me all my life long unto this day, the Angel which redeemed me from all evil, bless the lads. And let my name be named on them, and the name of my fathers Abraham and Isaac, and let them grow into a multitude in the midst of the earth."

Genesis 48:15-16

After much suffering, Job's supreme happiness came at the end of his long life when he "saw his sons, and his son's sons, even four generations" (Job 42:16). There was no keener delight in the evening of life than to rejoice in grandchildren, for "children's children are the crown of old men" (Proverbs 17:6). A grandchild could be, as in the case of Naomi and Ruth's son, "a restorer of thy life and a nourisher of thine old age" (Ruth 4:15).

From the point of view of grandchildren, it was and is a blessing to have a good grandfather, for as a wise saying declared, "A good man leaveth an inheritance to his children's children" (Proverbs 13:22), an inheritance of a respected name and traditions of upright living.

The only woman in the Bible specifically called a grandmother is Lois, whose grandson Timothy was a friend of Paul's and an important leader in the early Church. Lois herself must have been an outstanding woman, for she taught her grandson how to understand the Scriptures. She succeeded in the very delicate undertaking of communicating to a boy much younger than herself her sincere faith. Paul wrote to Timothy:

. . . I call to remembrance the unfeigned faith that is in thee which dwelt first in thy grandmother Lois and thy mother Eunice. . . . And that from a child thou hast known the holy scriptures which are able to make thee wise unto salvation through faith which is in Christ Jesus.

II Timothy 1:5; 3:15

## 5. FATHERS- AND MOTHERS-IN-LAW

The difficult relationship of fathers and mothers with their sons-in-law and daughters-in-law is illustrated by several notable biblical examples. We have already heard Rebekah's cry of irritation concerning her son's Hittite wives: "I am weary of my life because of the daughters of Heth" (Genesis 27:46).

Naomi was a far different kind of mother-in-law, for she was capable of inspiring such love and devotion in Ruth that the young woman could not bear to leave her. "Entreat me not to leave thee," pleaded Ruth, ". . . for whither thou goest, I will go; and where thou lodgest, I will lodge. Thy people shall be my, people, and thy God my God" (Ruth 1:16).

The vivid story of Jethro's visit to his harassed son-in-law Moses is narrated in Exodus 18. Jethro came to the Israelite camp in the wilderness, accompanied by his daughter Zipporah, who was Moses' wife, and Moses' two sons Gershom and Eliezer, who had been in his care while Moses was in Egypt. Moses had successfully led the whole company of Israelites out of Egypt, but Jethro now found him worn out by the great number of disputes brought to him for judgment. After studying Moses' predicament from a fresh viewpoint, Jethro offered a practical suggestion. "So Moses hearkened to the voice of his father-in-law, and . . . chose able men out of all Israel, and made them heads over the people. . . . And they judged the people at all seasons: the hard causes they brought unto Moses, but every small matter they judged themselves" (Exodus 18:24-26). Thus with a father-in-law's help Israel's civil government was established.

The most famous mother-in-law of the New Testament was Peter's, who, as we shall learn in a later chapter, was healed by Jesus one Sabbath day in Capernaum.

## 6. SERVANTS AND SLAVES

Servants, so frequently mentioned in the Bible, were important members of the family group in ancient times. These servants were rarely wage earners, free to come and go as they chose, but slaves, the property of their master, who protected and supported them and for whom they worked. Usually the condition of Hebrew slaves was neither humiliating nor irksome, for frequently a slave held a responsible position in his master's household, as did Eliezer in Abraham's (Genesis 15:2;24) and Joseph in Potiphar's (Genesis 39:1-5).

Besides Eliezer and Joseph, other slaves are mentioned in patriarchal times. Abraham's household included "all the men of his house, born in the house, and bought with money of the stranger" (Genesis 17:27), slaves, in short. Rebekah's nurse may also have been a slave, one of the "damsels" given to Rebekah as part of her dowry when she left home (Genesis 24:61) and mentioned years later, when the aged nurse died, as "Deborah, Rebekah's nurse" (Genesis 35:8).

Roland de Vaux, in his classic book on Old Testament sociology, entitled *Ancient Israel, Its Life And Institutions,* discusses the slave's position in Hebrew families as follows:

In everyday life the lot of a slave depended largely on the character of his master, but it was usually tolerable. In a community which attached such importance to the family, in which work was scarcely conceivable outside the framework of the family, a man on his own was without protection or means of support. The slave was at least assured of the necessities of life. More than that, he really formed part of the family; he was a "domestic" in the original sense of the word. . . . He joined in the family worship, rested on the sabbath (Exodus 20:10; 23:12), shared in the sacrificial meals (Deuteronomy 12:12, 18), and in the celebration of religious feasts . . . (p. 85).

It is noteworthy that family servants are mentioned in the Third Commandment, "Remember the sabbath day, to keep it holy. Six days shalt thou labour and do all thy work, but the seventh day is the sabbath of the Lord thy God. In it thou shalt not do any work, thou, nor thy son, nor thy daughter, nor thy manservant, nor thy maidservant . . ." (Exodus 20:8-10). Family servants are also mentioned as partaking in the great religous festivals with the family (Deuteronomy 16:11, 14).

Humane legislation in the Bible regulated the conditions of slavery and provided that a Hebrew slave was to be freed six years after his purchase (Exodus 21:2).

Job, the man of integrity, who lived according to a very high moral code, did not look upon his servants as "things," but as people with all the rights of human beings. Job's questions are soul-searching:

> If I ever ignored the rightful claim
>     of any servant, man or woman,
> what could I do when God rose up?
>     If he took me to task, what could I say? . . .
> Did not my Maker make my servant too,
>     and form us both alike within the womb?
>                 Job 31:13-15, Moffatt

One of the most charming stories in the Bible is that of the young Hebrew girl who served Naaman's wife. Though this Hebrew maid was a slave girl captured in war, she felt deep concern for her Syrian master who suffered from the dreadful disease of biblical times, leprosy. One day the little maid, remembering the wonder-working prophet of her own country, said to her mistress, "Would God my lord were with the prophet that is in Samaria, for he would recover him of his leprosy" (II Kings 5:3). Immediately acting upon this hopeful advice from his slave girl, Naaman set out to find Elisha and be healed in the waters of the Jordan.

Slavery persisted throughout Old Testament times, but in the Roman world of Jesus and the apostles it became one of the great social evils. Many early Christians were slaves. The best-known of these was Onesimus, the runaway slave of a Christian named Philemon, to whom Paul wrote a short, touching, and very personal letter. The apostle pleaded with the master to receive Onesimus back with forgiveness, saying, "If he hath wronged thee, or oweth thee aught, put that on mine account. I Paul have written it with my own hand——" One can imagine that at this point the scribe, who was writing the letter at Paul's dictation, paused, handed his pen to Paul, and waited while the great apostle added in his large, clumsy scrawl, "I will repay it" (Philemon 18-19).

Onesimus was in all likelihood forgiven by his master and also freed, for the preservation of the letter indicates a happy outcome to Paul's entreaty. According to tradition the former slave Onesimus became a bishop in the early Church, whose Founder had once assumed the role of a servant when He washed His disciples' feet.

## 7. FAMILY PETS

To the children of a family, and often to their parents as well, household pets seemed to be virtual members of the family, worthy of being tenderly cherished, fed, and protected. Pets brought variety, interest, and liveliness into homes that would otherwise have been drab, and provided endless hours of amusement and training for the children.

Though only a few pets are mentioned in the Bible, these brief clues indicate enjoyment of animals on the part of the Hebrews and a sense of companionship with dumb beasts. Noah's dove was no remote, wild creature, but a little scout entrusted with the family's welfare (Genesis 8:8-12). The story of Balaam's talking ass, who perceived an angel blocking the road, indicates an intimacy between a man and his trustworthy beast of burden (Numbers 22:22-35). Surely the most exotic of all biblical pets were the apes and peacocks brought to Solomon from the East and undoubtedly greatly enjoyed by the children of his many wives (I Kings 10:22). Elijah's ravens were hardly household pets, yet they do show wild creatures performing God's bidding and coming to the aid of a man (I Kings 17:4, 6). But the bird Job mentioned was a tame one, kept perhaps in a cage to amuse the family (Job 41:5). The ox and ass of Isaiah's prophecy, "The ox knoweth his owner, and the ass his master's crib" (Isaiah 1:3), were animals that through long association had become in some measure attached to the household.

Dogs in the Bible are usually of the wild or scavenger variety hunting in packs. But the Canaanite mother who begged Jesus to heal her daughter mentioned domesticated dogs who ate crumbs that fell from their masters' table (Matthew 15:27). In one of the Apocryphal stories, Tobias went on a journey "and the young man's dog was with him" (Tobit 5:15). Returning home, Tobias and his companion went ahead while "the dog went along behind them" (Tobit 11:4)—surely as clear a picture of a pet dog as biblical literature affords.

Finally, there were pet sheep so affectionately described in Nathan's parable:

> But the poor man had nothing, save one little ewe lamb, which he had bought and nourished up. And it grew up together with him and with his children. It did eat of his own meat, and drank of his own cup, and lay in his bosom, and was unto him as a daughter.
>
> II Samuel 12:3

Lambs made good family pets in biblical times. So close a sense of companionship developed with these appealing, dumb animals that the people of Israel sometimes identified themselves with a flock of sheep whose Good Shepherd was the Lord their God (Ezekiel 34:11-16). They sang, "For he is our God, and we are the people of his pasture and the sheep of his hand" (Psalm 95:7). While a prophetic announcement encouraged them with this idyllic picture:

> He shall feed his flock like a shepherd. He shall gather the lambs with his arm, and carry them in his bosom, and shall gently lead those that are with young.
>
> Isaiah 40:11

David never appeared in a more favorable light than in the story of his rescue of a lamb from the lion's mouth (I Samuel 17:34-35).

Though Jesus was not talking specifically about household pets in His parable of the Ninety-Nine Sheep (Luke 15:4-6) and in His question about the sheep rescued from a pit on the Sabbath (Matthew 12:11), the tone of His remarks indicated affectionate concern for creatures often treated as adopted members of the family group. That they were tenderly cared for is apparent in Jesus' final command to Peter, "Feed my lambs" (John 21:15).

# Family Breakdown

*

# CHAPTER 14

# Moral Laws Concerning the Family

Speak unto all the congregation of the children of Israel, and say unto them, "Ye shall be holy, for I the Lord your God am holy."

Leviticus 19:2

\*

## 1. FAMILY PURITY

The Israelites, whose civilization outlasted those of other ancient peoples, and whose ideals helped to form our present family traditions, upheld high standards of family purity. Believing that they were bound to the Lord their God in a unique relationship, the people of Israel tried to live in a manner worthy of their high calling. Because God is holy, their prophets told them that God's people also must be holy. Holiness implies goodness, moral excellence, and separation from all that is evil.

In order to insure family purity, so that all might "worship the Lord in the beauty of Holiness" (Psalm 29:2), strict laws were enacted to guard against all kinds of moral pollution. Ancient laws of the Israelites defended the sacred character of marriage, which, as we have seen, was from the beginning implicitly ordained by God as the lifelong union between one man and one woman.

Union with a close relative was a violation of the Law. It was believed that those who were, in a sense, already one flesh either by birth or by marriage, should not enter into a sexual union. This kind of relation with a parent, brother or sister, aunt or uncle, or any other near kinsman was forbidden (Leviticus 18:6-18; 20:11-21). Examples of incest include such crude old tales as that of drunken Lot and his daughters (Genesis 19:30-38) and Amnon and his half-sister, Tamar (II Samuel 13:6-14).

In New Testament times John the Baptist, with superb courage, sternly rebuked Herod Antipas, tetrarch of Galilee and Perea, for his marriage to his half-brother's divorced wife, Herodias, saying, "It is not lawful for thee to have thy brother's wife" (Mark 6:18). Herod's marriage was directly contrary to the Law (Leviticus 20:21), which declared that the union of a man with his brother's wife was incestuous. Relationships in the Herodian family were complicated, but it seems clear that Herodias had divorced her former husband, Herod Philip, in order to marry his half-brother, Herod Antipas, who was the stepbrother of her father Aristobulus.

Besides incest, sexual deviations of all kinds were prohibited. Drastic penalties were imposed upon those who, by engaging in such practices, sullied the holiness of the people of Israel. Though ancient Hebrew laws reflect a very different society and diverse conditions of life from ours, the purpose of the laws was timeless—to protect the purity of God's people and thus insure family stability and moral health throughout the nation.

The Bible's best summing up of laws relating to moral conduct inside the family appears in Leviticus 18, a part of the Holiness Code, so-called from its constant insistence upon holiness as a mode of conduct.

For whosoever shall commit any of these abominations, even the souls that commit them shall be cut off from among their people. Therefore shall ye keep mine ordinance, that ye commit not any one of these abominable customs, which were committed before you, and that ye defile not yourselves therein: I am the Lord your God.

Leviticus 18:29-30

## 2. THOU SHALT NOT COMMIT ADULTERY

Adultery, the union of a man with another man's wife, was prohibited in the Seventh Commandment (Exodus 20:14). The penalty for adultery was death: "And the man that committeth adultery with another man's wife . . . the adulterer and the adulteress shall surely be put to death" (Leviticus 20:10).

In the Bible intimacy outside marriage or between a married man and an unbetrothed, unmarried woman was not regarded as adultery and was usually called fornication. A man found guilty of such conduct had to pay a fine and marry the woman (Deuteronomy 22:19-21).

The warning against the dangers of adultery in Proverbs 6:24-35 contains the following: "But whoso committeth adultery with a woman lacketh understanding. He that doeth it destroyeth his own soul."

Job considered adultery "an heinous crime . . . a fire that consumeth to destruction" (Job 31:11-12). He described the secret wickedness of the adulterer, "The eye also of the adulterer waiteth for the twilight, saying, 'No eye shall see me'; and disguiseth his face" (Job 24:15).

Potiphar's disloyal wife, in her attempt to seduce Joseph, was a would-be adulteress. David repented of his adultery committed with Uriah's wife Bath-sheba, for he cried out when Nathan the prophet showed him the enormity of his guilt, "I have sinned against the Lord" (II Samuel 12:13).

In the New Testament account of the woman whom Jesus met at a well at Sychar in Samaria, He asked her to call her husband. When the woman admitted that she had no husband, Jesus replied, "Thou hast well said, 'I have no husband,' for thou hast had five husbands, and he whom thou now hast is not thy husband" (John 4:17-18).

A traditional story found in the Gospel of John concerns Jesus' answer to the scribes and Pharisees who brought before Him a woman accused of adultery. Knowing well His kindliness, His sympathy, and His forgiveness, they were sure He would not endorse the Law's harsh punishment for adultery, which was stoning to death. It would be easy, they thought, to trap Him into condemning their sacred Law. But Jesus turned the tables on the woman's accusers, challenging them, "He that is without sin among you, let him first cast a stone at her" (John 8:7).

Accused by their own consciences, the scribes and Pharisees one by one slunk away, leaving Jesus alone with the woman. He said to her, "Neither do I condemn thee. Go, and sin no more" (John 8:11).

Jesus did not regard adultery lightly, though He would not invoke the vindictive punishment prescribed for it by the Law. But in His Sermon on the Mount He went far beyond the requirements of the Law, for He taught that adultery lies not only in outward acts, but also in impure inner thoughts.

Ye have heard that it was said by them of old time, "Thou shalt not commit adultery." But I say unto you, That whosoever looketh on a woman to lust after her hath committed adultery with her already in his heart.

Matthew 5:27-28

Christ's foremost apostle to the Gentiles, Paul, whose teachings about the family will be discussed in a later chapter, was very specific about the spiritual result of adultery.

Walk in the Spirit, and he shall not fulfil the lust of the flesh. . . . Now the works of the flesh are manifest, which are those: adultery, fornication, uncleanness, lasciviousness, idolatry, witchcraft, hatred . . . and such like . . . they which do such things shall not inherit the kingdom of God.

Galatians 5:16, 19-21

## 3. WARNING AGAINST HARLOTS

The Canaanites and other ancient neighbors of the Israelites practiced ritual prostitution in connection with their debasing fertility worship, but the Israelites abhorred these pagan cults and the fornication associated with them. Amos declared that those who engaged in such pagan rites profaned the holy name of the Lord (Amos 2:7).

The folly and destructiveness of illegal sexual unions between unmarried pesons were greatly deplored by a people to whom the sacredness and permanence of the family were important. Warnings were uttered against harlots, the most graphic being those found in Proverbs 7:6-27.

The harlot or adventuress was described as one who "flattereth with her words" and entices "a young man void of understanding" (Proverbs 7:5,7). In Moffatt's translation she is "the loose woman with her words so smooth," who sees "a brainless youth strolling along near the street corner." The passage from Proverbs ends by warning that spiritual death befalls those taken in by the harlot's hypocrisy and flattery.

Let not thine heart decline to her ways,
  go not astray in her paths,
For she hath cast down many wounded.
  yea, many strong men have been slain by her.
Her house is the way to hell,
  going down to the chambers of death.

Proverbs 7:25-27

## 4. HONOR THY FATHER AND THY MOTHER

On the Fifth Commandment rested in large measure the happiness, stability, and solidarity of Hebrew families. This Commandment, given in Exodus 20:12 and again in Deuteronomy 5:16, became so much a part of the social pattern of Israel that even when parents became aged, helpless, and a burden to the family, they were still honored and tenderly cherished. The barbarous practice of abandoning or turning away from the home parents too old and feeble to work became unthinkable.

Isaac, though old and blind, was cared for and honored as the head of his clan (Genesis 27:1-40). Joseph showed deep concern for his aged father Jacob living in famine-stricken Canaan (Genesis 43:27). David, while an outlaw from Saul's court, showed affectionate concern for his parents by sending them to a safe place in Moab far from Saul's fury (I Samuel 22:3-4).

The Bible's best-known example of a son's loving care for His mother is found in Jesus' words from the cross committing His mother to the protection of the beloved disciple John.

When Jesus therefore saw his mother, and the disciple standing by, whom he loved, he saith unto his mother, "Woman, behold thy son!"
Then saith he to the disciple, "Behold thy mother!" And from that hour that disciple took her unto his own home.

John 19:26-27

Because honoring one's parents was so important, cursing them became a serious crime. In ancient Israel cursing was believed to be an effective way of doing harm. A curse was the opposite of blessing. To bless one's parents meant to invoke God's favor upon them so that they might be endowed with health, prosperity, success, strength, and wisdom. A curse called down upon them disease, failure, ruin, infirmity, and death. A son who cursed his parents was not merely expressing anger in a crudely unpardonable way; he was thought actually to strike a savage blow at his parents and the family solidarity they represented.

A law with a terrifying penalty for its violation forbade cursing one's parents. "For every one that curseth his father or his mother shall be surely put to death" (Leviticus 20:9; also Exodus 21:17). There is no record in the Bible that this law, which seems excessively cruel to us, was ever invoked.

## 5. THOU SHALT NOT COVET

The Tenth Commandment, like the Fifth and Seventh, conveyed great truths that insured the sanctity of the home and the preservation of the family. Recognizing the fact that covetous thoughts are far from harmless because they often produce acts that are morally wrong and destructive to family unity, this Tenth Commandment stated:

Neither shalt thou desire thy neighbour's wife, neither shalt thou covet thy neighbour's house, his field, or his manservant, or his maidservant, his ox, or his ass, or any thing that is thy neighbour's.

Deuteronomy 5:21

## 6. EVILS OF DRUNKENNESS

Alcoholic beverages made from grapes, apples, dates, and other products were served at festivals in the patriarchal families, and on such solemn occasions as Isaac's blessing of his son (Genesis 27:25). Wine was also used in religious ceremonies, as that of Melchizedek, the legendary priest-king of Salem who "brought forth bread and wine" (Genesis 14:18) when he came from his city to meet and bless Abraham.

The Psalmist considered wine, oil, and bread all beneficial products, for he wrote, "And wine that maketh glad the heart of man, and oil to make his face shine, and bread which strengtheneth man's heart" (Psalm 104:15).

Intemperate use of wine, however, was a recognized evil. Stories of the intoxication of Noah, of Lot, and of Abigail's churlish husband Nabal, plainly demonstrated that drunkenness could destroy a family's best interests. In the Persian period, King Ahasuerus' courtiers and guests drank heavily, for he set before them "royal wine in abundance" (Esther 1:7). At Belshazzar's feast wine was sacrilegiously drunk from the golden vessels looted from the Temple in Jerusalem (Daniel 5:1-4).

The people of Israel observed that, "Wine is a mocker, strong drink is raging, and whosoever is deceived thereby is not wise" (Proverbs 20:1). One of the great prophets declared that "whoredom and wine . . . take away the heart" (Hosea 4:11), while Isaiah cried out, "Woe unto them that rise up early in the morning, that they may follow strong drink; that continue until night, till wine inflame them" (Isaiah 5:11).

A vivid account of the degrading effects of intemperate drinking of wine stated that it "biteth like a serpent and stingeth like an adder" (Proverbs 23:29-35). In the same chapter of Proverbs occurs the advice, "Be not among winebibbers . . . for the drunkard and the glutton shall come to poverty" (Proverbs 23:20-21). Inevitably the drunkard's poverty created misery, not only for himself, but for his family.

These warnings against the evils of drunkenness, as well as other basic evils mentioned in this chapter, reveal that the early Hebrews were a people resolutely in earnest about the integrity of the family. They seemed to realize better than any ancient peoples that moral pollution begins inside the family and spreads throughout the nation.

# CHAPTER 15

# Divorce in Old Testament Times

For the Lord, the God of Israel, saith that he hateth putting away.

Malachi 2:16

✴

As we well know from the Genesis accounts of creation discussed in the first chapter, marriage was ordained as the lifelong union of a man and a woman. From earliest times, however, problems arising between husbands and wives often destroyed their partnership. Though divorces are not specifically mentioned in Genesis, many family difficulties and the tensions that create divorce are delineated, such as adultery, incompatibility, jealousy, desertion, and trouble with in-laws.

## 1. A SERIOUS PROBLEM

Today the problem of divorce assumes serious proportions, with one out of every four marriages in the United States ending in the divorce courts, and countless numbers of children living in broken homes. The old causes of divorce are still present, but our complex and rapidly changing modern society adds new strains to marriage. Unfortunately many people enter marriage with the idea that it is terminable and that a divorce is little different from trading in an old car.

Divorce, however, brings not only tragedy to individuals and to the homes concerned, but weakness to society as a whole. Broken families are a poor foundation for any society, but strong families are the very pillars of a strong nation. The family is the nursery of democracy. A home that recognizes the dignity and worth of its individual members and trains them to respect the rights of others is teaching the very elements of democracy. But if the home abdicates its responsibility, the state is endangered. As the well-known evangelist Billy Graham says, "The breaking up of American homes is eating away at the heart and core of our nation's structure."

An enduring marriage from which proceeds a strong, happy family is humanity's most important institution, deserving earnest thought and prayerful consideration. Since there is a deeply spiritual aspect to the lifelong union of a husband and wife, the Bible has much to say about marriage. What guidance does the Bible give on the problem of divorce?

## 2. ANCIENT BIBLE ORDINANCES

The oldest biblical references to divorce are found in Leviticus 21:7; 22:13; Numbers 5:12-31; 30:9-10; and Deuteronomy 22:19. The first reference in Numbers is to an ancient ordinance intended to remove suspicion of a wife's marital unfaithfulness. This primitive law subjected a wife to trial by ordeal, then a commonly accepted method of proving guilt, but now, of course, condemned by all civilized people as superstitious and grossly unfair.

If a husband suspected that his wife had been unfaithful to him in their marriage relationship, he took her to a priest. The priest sprinkled dust from the sanctuary on holy water in an earthen jar while he pronounced an oath. After writing down the oath, he dissolved the writing in the "bitter" water which he then gave to the woman to drink. If she were guilty, the water was believed to make her barren and thus a dreadful example to all; but "if the woman be not defiled, but be clean, then she shall be free, and shall conceive seed" (Numbers 5:28).

## 3. DIVORCE IN OTHER CIVILIZATIONS

The discovery of law codes dating back to the twentieth century B.C. shows that divorce was an ancient problem. In the Tigris-Euphrates region a century or two before the time of Abraham, a certain King Bilalama decreed that a husband who left his wife after she had borne him children had to give her his entire estate. The well-known eighteenth-century B.C. Code of Hammurabi permitted a wife to sue for divorce if she had suitable evidence of her husband's unfaithfulness.

In other Babylonian laws, however, the wife was given no protection, for a husband could merely say, "You are not my wife," pay a small sum of money, and be entirely free of the woman. One law specified that if a woman even suggested that she wanted a divorce, she was to be drowned in the river.


## 4. THE BILL OF DIVORCEMENT

Divorce had long been practiced in Israel, as the ancient ordinances concerning it indicate, when the Bible's first and only legal document dealing with the termination of a marriage was written (Deuteronomy 24:1-4). Samuel Rolles Driver, in his notable commentary on Deuteronomy, says of this statute, "Hebrew law does not institute divorce, but tolerates it, in view of the imperfections of human nature, and lays down regulations tending to limit it, and preclude its abuse." The law stated:

When a man hath taken a wife, and married her, and it come to pass that she find no favour in his eyes, because he hath found some uncleanness in her, then let him write her a bill of divorcement, and give it in her hand, and send her out of his house. And when she is departed out of his house, she may go and be another man's wife.

And if the latter husband hate her, and write her a bill of divorcement, and giveth it in her hand, and sendeth her out of his house; or if the latter husband die. . . . her former husband, which sent her away, may not take her again to be his wife. . . .

Deuteronomy 24:1-4

Bible scholars have long been uncertain of the exact meaning of "uncleanness" in the Hebrew divorce law. It may refer to adultery or to some indecency. Sometimes, however, as we shall see, the word was interpreted to cover trivial faults.

Divorce and remarriage after divorce are dealt with in this law. According to it a husband was required to bring a real case against his wife, presumably to appear before some public official, and to obtain from him a legal "bill of divorcement." A great prophet referred to this law in his question, "Where is the bill of your mother's divorcement, whom I have put away?" (Isaiah 50:1).

Hasty divorces were somewhat discouraged and wives given a slight amount of protection, for the time and money involved in obtaining a divorce made it less easy for a husband to get rid of his wife. As the Law made no provision for a wife to divorce her husband, it failed to solve all difficulties pertaining to this problem.

## 5. DIVORCE OF ALIEN WIVES

The many divorces among the Hebrews after the Exile in Babylon were the result of special circumstances posing a serious threat to the survival of Israel as a people. They might well have become mingled with other races and have disappeared from history, as was the fate of many ancient people. Undoubtedly the preservation of the Hebrews as a distinct race was due to drastic measures taken by the priest and scribe, Ezra.

In the fifth century B.C. Ezra secured from King Artaxerxes of Persia, then ruling in Babylon, an imperial edict empowering him to conduct a group of nearly fifteen hundred men of Israel and their families across the hazardous miles of desert to their former homes in the land of their fathers. This enthusiastic band of Jews planned to rebuild their ruined Temple in Jerusalem and restore the religious life of the people of God.

It seemed clear to Ezra that their plan to restore Israel would fail if Jewish men married "strange," meaning alien, wives who worshipped pagan gods. In his opinion these foreign women polluted the racial purity of Abraham's descendants and were a threat to Israel's religious integrity. It must be noted that in Ezra's time marriage was a far less personal matter than it is today. Wedlock concerned not only the man and woman intimately involved but the entire people of Israel.

Centuries earlier, when they entered the land of Canaan, the idea of marriage as the concern of the nation had been vividly expressed. In Canaan they were surrounded by Hittites, Amorites, Perizites, or Jebusites, and Girgashites (Nehemiah 9:8). The Israelites were commanded to shun all these neighbors.

Thou shalt make no covenant with them, nor show mercy unto them.

Neither shalt thou make marriages with them. Thy daughter thou shalt
not give unto his son, nor his daughter shalt thou take unto thy son. For
they will turn away thy son from following me, that they may serve
other gods. . . .

Deuteronomy 7:2-4

In the court of the restored Temple, Ezra publicly mourned when
he saw that "the people of Israel . . . have not separated themselves
from the people of the lands . . . so that the holy seed have mingled
themselves with the people of those lands" (Ezra 9:1-2).

The huge crowd of men, women, and children gathered around
their revered leader Ezra were shocked and amazed to see him rend
his garments, pluck out his hair, and sit in appalled silence until the
evening sacrifice. When he poured out his soul's anguish and despair
to God in prayer, the crowd became hushed, listening to his every
word (Ezra 9:6-15).

At the end of his fervent prayer, while the people wept for their
iniquities, a man rose up and spoke in behalf of them all, saying:

"We have trespassed against our God, and have taken strange wives of
the people of the land. . . . Now therefore let us make a covenant with
our God to put away all the wives and such as are born of them, according to the counsel of my lord, and of those that tremble at the commandment of our God. And let it be done according to the law."

Ezra 10:2-3

It was proclaimed throughout the land that all Jews should as-
semble in Jerusalem on pain of forfeiting their lands and losing their
citizenship. Everyone came and was thoroughly miserable for they all
"sat in the street of the house of God, trembling because of this matter and for the great rain" (Ezra 10:9). Ezra, who by common consent had been put in charge, addressed the wet and shiveringly
apprehensive people:

"Ye have transgressed, and have taken strange wives, to increase the
trespass of Israel. Now therefore make confession unto the Lord God of
your fathers, and do his pleasure, and separate yourselves from the
people of the land and from the strange wives."

Ezra 10:10-11

With loud voices the people shouted their assent. Though four
leading men boldly tried to oppose Ezra's demand, no one supported
them. The task of dissolving all marriages to non-Jewish wives was
undertaken by a commission that went from town to town.

The list of those who were compelled to divorce their wives included many influential people: seventeen priests, six Levites, one singer, three doorkeepers, and eighty-six laymen. Bitter unhappiness and great social upheaval must have ensued. Nothing is recorded of measures taken for the welfare of the wives and their children thrust from their homes and deprived of the protection of their former husbands, but some fair arrangement must have been made for their support.

The prevention of mixed marriages was a problem that occupied the attention of Nehemiah also, the famous governor who rebuilt the walls of Jerusalem (Nehemiah 13:23-28). He even went so far as to drive out of the city the high priest's grandson who had married a daughter of Sanballat, a Horite leader and bitter enemy of Nehemiah's.

Some scholars believe that the tender story of Ruth, the foreign girl from Moab who became ancestress of David, was written in the period of Nehemiah and Ezra as a protest against the harsh views about marrying aliens.

The Book of Daniel, referring to events in the second year of King Nebuchadnezzar, long before the return of the exiles, contains the Bible's first meaningful metaphor on the dire results of marriage with aliens. Daniel, deported into Babylonia as a youth, probably witnessed at first hand the problems involving marriage with alien wives, all leading to divorce and so he wrote:

"As you saw the iron mixed with miry clay, so they will mix with one another in marriage, but *they* will not hold together, just as iron does not mix with clay."

Daniel 2:43, RSV

Whether *they* here refers to the kings, the Ptolemies and Seleucids, or the people, translators are not certain. But that is of small consequence. The metaphor itself is better than a whole sermon on intermarriage between those with unrelated religious and ethical backgrounds. Marriage between the God-loving and the godless presents a real threat to a stable family life, and is one of the main causes of divorce.

## 6. MALACHI'S OPPOSITION TO DIVORCE

Another marital problem occurred in the time of the prophet Malachi, shortly before the marriage reforms of Nehemiah and Ezra.

Jewish men were divorcing their Jewish wives, with whom they had been living for years, in order to marry attractive, young, alien women. Ritually this was repugnant to Malachi, for like Ezra and Nehemiah, he believed that marriage to "the daughter of a strange god," meaning a woman who worshipped a pagan god, inevitably "profaned the holiness of the Lord" (Malachi 2:11). Heathen wives in their midst not only destroyed the physical unity of Israel but its religious purity as well.

The problem, however, had, what seems to us, a deeper aspect. Divorce meant breaking faith with the first wife and repudiating sacred obligations to her. Malachi was absolutely opposed to this. To him the marital union was sacred and indissoluble. Fleming James, in his *Personalities of the Old Testament,* interprets Malachi's teaching as follows:

Finally, Malachi's conception of the marriage relation was singularly beautiful. A man enters into a covenant with his wife when she is young and fair and he must keep true to it after she has faded with advancing years. She must still be his companion, bound to him by intimate and sacred ties. She has trusted him and he must not deal treacherously with her by turning from her and seeking a younger face. . . . Wedlock was under God's special protection, and the preservation of the home His passionate concern: "I hate putting away, saith Yahweh." Evidently Malachi rejected the "liberality" of the Deuteronomic provision for divorce (Deut. 24:1 ff) which permitted a man to let his wife go "if she find no favour in his eyes, because he hath found some unseemly thing in her"—and when could a man not find such unseemliness if his heart was set on it? Malachi's sympathies were all on the side of the woman. And so, he believed, were God's (pp. 423-424).

The Old Testament's final words on divorce are those of Malachi in which he surpassed the Old Testament's previous teachings and in large measure anticipated those of Jesus.

Because the Lord was witness to the covenant between you and the wife of your youth, to whom you have been faithless, though she is your companion and your wife by covenant. . . . So take heed to yourselves, and let none be faithless to the wife of his youth. For I hate divorce, says the Lord God of Israel. . . . So take heed of yourselves and do not be faithless.

Malachi 2:14-16, RSV

# CHAPTER 16

# Christian Teachings on Divorce

What therefore God hath joined together, let not man put asunder.
                                                          Mark 10:9

*

## 1. DIVORCE IN JESUS' WORLD

Divorce was very common among both Jews and Gentiles in the first century A.D. In the Gentile world a woman could divorce her husband, but this was unknown among the Jews. The rabbis agreed that divorce, though not desirable, was lawful. Two different schools of thought disputed what constituted a valid reason for terminating a marriage.

Rabbi Hillel and his followers interpreted the Law (Deuteronomy 24:1) very leniently in the husband's favor. Hillel, who had been born in the Jewish community in Babylon about 70 B.C. of parents descended from David, went to Jerusalem to study law. There he became a leader of the scribes of the Sanhedrin and a notable teacher of the virtues of charity, humility, patience, and piety. Many of his rules for living were wise and good, but his teachings on divorce were lax and involved cruel injustice to wives. He declared that if a wife so much as spoiled her husband's dinner by burning the bread, he had sufficient ground for divorcing her. If a husband became tired of his wife or preferred another woman to her, he was entitled to a divorce. Mere caprice could thus destroy the union between a man and a woman. Family life became insecure and men could tyrannize over their wives.

Opposed to Rabbi Hillel were Rabbi Shammai and his followers who interpreted the Law very strictly. They declared that only if a husband found his wife guilty of shameful behavior, such as adultery, could he be granted a divorce.

## 2. JESUS' TEACHING ON DIVORCE (Mark 10:2-12)

Jesus was in the populous region beyond the Jordan teaching crowds of people who were eager to hear His words, when some Pharisees came to Him. Hoping to trap Him into making a statement they could use to discredit Him, they asked, "Is it lawful for a man to put away his wife?" (10:2).

These Pharisees may have belonged to the liberal school of Hillel or to the strict school of Shammai. In either case they undoubtedly enjoyed arguing and felt confident of their ability to put Jesus in the wrong with the people. The crowd must have pressed closer to hear Jesus' answer to the Pharisees' question, which involved a difficult problem of living.

In His customary way, Jesus first asked His own question to determine what was on their minds, "What did Moses command you?" (10:3). From their long familiarity with the Law the Pharisees quickly replied, "Moses suffered [allowed] a man to write a bill of divorcement and to put her away" (10:4).

Divorce, then, was clearly permitted by the Law. But how would Jesus interpret the Law? The people expected Him to pronounce valid reasons for divorce, but He surprised them. Instead of becoming involved in a morass of legalistic controversy, Jesus moved to the much higher plane of spiritual principles.

Moses, He explained, allowed a man to divorce his wife, not because it was right, but because of "the hardness of your hearts." The Law was a concession unwillingly given in view of man's weak, imperfect nature and his ignorance of the true meaning of love. With inspired insight and superb courage Jesus then taught the people God's eternal purpose in the institution of marriage, already cited in the chapter on marriage but still important to this chapter on divorce.

But from the beginning of the creation God made them male and female. For this cause shall a man leave his father and mother and cleave to his wife. And they shall be one flesh: so then they are no more twain, but one flesh. What therefore God hath joined together, let not man put asunder.

Mark 10:6-9

Nothing remained for the Pharisees with their futile arguments but to sneak away while Jesus' sublime words still echoed over the silent crowd, awed by the majesty and truth of His teaching.

Afterwards, when the disciples reached the house where they were staying, they questioned Him further. Jesus replied:

"Whosoever shall put away his wife, and marry another, committeth adultery against her. And if a woman shall put away her husband, and be married to another, she committeth adultery."

Mark 10:11-12

## 3. THE ONE EXCEPTION IN MATTHEW

Matthew 19:3-9 records substantially the same teaching as that in Mark. In the ninth verse, however, Matthew added a phrase, not found in Mark, which reads: "except it be for fornication [unchastity]." This one allowable exception in Matthew does not make divorce easy, but rather prevents trivial grounds being used as an excuse for irresponsibility terminating a marriage:

"And I say unto you, Whosoever shall put away his wife, except it be for fornication, and shall marry another, committeth adultery; and whoso marrieth her which is put away doth commit adultery."

Matthew 19:9

Was Jesus' repudiation of divorce absolute, or did He indeed give the one exception reported in the verse from Matthew above? In Luke 16:18 as in Mark, no grounds for divorce are reported, a fact which leads many scholars to conclude that Matthew contributed the phrase, "except it be for fornication," to the original tradition in an effort to guide the early Church in judging difficult marital cases.

## 4. THE APPLICATION OF JESUS' TEACHING

Discussion of this scholarly point, however, can lead to the danger of using Jesus' words legalistically, in the same manner as the Pharisees long ago interpreted the words of the Law. L. H. Marshall, in his book *The Challenge of New Testament Ethics,* avoids this danger when he comments on Jesus' teachings and their application as follows:

. . . it must be clearly recognized that Jesus was not framing any law for the statute book of the State. His teaching about the indissolubility of marriage, like other hard sayings of His, is fully applicable only to those who are citizens of the Kingdom of God, who spontaneously accept God's will as the law of their lives, and who consequently adopt the divine idea of marriage. In this imperfect and sinful world where the human weaknesses and "hardness of heart" which led Moses to make legal provision for divorce still persist, . . . the ideal view of marriage cannot be made compulsory. A view of marriage voluntarily adopted *within* the Kingdom of God cannot be enforced by legal sanctions *outside* (pp. 146-147).

Jesus' fearless, uncompromising teaching on divorce made it abundantly clear to all who heard Him that women are not man's possessions, but persons with marriage rights which in God's sight are equal to those of men. He swept away the old notion of male dominance and the idea that a marriage could be quickly dissolved by reason of a husband's caprice, desire, or a trumped-up charge against his wife. He taught that God Himself creates a lifelong bond in marriage.

## 5. PAUL'S POSITION

Paul, the great apostle who carried the Christian message far and wide throughout the Gentile world, based his teachings about divorce upon the words of Jesus. Various difficulties were encountered by Paul's converts in Corinth as they attempted to live Christian lives in that large, pagan, commercial city. Their letter to Paul has been lost, but his reply to them is the First Epistle to the Corinthians. In it he advised them in their difficulties, one of which was the problem of divorce.

With beautiful clarity *The New English Bible* translates Paul's advice to married people belonging to the church in Corinth as follows:

To the married I give this ruling, which is not mine but the Lord's: a wife must not separate herself from her husband; if she does, she must either remain unmarried or be reconciled to her husband; and the husband must not divorce his wife.

I Corinthians 7:10-11, NEB

There were Christian husbands in Corinth who were married to pagan wives and vice versa. Should these Christians divorce their unbelieving spouses? Paul, in his earnest attempt to help his converts with this urgent and very troublesome local problem, was careful to state that he gave his own opinion, not Christ's command.

To the rest I say this, as my own word, not as the Lord's: if a Christian has a heathen wife, and she is willing to live with him, he must not divorce her; and a woman who has a heathen husband willing to live with her must not divorce her husband. For the heathen husband now belongs to God through his Christian wife, and the heathen wife through her Christian husband. Otherwise your children would not belong to God, whereas in fact they do. If on the other hand the heathen partner wishes for a separation, let him have it. In such cases the Christian husband or wife is under no compulsion; but God's call is a call to live in peace. Think of it: as a wife you may be your husband's salvation; as a husband you may be your wife's salvation.

I Corinthians 7:12-16, NEB

After writing his letters to the Corinthians, Paul made them a personal visit. While in Corinth, probably in the winter months of A.D. 55-56, Paul wrote his most important letter, the Epistle to the Romans, called "the first great work of Christian theology." In explaining the meaning of the Christian's new life in Christ, Paul made use of a marriage metaphor.

In Romans, Paul assumed that the marriage bond is so sacred that only death can dissolve it. Fidelity in marriage must continue to the very end of life, after which the bond no longer exists.

For the woman which hath an husband is bound by the law to her husband so long as he liveth; but if the husband be dead, she is loosed from the law of her husband. So then if, while her husband liveth, she be married to another man, she shall be called an adulteress: but if her husband be dead, she is free from that law; so that she is no adulteress, though she be married to another man.

Romans 7:2-3

From the lofty teachings of Jesus, the letters of Paul, and the life of innumerable dedicated Christians, marriage attained a new status, higher than that of Old Testament days. Divorce, a tragedy of the centuries that unfortunately continues to plague the Church and the family, was repudiated by Jesus. Lifelong monogamy, recognized as fulfilling the purpose of God, became the Christian principle of marriage. An Old Testament prophet's insight was upheld: "For the Lord, the God of Israel, saith that he hateth putting away" (Malachi 2:16).

# Family Strength

*

# CHAPTER 17

# Family Worship

And thou shalt rejoice before the Lord thy God, thou, and thy son, and thy daughter, and thy manservant, and thy maidservant, and the Levite that is within thy gates, and the stranger, and the fatherless, and the widow that are among you. . . .

Deuteronomy 16:11

✱

## 1. ALL OF THE FAMILY

One of Israel's greatest sources of strength was its worship of God by the entire family, as commanded in the verse above. In this excellent tradition of adoration and humble confidence, Israel's families felt "God's greatness yet nearness, His Holiness and His Presence."

From the first altars to the tabernacles, temples, and religious festivals, we see Israel's families united together, with the hand of God ever leading the way and with the people realizing that God was molding them to His will. These primitive people bear a striking contrast to many of today's families, who have no time for worship together, and consequently walk toward many dangers.

Family worship must have begun long before recorded history when, in the time of Seth's son Enos, "began men to call upon the name of the Lord" (Genesis 4:26). The first altar mentioned in the Bible, however, was built by Noah after the Flood, when all of his family came out of the ark. Planting their feet once again upon firm, dry land, they began to pile stones one upon another to make "an altar unto the Lord" (Genesis 8:20). There, doubtless as a family they offered a sacrifice to the Lord, Who blessed them and said, "Be fruitful and multiply and replenish the earth" (Genesis 9:1). After their terrifying experience in the storm, Noah's family was reassured that never again would the Lord send a flood to destroy the earth.

## 2. ALTARS OF PATRIARCHAL FAMILIES

Abraham built his first altar at Shechem in the Promised Land of Canaan at the place where the Lord appeared to him and promised, "Unto thy seed will I give this land" (Genesis 12:7). At Abraham's altar, as at Noah's, the Lord's words embraced the entire family, and indicate that family worship in patriarchal times centered around the altar. Here began the tradition of God-centered families handing down from one generation to another their devotion to the Lord.

Abraham built altars wherever he went, usually at the place where the Lord spoke to him, as at Bethel, Hebron, and in the "land of Moriah." His structures may have been crude and rough, sometimes merely a simple mound of earth, a naturally flat rock, or a pile of stones with a rock slab on top where the sacrificial animal could be slaughtered and burned.

At Beer-sheba Abraham's son Isaac built or rededicated an altar originally erected by his father, who had spent many years with his family in that arid place (Genesis 26:25). Isaac's son Jacob rebuilt his grandfather's and father's altars at Shechem and Bethel. With positive assurance, Jacob directed the worship of all of his family as he started back toward Bethel from his mother's homeland in Mesopotamia, where he had spent twenty years. He commanded his household and all that were with him:

"Put away the strange gods that are among you . . . And let us arise, and go up to Beth-el, and I will make there an altar unto God, who answered me in the day of my distress, and was with me in the way which I went."

Genesis 35:2-3

And God went before Jacob's family as they journeyed homeward. The rhythmic movement of patriarchal families from altars at Shechem, Bethel, Hebron, Moriah and Beer-sheba, all sites of some special revelation of Jehovah, assure us of the significance of these altars in patriarchal families. It is no wonder that they, moving together from one altar to another, were recognized in ancient times as a people of destiny, who had God-centered goals, and who moved steadfastly toward them.

## 3. ALTARS OF MOSES AND AARON

The next eventful record of the building of altars came in the time of Moses, who called his altar "Jehovah-nissi" (Exodus 17:15), meaning "Jehovah is my banner." Due to the influence of Egyptian culture, tabernacle altars became quite elaborate. The first tabernacle, built to the pattern given to Moses on Mount Sinai, arose according to God's command. Every member of the family, it appears, assisted in the building of this tabernacle.

And they came, both men and women, as many as were willing-hearted, and brought bracelets, and earrings, and rings, and tablets, all jewels of gold. . . . And every man, with whom was found blue, and purple, and scarlet, and fine linen, and goats' hair, and red skins of rams, and badgers' skin, brought them . . . and every man, with whom was found shittim wood. . . . And all the women that were wise-hearted did spin with their hands, and brought that which they had spun, both of blue, and of purple, and of scarlet, and of fine linen. And all the women whose heart stirred them up in wisdom spun goats' hair.

Exodus 35:22-26

Not Aaron alone but Aaron and his sons first anointed and sanctified the tabernacle (Exodus 40:12-14). Of the sons, God said to Moses, "thou shalt anoint them, as thou didst anoint their father . . . for their anointing shall surely be an everlasting priesthood throughout their generations" (Exodus 40:15). "And the Lord spake unto Aaron, saying, Do not drink wine nor strong drink, thou, nor thy sons with thee, when ye go into the tabernacle of the congregation, lest ye die: it shall be a statute for ever throughout your generations" (Leviticus 10:8-9).

When the first poll of the Children of Israel was made Moses, standing in the tabernacle, received this divine command:

"Take ye the sum of all the congregation of the children, after their families, by the house of their fathers, with the number of their names, every male by their polls"

Numbers 1:2

"Every man of the children of Israel shall pitch by his own standard, with the ensign of their father's house: far off about the tabernacle of the congregation shall they pitch"

Numbers 2:2

We see here that the tabernacle was the very center of family life during the time of Moses and Aaron. These worshiping families—brothers, fathers, sons and all within their father's house—experienced together a growing revelation of His Holiness, and sensed the unspeakable mystery of His hidden Being. Worship that was family fostered thus became truly personal.

## 4. AN ALTAR TO A FAMILY'S ONENESS

The next mention of family worship around an altar came in the time of Joshua, Moses' successor. The children of Reuben and the children of Gad and the half-tribe of Manasseh built an altar by the Jordan, described as "A great altar . . . a witness between us that the Lord is God" (Joshua 22:10, 34).

In order to keep alive and strong their tribal ties, forged by long years of adversity and struggle, this "great altar" was set up as a testimony to God after these two and a half tribes returned from battle.

Thinking these two and a half tribes had set up the altar for a burnt offering and a sacrifice, the other nine and a half tribes challenged them for putting the altar to the wrong use. But the representatives of the two and a half tribes told agents of the other tribes that they had set up this altar as "a witness, between us, and you, and our generations after us, that we might do the service of the Lord . . . that your children may not say to our children in time to come, Ye have no part in the Lord" (Joshua 22:27). The rebelling brothers from the other tribes answered, "This day we perceive that the Lord is among us" (22:31).

This "great altar," which had first seemed to divide the two and a half tribes of Israel from the other nine and a half tribes, became a monument to the oneness of the twelve tribes, and to their belief in the Lord God.

## 5. A FATHER'S AND A SON'S DREAM FOR AN ALTAR

While living in his palace of cedar, David was the first to realize that the Ark of the Covenant must rest in something stronger than a tent on Zion. The dwelling of Jehovah, he said, should be a magnificent temple in Jerusalem, at the center of the nation's life. And David heard a voice speak:

"Behold a son shall be born to thee, . . . for his name shall be Solomon,

and I will give peace and quietness unto Israel in his days. He shall build
an house for my name; . . . and I will establish the throne of his kingdom over Israel for ever."

I Chronicles 22:9-10

David purchased the site for the temple altar from Araunah, who
had once used it for a threshing floor (II Samuel 24:16-24). Legend
claims that the site, now covered by the Moslem Dome of the Rock,
was where Abraham sacrificed a ram instead of his son (Genesis
22:1-14).

As the people of Tyre and Zidonia brought cedar trees in abundance David directed them:

"Solomon my son is young and tender, and the house that is to be builded
for the Lord must be exceedingly *magnifical,* of fame and of glory
through all countries: I will therefore now make preparations for it. So
David prepared abundantly before his death. Then he called for Solomon
his son, and charged him to build an house unto the name of the Lord
God of Israel."

I Chronicles 22:5-6

David afterward set masons to hewing the wrought stones, as-
sembling iron in abundance for nails and doors and other supplies
such as brass, gold, and silver. And David spoke to his son Solomon
of his plans for this great temple, which Solomon saw through to its
completion.

The divine word concerning Solomon, first revealed to his father,
sounded in Solomon's ears as he went forth with a spirit of thankful-
ness and obedience to do God's will. In his eloquent dedicatory address (I Kings 8:22-54), Solomon thrice mentioned his father in the
beginning words of that address (verses 24-26).

This revelation of the temple, handed down from father to son, is
a heart-warming example of a Hebrew family which from one generation to another was dominated by a thirst for God and a sense of
obligation to God.

## 6. THE PASSOVER—A FAMILY FESTIVAL

Many of Israel's chief religious festivals were family celebrations
of prayer and thanksgiving to the God of their fathers.

The ancient festival of the Passover, as recorded in Exodus, was a family feast presided over by the father. It was celebrated at the first full moon after the spring equinox, in remembrance of Israel's deliverance by the Lord from Egyptian bondage. Each family in its own home carried out the specific directions for the feast as outlined in Exodus 12:3-8, 11.

One can well imagine each member of the family having a part in the preparation for this feast. The father and his eldest son would select a lamb from the flock and perhaps invite a neighbor who lived alone with his old father to join their celebration. The mother would grind the meal, bake the unleavened bread, and light a fire for the roast. Meanwhile the children would bring in more firewood, sweep out the house, gather bitter herbs, and find their father's shoes and staff. Even the small children knew from the scriptural words they had been taught that this feast was a sacred one celebrated throughout all generations: "And ye shall observe this thing for an ordinance to thee and to thy sons for ever" (Exodus 12:24).

Eagerly the youngest child, or in some families the eldest son, waited for his special part in the ritual of the feast. It was his privilege to ask the age-old question, "What mean ye by this service?" (Exodus 12:26). His father, as the chief celebrant, replied, "It is the sacrifice of the Lord's passover, who passed over the houses of the children of Israel in Egypt, when he smote the Egyptians and delivered our houses" (Exodus 12:27).

Thus every year, century after century, the immemorial feast was celebrated and the old, yet ever new, story of God's love, mercy, and deliverance was retold by each father as he sat at table surrounded by his family.

## 7. PILGRIMAGE TO JERUSALEM

The celebration of the Passover changed somewhat in the seventh century B.C. after the reforms of King Josiah. From then on families journeyed up to Jerusalem to sacrifice their Passover lamb, for the new law decreed that only on the altar of the great Temple could sacrifices be offered. To the solemn family meal and the ritual celebrating the Lord's salvation of His people was added the excitement and wonder of a pilgrimage to the Holy City.

The journey was made by family groups, often accompanied by their kindred and neighbors. Though the pilgrimage was religious in intent, it had other aspects. One can vividly imagine, with Mary Ellen Chase in her book *The Psalms for the Common Reader,* some of these other aspects:

> They were, without doubt, the dreams of excited children for months before entire families set forth with friends and neighbors, mules and asses, bags and baskets of provender, sheep and lambs for sacrifice. . . . Here was the one chance during the year to see new or perhaps old faces, to exchange tidings, to indulge in talk and storytelling around campfires, and to enjoy, as on all such journeys, the sights and sound of an unfamiliar countryside. And whenever houseworn and tired women who longed for a change of scene felt obliged to give up a coveted outing, as did Hannah, the beloved of Elkanah's two wives, who forfeited her pilgrimage to stay at home with her baby, it must have seemed a sacrifice indeed! . . . There were the old to care for and children to be watched over and tended. There was always the weariness of long days spent in plodding forward . . . the asses and the mules being used largely for the necessary provisions, or for the aged and the very young (pp. 58-59).

The Passover was indeed a family festival binding together young and old in a solemn yet joyous celebration of those mighty acts by which the Lord made Himself known as the Savior of His people. As the expectant travellers approached the Holy City and beheld, high on its hill, their splendid Temple shining in the sun, parents and children joined in the time-honored, pilgrim song (Psalm 122:1-4, 6-8).

The beautiful story of the boy Jesus going up to Jerusalem with His parents to celebrate his first Passover illuminates one of the family aspects of Hebrew worship.

## 8. OTHER RELIGIOUS FESTIVALS

Hebrew families played an important part in other great religious celebrations. After the Passover came the second annual festival, the Feast of Weeks, which was a thanksgiving for the wheat harvest gathered seven weeks to fifty days after the beginning of the barley harvest. The Feast of Weeks on the "fiftieth" day became known as Pentecost, from the Greek word for "fiftieth."

All the members of a family might well be employed in preparations for the Feast of Weeks, as the ritual for it in Leviticus 23:15-21 specified that two ordinary loaves of bread were to be offered to the

Lord. Though the mother and her daughters ground the meal, measured it, made a fire in the oven, procured yeast, kneaded the dough,
formed loaves and baked them, the father and his sons first had to
harvest the wheat and thresh it, all according to the Law: "You shall
bring from your dwellings two loaves of bread to be waved, made of
two tenths of an ephah; they shall be of fine flour, they shall be
baked with leaven, as first fruits to the Lord" (Leviticus 23:17, RSV).

The third great festival of the year, the Feast of Tabernacles, was
a week-long religious picnic during which families left their ordinary
homes to live in temporary shelters variously called booths, huts,
tents, or tabernacles, made of branches (Leviticus 23:34-43). This
joyous harvest festival and family outing came in the autumn after
crops had been cut and gathered, grain threshed, and grapes and
olives pressed.

Throughout the entire celebration, however, children and parents
were aware of the religious aspect of the feast: "That your generations may know that I made the children of Israel to dwell in booths,
when I brought them out of the land of Egypt: I am the Lord your
God" (Leviticus 23:43).

Hanukkah, the joyful Feast of Dedication or the Feast of Lights,
was instituted by Judas Maccabeus in memory of the rededication of
the Temple in 165 B.C. after it had been profaned by the worship of
the pagan god Zeus. Still celebrated by the Jews, as are the three
ancient feasts, Hanukkah is a December festival mentioned in connection with Jesus' visit to Jerusalem (John 10:22).

The Feast of Dedication included the lighting of lamps in front of
each house, feasting, a procession with palms, and the singing of the
Hallel (Psalms 113-118), which was also sung by family groups at
the other great festivals.

The three great festivals enjoined by the Law—Passover, the Feast
of Weeks, and the Feast of Tabernacles—with the later Feast of
Lights thus afforded old and young in Hebrew families, from Old to
New Testament times, an opportunity to worship and rejoice together.

Sometimes nursing infants were included in religious services, for
in his call to prayer and repentance the prophet Joel cried:

> Blow the trumpet in Zion
>   sanctify a fast,
> call a solemn assembly.

> Gather the people,
> sanctify the congregation,
>    assemble the elders,
> gather the children,
>    and those that suck the breasts.
> Let the bridegroom go forth of his chamber,
>    and the bride out of her closet.
>                                   Joel 2:15-16

Today, looking back upon centuries of family worship, it becomes clear that a general restoration of family worship would surely deepen individual lives and enrich home life. Pauline and Elton Trueblood, in their book *The Recovery of Family Life,* say: "If we can believe that a home is potentially as much a sanctuary as any ecclesiastical building can ever be, we are well on the way to the recovery of family life which our generation sorely needs" (p. 120).

# CHAPTER 18

# Faith Sustaining the Family

Now faith is the substance of things hoped for, the evidence of things not seen.

Hebrews 11:1

Dramatic instances of families protected and sustained by the power of faith can be found in the stories of Noah, Abraham, and Jacob. All of these heads of families reached forward toward unseen goals for themselves and their loved ones, assured by their direct, personal relationship with God of the reality of His promises. In the superb eleventh chapter of Hebrews the heroes mentioned above, and many others are honored in the triumphant roll call of the victors of faith.

## 1. "NOAH WALKED WITH GOD"

In Noah's story, coming down to us from the ancient past, signs of the impending catastrophe were evident: "The earth also was corrupt before God, and the earth was filled with violence" (Genesis 6:11). Yet only Noah, sensitively aware of the signs of the times, heard the voice of the Lord, for "Noah was a just man and perfect in his generations, and Noah walked with God" (Genesis 6:9).

By faith Noah, being warned of God of things not seen as yet, moved with fear, prepared an ark to the saving of his house; by the which he condemned the world, and became heir of the righteousness which is by faith.

Hebrews 11:7

The account of how Noah and his three sons built a huge ark of gopherwood and brought aboard it two of every kind of beast, cattle, creeping thing, and bird, is enthralling to old and young alike. Everyone can imagine how Noah's neighbors must have scoffed at him as they pointed to his huge ship resting incongruously in a green meadow while the sun shone above it in a cloudless sky. But Noah and his sons hammered away at their immense craft and covered with pitch each seam and joint where the sea might pour in. When clouds began to form in the sky, they hurried their work, finishing it as the first big, ominous drops of rain began to fall.

For forty days the rain continued, but safe inside the ark with the animals, Noah's family drew up the gangplank and closed the port. Outside "were all the fountains of the great deep broken up, and the windows of heaven were opened" (Genesis 7:11). Even the mountains were covered by the disastrous flood in which every living creature perished except Noah, his wife, his three sons, and their wives and the creatures with them in the ark which floated high upon the raging waters.

After many days God remembered Noah and caused the rain to cease, and the waters to recede, until finally the ark with its living cargo grounded upon a mountain top. Over the vast expanse of water Noah sent out a raven which vanished from sight, for its great powers of flight enabled the large bird to fly to and fro until the earth was dry. Noah next sent out a dove which soon returned to the ark, for no dry land had yet appeared on which the bird could alight. After seven days of impatient waiting Noah again sent out the dove which returned carrying in its bill a freshly plucked olive leaf, the happy symbol that God had made peace with man and that the earth would once more welcome him.

A week later when a dove was again sent out, it failed to return to the shelter of the ark, thus indicating to Noah that the flood waters had entirely receded, making the earth safe for his family. Over the altar which they thankfully built, appeared the rainbow of God's everlasting covenant with Noah and his descendants. The brightly colored arch in the heavens was a sign that the orderly round of the seasons and the alternation of day and night will never cease.

The God Who had moved in judgment in the storm was the God Whose promise of mercy and life embraced Noah and his family. Though they did not see the Lord face to face, they were assured of His covenant in the shining rainbow as they walked forth unafraid. Noah's faith was abundantly justified, as the following prophecy states:

> "For this is as the waters of Noah unto me;
>   for as I have sworn that the waters of Noah
>     should no more go over the earth,
> so have I sworn that I would not be wroth with thee,
>   nor rebuke thee.
>
> "For the mountains shall depart
>   and the hills be removed,
> but my kindness shall not depart from thee,
>   neither shall the covenant of my peace be removed."
>     saith the Lord that hath mercy on thee.
>
> Isaiah 54:9-10

## 2. ABRAHAM'S FAITH IN GOD'S PROMISES

It would have been so much easier for Abraham and Sarah to remain safely at home with their kinsfolk than to venture forth across deserts into an unknown, perilous land. They could have enjoyed the many comforts and pleasures of the sophisticated civilization at Ur or at Haran in northern Mesopotamia. In that case, however, their names would have been forgotten millenniums ago, history would have been different, and one of the most glorious chapters of faith would not have been written.

When Abraham received the Lord's call to leave his country and kindred and father's house, he responded with all the resources of his being, certain of the reality of God's command and God's promise.

> By faith Abraham, when he was called to go out into a place which he should after receive for an inheritance, obeyed; and he went out, not knowing whither he went. By faith he sojourned in the land of promise, as in a strange country, dwelling in tabernacles with Isaac and Jacob, the heirs with him of the same promise; for he looked for a city which hath foundations, whose builder and maker is God.
>
> Hebrews 11:8-10

Abraham's family was involved in God's three promises. First Abraham was assured, while he was still childless, that the Lord would make of his descendants a great nation. One night as Abraham sat in his tent, pitched in the plain of Mamre, the Lord appeared to him in a vision and "brought him outside and said, 'Look toward heaven, and number the stars, if you are able to number them.' Then he said to him, 'So shall your descendants be.' And he believed the Lord; and he reckoned it to him as righteousness" (Genesis 15:5-6, RSV).

When the Lord made a covenant with Abraham, He promised, as we have seen, to give his descendants the entire Promised Land lying between the Nile and the Euphrates rivers. Though Abraham continued to be a wanderer and a sojourner all his days, and his burial place was the only plot of ground he owned in the Promised Land, he trusted that the Lord would indeed give the entire region to his descendants.

The Lord's third promise concerning Abraham's son and heir, "But my covenant will I establish with Isaac, which Sarah shall bear unto thee at this set time in the next year" (Genesis 17:21), was the only promise actually fulfilled in Abraham's lifetime. As the exalted chapter on faith declares, "These all died in faith, not having received the promises, but having seen them afar off, and were persuaded of them, and embraced them, and confessed that they were strangers and pilgrims on the earth" (Hebrews 11:13).

Hindrances, hardships, disappointments, perplexities, seemingly impossible commands tested his faith, yet Abraham did not falter. Such was the quality of the man the Hebrews called their father. Paul said of him, "No distrust made him waver concerning the promise of God, but he grew strong in his faith, as he gave glory to God, fully convinced that God was able to do what he had promised" (Romans 4:20-21, RSV). No wonder that Paul held up Abraham as a shining example of faith and exhorted Christians to "walk in the steps of that faith of our father Abraham" (Romans 4:12).

## 3. JACOB'S FAITH IN HIS FAMILY'S FUTURE

Though Abraham's grandson Jacob lived to be very old, he could never forget his awe-inspiring dream at Bethel when he was a young man journeying toward northern Mesopotamia for a wife. When his sight failed, he could still see in his mind's eye the amazing ladder on which angels from heaven descended and ascended. During his long life Jacob experienced, as we know, many joys and sorrows. The members of his family, torn apart by jealousy, fear, hatred, and violence, were finally reunited in Egypt by the forgiveness and family loyalty of his beloved son Joseph. But even when Jacob's troubles were at their worst, there continued to echo in his ear God's promise to him at Bethel:

"I am the Lord God of Abraham thy father, and the God of Isaac. The land whereon thou liest, to thee will I give it, and to thy seed. And thy seed shall be as the dust of the earth . . . and in thee and in thy seed shall all the families of the earth be blessed. And behold I am with thee, and will keep thee in all places whither thou goest, and will bring thee again into this land. For I will not leave thee until I have done that which I have spoken to thee of."

Genesis 28:13-15

On his deathbed in Egypt Jacob was far from the Promised Land, yet he still believed that the Lord would give all He had promised. Jacob's descendants were already so numerous that many wagons had been required to transport them all to the strange, alien land of Egypt where the Lord was indeed with them all. Remembering, perhaps, those years when his faith had been sorely tested, Jacob exclaimed to his beloved son Joseph, "I had not thought to see thy face, and, lo, God hath showed me also thy seed! . . . Behold, I die; but God shall be with you, and bring you again unto the land of your fathers" (Genesis 48:11, 21).

His little grandsons represented another generation, and as Jacob blessed them he was strangely moved. He believed that these two boys would become illustrious, so that in later times the people of Israel would call upon their blessing. Jacob said, "The Israelites will invoke your blessing for themselves; they will say to a man, 'God make you like Ephraim and like Manasseh!'" (Genesis 48:20, Moffatt).

Today pious Jewish fathers and grandfathers in a sabbath eve family service re-enact Jacob's blessing, laying their hand on the heads of their sons and saying, "God make you as Ephraim and Manasseh."

Jacob saw in the faces of his grandsons tokens of God's promises.

Abraham believed that the stars signified God's covenant. Noah saw it in the rainbow. What the future actually held for their families none of the patriarchs could be sure, but all believed that God would fulfill His word.

## 4. THE FRUITS OF DOUBT AND OF FAITH

A prophet described the quality of these patriarchs and of other men of faith when he said, "Thou wilt keep him in perfect peace, whose mind is stayed on thee, because he trusteth in thee" (Isaiah 26:3).

It sometimes happened that faith, unnourished by prayer, died from careless indifference, materialistic living, or craven fear. Whenever their faith succumbed, people were warned that they would experience

a trembling heart, and failing of eyes, and sorrow of mind. And thy life shall hang in doubt before thee, and thou shalt fear day and night, and shalt have none assurance of thy life. In the morning thou shalt say, "Would God it were even!" and at even thou shalt say, "Would God it were morning!" for the fear of thine heart wherewith thou shalt fear, and for the sight of thine eyes which thou shalt see.

Deuteronomy 28:65-67

This picture of the consequences of doubt and unbelief contrasts sharply with the stories of the biblical heroes of faith we have been considering in the eleventh chapter of Hebrews. Because of a close relationship with God, these heroes and heroines gained for themselves and their families such firm confidence in His promises that they were enabled to perform extraordinary deeds. They were the believing ones

who through faith subdued kingdoms, wrought righteousness, obtained promises, stopped the mouth of lions, quenched the violence of fire, escaped the edge of the sword, out of weakness were made strong, waxed valiant in fight, turned to flight the armies of the aliens.

Hebrews 11:33-34

These triumphant men and women of faith have inspired innumerable families to place their own quiet confidence and trust in the Lord.

CHAPTER 19

# Love in the Family

Beloved, let us love one another, for love is of God; and every one that loveth is born of God, and knoweth God. He that loveth not knoweth not God, for God is love.

I John 4:7-8

The family at its best is a nursery of love. This natural aspect of a family is perhaps its highest reason for being. To begin life as one who is loved and to grow up surrounded by the warmth and tenderness of family affections is to be supremely fortunate. Love flourishes in a happy home where parents, children, sisters, brothers, wives, and husbands care for each other and express affectionate interest in the well-being of all.

## 1. THE RICHNESS OF FAMILY AFFECTIONS

Unforgettable examples of the many-faceted nature of love in the family are found in the Bible stories we have already examined. Is any instance of romantic love more beautiful than that of Jacob's for Rachel, the lovely girl for whom he served seven years, "and they seemed unto him but a few days, for the love he had to her" (Genesis 29:20)? Is not the mature and understanding love of a husband for his wife perfectly expressed in Elkanah's love for Hannah? Hosea's love for his erring wife Gomer is a classic example of forgiving and enduring love.

The Bible contains many instances of a parent's devotion to his child, such as: Abraham's grieving love for the son he felt called upon to sacrifice; Rebekah's love for Jacob—a love that became harmful favoritism; Jacob's unwise preference for Joseph; Jochebed's loving determination that her little Moses should not die; Hannah's unselfish love for her child Samuel, whom she left to be educated at the temple in Shiloh; David's enduring love for his worthless son Absalom; Rizpah's heroic devotion to her dead sons; the Shunammite mother's love that defied death. All these stories and many others sprang from the deep, rich soil of a father's or a mother's love. Some of these loves are stained with human failings, but Jesus in His parable of the Prodigal Son depicted a father whose love was flawless.

Those who expressed filial love in the Bible include such people as: Noah's two sons, Shem and Japheth, who loyally concealed their father's shame; Isaac and Ishmael, who buried their father Abraham, according to his wish, beside Sarah in the cave of Machpelah; Joseph, who used the wealth and prestige of his high position in Egypt to aid his father Jacob; Gideon, who threshed his father's grain; and Ruth, who gleaned in the fields to support her mother-in-law Naomi, whom Ruth loved as her own mother.

Of brotherly and sisterly love, we have already found numerous examples, such as: Joseph's tender concern for his full brother Benjamin; the protection and help Miriam and Aaron gave to their brother Moses; Mary's and Martha's love for their brother Lazarus; and the loyalty and co-operation between the famous pairs of brothers, the disciples Peter and Andrew, James and John.

## 2. LOVE EXTENDING BEYOND THE FAMILY CIRCLE

Love characteristically spreads beyond the narrow bounds of a family, especially one in which father and mother, parents and children, brothers and sisters are bound together in affectionate concern for one another, and in which children are taught to love the Lord.

Among the many people in the Bible whose love and protection extended beyond the circle of their immediate family should be mentioned: Abraham, who gave his nephew Lot the opportunity of journeying with him to the Promised Land and there rescued him from his enemies; David, who granted kingly favors to the lame prince Mephibosheth, son of his friend and brother-in-law Jonathan

(II Samuel 9:3-13); Joash's aunt who rescued him from a murderous plot and hid him and his nurse in her house for six years until the boy could be proclaimed rightful king of Judah (II Kings 11); and Mordecai, who adopted his uncle's orphaned daughter Esther.

The New Testament records the tender love and understanding between two cousins, Elisabeth, mother of John the Baptist, and Mary, mother of Jesus. It also relates that Barnabas took his nephew, John Mark, on the first missionary journey and loyalty defended the young man in his misunderstanding with Paul. Paul himself benefited from the family affection and loyalty of his nephew, his sister's son, living in Jerusalem, who warned Paul of the plot to kill him (Acts 23:12-22).

All these aspects of family loyalty are so convincingly portrayed in the Bible that they give us unforgettable and inspiring examples of the power of love to bind the members of a family together and to include in its protective sphere relatives, friends, and acquaintances.

## 3. "LOVE IS OF GOD"

As the First Epistle of John declares, "love is of God." "We love him, because he first loved us" (I John 4:19). Our love for others is but an overflowing of the love God pours into our hearts. Even family affections may fail unless the channels are open for father, mother, and child to receive the abundant love of God. "God is love; and he that dwelleth in love dwelleth in God, and God in him" (I John 4:16). A family in which the indwelling love of God is present is a Christian family indeed.

When Jesus was asked to name the greatest commandment, He answered in words from Deuteronomy 6:4-5 and Leviticus 19:18 which express the deepest insights of Judaism:

"Hear, O Israel, The Lord our God is one Lord. And thou shalt love the Lord thy God with all thy heart, and with all thy soul, and with all thy mind, and with all thy strength: this is the first commandment.

"And the second is like, namely this, Thou shalt love thy neighbor as thyself. There is none other commandment greater than these."

Mark 12:29-31

Christianity's central teaching proclaims that at the heart of the universe there is love—a love that becomes evident when men look at

Christ. "For God so loved the world, that he gave his only begotten Son, that whosoever believeth in him should not perish, but have everlasting life" (John 3:16). Christ, then, is the manifestation of God's love for us. In the life and teachings of Jesus, as these are recorded in the four Gospels, we behold love perfectly incarnated in a man.


## 4. PAUL'S HYMN OF LOVE

The great apostle Paul, in a letter to the Christians in Corinth, wrote the most moving description of love in the Bible (I Corinthians 13). Paul's original Greek word for love, *agape,* is translated in the King James Version as "charity," in the rich, full, old meaning of that word, but newer versions of the Bible generally use the word "love."

An illuminating way to study Paul's beautiful and very familiar chapter on love and to gain fresh insight into its meanings is to read it in one of the newer translations. Here is James Moffatt's rendering of the elements of love expressed in a modern idiom:

Love is very patient, very kind. Love knows no jealousy; love makes no parade, gives itself no airs, is never rude, never selfish, never irritated, never resentful; love is never glad when others go wrong, love is gladdened by goodness, always slow to expose, always eager to believe the best, always hopeful, always patient.

I Corinthians 13:4-7

Henry Drummond in his essay on love, entitled *The Greatest Thing in the World,* comments that as a beam of light is passed through a prism to show its component colors of red, orange, yellow, green, blue, and violet, so Paul passed love "through the magnificent prism of his inspired intellect, and it comes out on the other side broken up into its many elements." Here, according to Henry Drummond, are the nine elements of love corresponding to Paul's analysis:

| | | |
|---|---|---|
| Patience | ——— | Love suffereth long |
| Kindness | ——— | And is kind |
| Generosity | ——— | Love envieth not |
| Humility | ——— | Love vaunteth not itself, is not puffed up |
| Courtesy | ——— | Doth not behave itself unseemly |

| | | |
|---|---|---|
| Unselfishness | ——— | Seeketh not her own |
| Good Temper | ——— | Is not easily provoked |
| Guilelessness | ——— | Thinketh no evil |
| Sincerity | ——— | Rejoiceth not in iniquity, but rejoiceth in truth |

Paul contrasted love with eloquence—"the tongues of men and of angels"—with prophecy, with faith, with benevolence, with sacrifice, even with martyrdom, yet found that of all these, love is greatest. Without love, Paul said, "I am become as sounding brass, or a tinkling cymbal" (I Corinthians 13:1).

Though Paul was indeed a man of towering intellect, even he could not have conceived his superb picture of love by rational processes alone. Must he not have been inspired by someone whose life incarnated love at its best? Brought up, as he was, in a devout Jewish family and early in his life trained in the love of God, Paul experienced many aspects of love. But his chapter in Corinthians contains deeper elements than those he received from his early religious background. As we study his words a familiar portrait begins to emerge. Is Paul describing with penetrating power someone he knew? To whom do these qualities best refer? Is not the thirteenth chapter of I Corinthians a perfect summary of the character of Jesus?

All family love is an echo of His transcendent love and all Christian families seek to obey Him: "This is my commandment, That ye love one another, as I have loved you" (John 15:12).

CHAPTER 20

# Sources of Family Unity

---

Behold, how good and how pleasant it
is for brethren to dwell together in unity!
Psalm 133:1

---

\*

## 1. LOVE OF THE LAND

In addition to the forces acting to unify the family discussed in the three previous chapters, love of the land, the cradle of their faith, was a potent factor in molding families in ancient Israel. Their dependence upon the products of the land tended to hold Hebrew families together. It seemed to them after the rigors of the desert "a good land and a large . . . a land flowing with milk and honey" (Exodus 3:8). They described their country in glowing terms as

a land of brooks of water, of fountains and depths that spring out of valleys and hills; a land of wheat and barley and vines and fig trees and pomegranates; a land of olive oil and honey; a land wherein thou shalt eat bread without scarceness, thou shalt not lack any thing in it; a land whose stones are iron, and out of whose hills thou mayest dig brass [copper].

Deuteronomy 8:7-9

The people who lived there loved its deserts and mountains, plateaus and plains, wildernesses and fertile fields, the Sea of Galilee bordered with mountains, the winding river Jordan, the rough, stony hills of Judea, and the farm land of the valleys. Love of country was profoundly significant in binding the members of a family together and in uniting all the families of Israel.

## 2. OBEDIENCE TO THE LAW

The Law of Moses enshrined in the Pentateuch as the will of God fostered family solidarity and wholeness, insofar as this Law was faithfully obeyed. The Psalmist in a lengthy and enthusiastic tribute to the Law joyfully exclaimed, "O how I love thy law! It is my meditation all the day! . . . Therefore I love thy commandments above gold, yea, above fine gold" (Psalm 119:97, 127).

As soon as a child was able to learn anything, he was taught the *Shema,* Israel's confession of faith in one God, beginning, "Hear, O Israel: The Lord our God is one Lord" (Deuteronomy 6:4). This supreme truth with its following command to love the Lord was recited twice each day by every faithful Israelite. It prefaced every synagogue service, and was inscribed on the doorposts of Hebrew homes.

The child next learned the Decalogue, or Ten Commandments, which express God's character and will and are the very foundation of the Law. These ten simple but profound rules have knit Hebrew families together throughout history, for they contain the quintessence of Israel's moral and spiritual life. Being universal in scope, they are as valid today as in the time of Moses.

After the Exile, synagogues became centers for teaching and studying the Law. Today when Jewish families attend the synagogue they hear the Law read to them from sacred scrolls kept in an ark over which burns a perpetual light. Their faithful love and observance of the Law during thousands of years is largely responsible for the unity of Jewish families.

## 3. BELIEF IN THEIR DESTINY AS THE PEOPLE OF GOD

A powerful factor contributing to family unity was the Israelites' belief that as descendants of Abraham and the people with whom God made His covenant at Sinai, they had an especially close personal relationship with the Lord. They were His people. He was their God. He had chosen their fathers long ago. "Only the Lord had a delight in thy fathers to love them, and he chose their seed after them, even you above all people, as it is this day" (Deuteronomy 10:15).

In the exalted words of a prophet, speaking for the Lord:

> "But thou, Israel, art my servant,
>   Jacob whom I have chosen,
>   the seed of Abraham my friend.
> Thou whom I have taken from the ends of the earth, . . .
>   fear thou not, for I am with thee;
>   be not dismayed, for I am thy God;
> I will strengthen thee, yea, I will help thee;
>   yea, I will uphold thee with the right hand
>       of my righteousness."
>
> Isaiah 41:8-10

## 4. FAITH IN GOD

Faith in God was doubtless the greatest source of unity in Israel's families. God seemed very near to them. He was One to whom they could speak and Who in turn spoke to them. From the beginning He had been with them, for, as He revealed from the burning bush to Moses, "I am the God of thy father, the God of Abraham, the God of Isaac, and the God of Jacob" (Exodus 3:6).

As their experience of God deepened, they discerned that He is all-powerful, infinitely wise, holy, good, loving, merciful, changeless, perfect, and eternal. He was their rock of defense, their shield against danger, their stronghold in time of trouble.

Faith in such a God was part of the family atmosphere enfolding Hebrew children during their impressionable early years. Because God was real to them from childhood, He seemed to them as integral a part of their family as their father himself. In family suffering they felt God's presence giving them courage to endure.

> Then they cry unto the Lord in their trouble,
>   and he saveth them out of their distresses.
> He sent his word, and healed them,
>   and delivered them from their destructions.
> Oh that men would praise the Lord for his goodness,
>   and for his wonderful works to the children of men!
>
> Psalm 107:19-21

## 5. KNOWLEDGE OF THE SCRIPTURES

Israel's faith in God was nourished by prayer and, as we have already seen, by the rich and many-sided aspects of family worship, one of which included the study of the Scriptures. As one of the psalmists sang, "Thy word is a lamp unto my feet and a light unto my path" (Psalm 119:105).

Before the Scriptures were written, many of their stories circulated in oral form. The patriarchs must have passed on from father to son stories of the Creation, the Garden of Eden, the Flood, and the Tower of Babel, all doubtless brought from Abraham's homeland in Haran.

The events leading to Israel's deliverance from Egypt long remained in oral story, like the ancient ones in Genesis, retold from father to son, for the Lord had commanded Moses, saying, "tell in the ears of thy son, and of thy son's son, what things I have wrought in Egypt, and my signs which I have done among them; that ye may know how that I am the Lord" (Exodus 10:2). As each new generation listened to the wonderful old narrative, the children felt a deeper bond with their parents and their hearts were uplifted with pride in their ancestors.

Even after the books of Scripture were written, few but priests and scribes were able to read them, nor could many people afford to have scrolls hand-copied from the original manuscripts. The ancient stories and the laws of God were of such absorbing and vital interest to the Hebrews, however, that the scribes read portions of the books to the people, who then discussed the chief ideas at home and taught them to their children, as the Lord commanded: "And thou shalt teach them diligently unto thy children, and shalt talk of them when thou sittest in thine house, and when thou walkest by the way, and when thou liest down, and when thou risest up" (Deuteronomy 6:7).

The scribe Baruch read Jeremiah's prophecies to the people of Judah assembled in the Temple at Jerusalem on a fast day (Jeremiah 36:6, 8). Similarly, when the first version of Deuteronomy was discovered in the Temple during repairs made in Josiah's reign, 640-609 B.C., the king summoned "all the people, both small and great, and he read in their ears all the words of the book of the covenant which was found in the house of the Lord" (II Kings 23:2).

A century later entire families who had returned from the Exile gathered in Jerusalem to hear Ezra read the Law of Moses to them.

Those attending his huge Bible class included "men and women, and all that could hear with understanding" (Nehemiah 8:2), doubtless meaning all children old enough to listen intelligently and quietly. From early morning until the hot noonday sun drove them into the shade, the congregation stood in the open space in front of the gate, listening attentively. Assisted by certain Levites, Ezra translated and explained the text as he read it. "So they read in the book in the law of God distinctly, and gave the sense, and caused them to understand the reading" (Nehemiah 8:8).

This story is a picturesque instance of how the Israelites obeyed the law in Deuteronomy which enjoined Bible study.

Gather the people together, men, and women, and children, and thy stranger that is within thy gates, that they may hear, and that they may learn, and fear the Lord your God, and observe to do all the words of this law. And that their children, which have not known any thing, may hear, and learn to fear the Lord your God, as long as ye live in the land whither ye go over Jordan to possess it.

Deuteronomy 31:12-13

The tradition of discussing, if not reading, the Scriptures in Hebrew homes continued in New Testament times. In Jerusalem after the Crucifixion, the risen Christ appeared to a little group including His eleven disciples in a house where they were staying. "Then opened he their understanding, that they might understand the scriptures" (Luke 24:45). Earlier in the evening on the road to Emmaus, He had likewise explained the Scriptures to Cleopas and his companion.

Family Bible study as well as study by individuals became a factor in uniting people in understanding and devotion to the rapidly expanding Church. At Thessalonica in Macedonia, the Christians in one house or another, "searched the scriptures daily" (Acts 17:11). In Rome, where Paul went for his trial, he received in his lodging many Jews "to whom he expounded and testified the kingdom of God, persuading them concerning Jesus, both out of the law of Moses, and out of the prophets, from morning till evening" (Acts 28:23).

Paul, convinced that the Jewish Scriptures, the books of the Old Testament, contained valuable spiritual instruction and encouragement for Christians, wrote, "For whatsoever things were written aforetime were written for our learning, that we through patience and comfort of the scriptures might have hope" (Romans 15:4).

Clear proof of the importance of Bible study in early Christian families is furnished by Paul's words to his young companion Timothy, who, as we have already seen, was taught by his grandmother Lois and his mother Eunice:

And that from a child thou hast known the holy scriptures, which are able to make thee wise unto salvation through faith which is in Christ Jesus. All scripture is given by inspiration of God, and is profitable for doctrine, for reproof, for correction, for instruction in righteousness.

II Timothy 3:15-16

The Church Paul and Timothy knew was, at its best, a unified family. As Paul declared, "For ye are all the children of God by faith in Christ Jesus. . . . There is neither Jew nor Greek, there is neither bond nor free, there is neither male nor female, for ye are all one in Christ Jesus" (Galatians 3:26, 28).

# Family Concerns

*

# CHAPTER 21

# Food and Clothing
# for the Family

And having food and raiment let us be therewith content.
I Timothy 6:8

✱

The Bible recognizes that food, clothing, and shelter, three basic physical needs of the family, are essential. Most biblical stories, dealing as they do with the life of actual people, contain some reference to eating, drinking, wearing garments, or living in houses. Even the story of Adam and Eve mentions the fruits and vegetables they ate and the animal skins they used for clothing. Their sons labored to supply the family with essentials, for Cain was a farmer, "a tiller of the ground," while Abel kept sheep.

Though a complete study of all the food and clothing mentioned in the Bible would reveal many fascinating aspects of life in ancient times, this chapter will be confined to a discussion of how families obtained their necessities and how God in His care and bounty provided all that the people needed. "Thou givest them their meat in due season. Thou openest thine hand and satisfiest the desire of every living thing" (Psalm 145:15-16).

## 1. FAMILY FOOD PRODUCTION

In patriarchal times the family was an industrial group principally engaged in the production of food and fiber. Father, mother, and older children all joined in the ceaseless tasks of feeding and clothing the family. To obtain meat, milk, butter and cheese from their flocks and herds required the labor and skill of many hands. Domestic animals had to be driven to green pastures, such as those at Shechem found by Jacob's sons. There was the daily chore of watering the sheep, a task entrusted to Rachel on the memorable day when she met Jacob at the well. Butchering and sheepshearing were probably done by the men, while milking and butter and cheese making were women's work.

Though Isaac was rich in cattle, he planted vegetable and grain crops at Gerar. Figs, dates, olives, and pomegranates were gathered from trees. Noah is said to have introduced the cultivation of grapes. All these products of the land required planting, harvesting, and processing before they were ready for cooking and eating. We know that Gideon threshed grain secretly in a wine press. From morning until dark whole families must have labored to produce their food, while the mother's task of cooking was continual.

Even when the Hebrews moved into the Promised Land and settled in towns and villages, many families planted their own grapevines and fig trees (I Kings 4:25), and often kept their own sheep or goats. The fertile soil of Palestine yielded lentils, cucumbers, and squash, peas, lettuce, and onions. Fish from the Sea of Galilee supplied families in the neighborhood and as far away as Jerusalem. From caravans of traders they purchased salt, spices, and honey. Though markets sprang up in larger towns where a variety of produce was sold, most families raised and processed their own food.

As large numbers of court officials and servants ate at a king's table (Queen Jezebel fed four hundred prophets of Baal at her table), the produce of many farms and pastures was necessary to supply royal needs. "And Solomon's provision for one day was thirty measures of fine flour, and threescore measures of meal, ten fat oxen, and twenty oxen out of the pastures, and an hundred sheep, beside harts, and roebucks, and fallowdeer, and fatted fowl" (I Kings 22:23).

Five centuries later, when Nehemiah was governor of Jerusalem, he entertained daily one hundred and fifty Jews. Though his provisions were far less lavish than Solomon's, they were still impressive. Nehemiah wrote: "Now that which was prepared for me daily was one ox and six choice sheep; also fowls were prepared for me, and once in ten days store of all sorts of wine" (Nehemiah 5:18).

Lest these commissary department records give us a false idea of plenty in Israel, we should bear in mind that these lavish lists are those of a fortunate ruler and the most splendid of their kings. For the average family of biblical times hunger was always just around the corner. Even in the rich land of Egypt bordering the Nile, seven years of plenty had been followed by seven years of relentless famine. Armies periodically marched across Israel's most fertile lands, plundering the harvest and laying waste the fields. Natural disasters took their toll of crops: high winds flattened the grain, flash floods washed away good soil, droughts parched the fields, and insect pests chewed their way through every green leaf.

During a drought in King Ahab's reign, the king and his palace official, Obadiah, were reduced to a frantic search for any hidden spring around which they might find a little green grass for their starving beasts. Ahab said, " 'Go into the land, unto all fountains of water, and unto all brooks. Peradventure we may find grass to save the horses and mules alive, that we lose not all the beasts.' So they divided the land between them . . . Ahab went one way by himself, and Obadiah went another way by himself" (I Kings 18:5-6).

Joel, the prophet, mourning the effects of a locust plague, describes its dire results:

> The fields are laid waste,
>     the ground mourns;
> because the grain is destroyed,
>     the wine fails,
>     the oil languishes.
> Be confounded, O tillers of the soil,
>     wail, O vinedressers,
> for the wheat and the barley;
>     because the harvest of the field has perished.
> The vine withers,
>     the fig tree languishes.
> Pomegranate, palm, and apple,
>     all the trees of the field are withered. . . .
> How the beasts groan!
>     The herds of cattle are perplexed
> because there is no pasture for them;
>     even the flocks of sheep are dismayed.
>                     Joel 1:10-12, 18, RSV

These disasters, with their accompanying times of want, reminded the Hebrews that, despite all their labor in field and pasture, at oil press and threshing floor, it was ultimately the Lord Who fed and sustained them.

## 2. THE LORD PROVIDES

Beginning with the old story of the rainbow after the Flood, many events in their long history gave the Hebrews assurance that the Lord would supply all human needs, forever upholding the order and stability of nature by which summer follows winter and crops ripen for the harvest. In His covenant with Noah, the Lord had said, "While the earth remaineth, seedtime and harvest, and cold and heat, and summer and winter, and day and night shall not cease" (Genesis 8:22).

If ever there were a time when starvation seemed imminent, however, it was during the wanderings of the people of Israel in the barren, dry wilderness. In their hunger they complained bitterly to Moses and Aaron, saying, "Would to God we had died by the hand of the Lord in the land of Egypt, when we sat by the flesh pots and when we did eat bread to the full. For ye have brought us forth into this wilderness, to kill this whole assembly with hunger" (Exodus 16:3). But the Lord sent them quails for meat and a small, sweet, wafer-like substance called manna for bread, and they ate and were satisfied.

> He rained flesh also upon them as dust,
>     and feathered fowls like as the sand of the sea;
> and he let it fall in the midst of their camp,
>     round about their habitations.
> So they did eat, and were well filled,
>     for he gave them their own desire.
>                     Psalm 78:27-29

The story of manna in the wilderness taught the Israelites a profound lesson which was enshrined in the Law and quoted by Jesus during His temptation. "And he humbled thee and suffered thee to hunger, and fed thee with manna . . . that he might make thee know that man doth not live by bread only, but by every word that proceedeth out of the mouth of the Lord doth man live" (Deuteronomy 8:3).

Though their hunger was satisfied in the wilderness, they could find no water to drink and they feared lest they and their children and all their cattle die of thirst. God spoke to Moses, saying, "Behold, I will stand before thee there upon the rock in Horeb, and thou shalt smite the rock, and there shall come water out of it, that the people may drink" (Exodus 17:6). Again God supplied the needs of the wandering families of Israel.

Centuries later the prophet Elijah was twice miraculously supplied with food: once while in hiding at the brook Cherith where ravens fed him (Kings 17:3-7), and a second time on his journey to Horeb when an angel baked a cake on hot stones for him and provided a jar of water (I Kings 19:5-8). During the famine, while Elijah lodged with the widow of Zarephath and her son, their "barrel of meal wasted not, neither did the cruse of oil fail," so that "she, and he, and her house did eat many days" (I Kings 17:15, 16).

In a psalm praising God's loving kindness, the Hebrews described how He makes the land fruitful for men:

> He turneth the wilderness into a standing water,
>     and dry ground into watersprings.
> And there he maketh the hungry to dwell,
>     that they may prepare a city for habitation,
> and sow the fields and plant vineyards,
>     which may yield fruits of increase.
> He blesseth them also, so that they are multiplied greatly,
>     and suffereth not their cattle to decrease.
>
> Psalm 107:35-38

Another psalm, possibly the best known and best loved of all, sings of God's tender care in providing His people with their necessities:

> The Lord is my shepherd; I shall not want. . . .
> Thou preparest a table before me. . . .
> Thou anointest my head with oil,
>     my cup runneth over.
> Surely goodness and mercy shall follow me
>     all the days of my life,
> and I will dwell in the house of the Lord
>     for ever.
>
> Psalm 23:1, 5-6

## 3. GRACE AT TABLE

The people of Israel expressed their profound gratitude to the Lord at their harvest festivals and also in daily prayers of thanksgiving. These prayers, often called blessings, were offered with their food, according to the Law. "When thou hast eaten and art full, then thou shalt bless the Lord thy God for the good land which he hath given thee" (Deuteronomy 8:10).

Customarily a Jewish father offered a thanksgiving before the family ate, saying as he broke bread, "Blessed art thou, O Lord, God of the universe, Who dost bring forth bread from the earth." At the conclusion of the common meal he blessed the cup of wine, thanking the Lord Who "dost create the fruit of the vine." After drinking from the cup, the father passed it to each person at the table in turn.

The Gospels record three occasions when Jesus offered the traditional blessing. The first was at the repast of loaves and fishes when He "took the seven loaves, and gave thanks, and brake, and gave to his disciples to set before them, and they did set them before the people. And they had a few small fishes; and he blessed, and commanded to set them also before them. So they did eat, and were filled. . . . And they that had eaten were about four thousand" (Mark 8:6-9).

The blessings of the bread and the wine at the Last Supper were again the table thanksgiving of the Jews transformed by Jesus into an act of profound meaning. "And as they did eat, Jesus took bread and blessed and brake it and gave to them and said, 'Take, eat, this is my body.' And he took the cup, and when he had given thanks, he gave it to them, and they all drank of it" (Mark 14:22-23).

When the stranger, whom Cleopas and his companion met on the road to Emmaus, accompanied them home for supper, "he took bread and blessed it and brake and gave to them. And their eyes were opened and they knew him" (Luke 24:30-31). Having seen Jesus perform this reverent act, they suddenly recognized the stranger as the risen Christ.

From these biblical records it becomes evident that today's custom of grace at the family table is derived from the ancient Jewish table blessings which gave thanks to God as the Giver of all our food.

The "Wesley Grace," sung at table, goes as follows:

> Be present at our table, Lord,
>   Be here and everywhere adored.
> These mercies bless and grant that we
>   May feast in fellowship with thee.

A prayer often used in Christian families recognizes that in our infinite indebtedness to Him we should be stewards of His bountiful goodness, especially to those in need.

Give us grateful hearts, our Father, for all thy mercies, and make us mindful of the needs of others; through Jesus Christ our Lord. Amen

## 4. BIBLICAL GARMENTS

The earliest garments were probably made of animal skins such as those with which the Lord clothed Adam and Eve (Genesis 3:21), but at an early period cloth made from sheep's wool, goat's hair, or camel's hair was widely used. After shearing, the wool or hair was beaten to free it from embedded dirt or leaves. Then the mother of the family, assisted by her daughters, combed the wool, spun it into thread, wove it on the family loom, and sometimes dyed the cloth in a vat. Black dye was obtained from pomegranate bark, yellow dye from almond leaves, and other colors from combinations of vegetable matter with such substances as potash and lime. The famous purple-red dye sold by Lydia (Acts 16:14), came from murex shellfish of the Mediterranean. The color of apparel seems to have had great significance.

Flax was raised in Canaan before the twelve tribes entered the land. At Jericho, Rahab hid the Israelite spies on her rooftop amid stalks of drying flax (Joshua 2:6). Fine linen for the priests' elaborate garments was made from flax (Exodus 39:22-29). Solomon imported linen yarn from Egypt "at a price" (II Chronicles 1:16). Isaiah tells of workers combing flax (19:9), and the Book of Esther describes Mordecai as being dressed "in a garment of fine linen and purple" (8:15).

Silk, a luxury fabric, may have been imported from China. Cotton was apparently not introduced until the end of the Old Testament period. Sackcloth, a coarse fabric, was worn to signify mourning (Jonah 3:5).

The good wife of Proverbs, as mentioned earlier, worked industriously to clothe her family in suitable garments for all seasons. She also had a little business making linen clothing and leather girdles. Dorcas made coats and garments for widows and orphans in the upper room of her house at Joppa (Acts 9:39).

The garments women made for their families included: a loincloth, a tunic of linen or wool reaching from neck to ankles, and a long mantle or cloak of wool or goat's hair seamed at the shoulders. Sandals were made of leather, but girdles, though usually of leather, were sometimes of fabric with pockets for carrying such articles as coins and knives. A cloth veil or turban was worn as a headdress for protection against the sun.

Infants were bundled in a cloth tied around with swaddling bands, while the dead were wrapped in linen graveclothes, as in the story of Lazarus (John 11:44). Joseph of Arimathaea bought fine linen and after wrapping Jesus' body in it laid Him in the sepulchre (Mark 15:46). These linen graveclothes lying in the tomb became evidence to Peter and the other disciples of the reality of the Resurrection (John 20:5-8).

Most of the garments of Bible times, worn by men and women, appear to have been loose. The majority of them do not appear to have had sleeves, buttons, collars, or cuffs. With these garments the people wore scarves draped about the head and over the shoulders.

Some of the noteworthy garments mentioned in the Bible include: Joseph's princely coat of many colors; Samuel's little robe, lovingly made for him each year by his mother; Elijah's wonder-working mantle; John's garment of camel's hair; Jesus' seamless tunic for which His executioners cast lots (John 19:23-24); and the cloak Paul requested Timothy to bring to him from Troas (II Timothy 4:13).

## 5. ELABORATE *vs.* SEEMLY ATTIRE

From a modern point of view, most people in biblical times were rather shabbily dressed. Few had more than one change of garments and many people lacked a warm covering. John the Baptist exhorted his hearers to share their extra food and clothing: "He that hath two coats, let him impart to him that hath none. And he that hath meat, let him do likewise" (Luke 3:11).

Clothing was often passed down in a family and its torn fabric was frequently mended and patched (Mark 2:21). Fullers used soap in cleansing dirty garments (Malachi 3:2), for they carried on a thriving trade in cleaning as well as in bleaching and dyeing cloth.

A few fortunate women of Jerusalem dressed elaborately, according to the list of their finery itemized by Isaiah. The articles he enumerates have been interpreted as:

anklets, tiaras, necklaces, earrings, bracelets and veils, headbands, arm-
lets, and sashes, scent-bottles, charms, signet-rings and nose-rings, robes
of state, mantles, shawls and purses, gauze, linen turbans, and wrappers.

Isaiah 3:18-23, Moffatt

Another luxurious wardrobe is described in Ezekiel's allegory of
Israel as a beautiful woman:

I decked you with embroidered robes, I shod you with Egyptian
leather, I swathed you in fine linen, I clothed you in silk; I adorned you
with finery, bracelets on your arms, a necklace round your throat, a ring
on your nose, earrings in your ears, and a lovely crown upon your head.

Ezekiel 16:10-12, Moffatt

Proper attire was the subject of various regulations. In the early
period it was decreed that a garment made of both linen and wool
was not to be worn (Leviticus 19:19). A man was not to wear a
woman's garment, nor a woman, a man's (Deuteronomy 22:5). One
did not wear unseemly clothes to a wedding, but, out of courtesy to
the bride and groom, put on a "wedding garment" (Matthew 22:11).

In Christian times women were advised to "adorn themselves
modestly and sensibly in seemly apparel, not with braided hair or
pearls or costly attire but by good deeds, as befits women who pro-
fess religion" (I Timothy 2:9-10, RSV).

## 6. JESUS' TEACHINGS CONCERNING MATERIAL NEEDS

Jesus taught His disciples to pray for human needs: "Give us this
day our daily bread" (Matthew 6:11). For fearful and worried
people who dreaded the next day with all its cares and troubles, Jesus
had words of serene courage and faith. Like the good father of a
family, God, in providing for His children, both clothes and feeds
them, for "they that seek the Lord shall not want any good thing"
(Psalm 34:10). Jesus told those who were troubled in their hearts
not to be anxious about

. . . what ye shall eat, or what ye shall drink, nor yet for your body,
what ye shall put on. Is not the life more than meat, and the body more
than raiment? . . . And why take ye thought for raiment? Consider the
lilies of the field, how they grow; they toil not, neither do they spin, and
yet I say unto you that even Solomon in all his glory was not arrayed

like one of these. Wherefore, if God so clothe the grass of the field, which today is and tomorrow is cast into the oven, shall he not much more clothe you, O ye of little faith?

Therefore take no thought, saying, What shall we eat? or, What shall we drink? or, Wherewithal shall we be clothed? . . . For your heavenly Father knoweth that ye have need of all these things. But seek ye first the kingdom of God, and his righteousness, and all these things shall be added unto you.

Matthew 6:25, 28-33

# CHAPTER 22

# The Family Home

And if a house be divided against itself, that house cannot stand.
                                                    Mark 3:25

*

The words *home, house, abode, habitation, dwelling, tent, resting place,* so widely and frequently used throughout the Bible, indicate to what a great extent the Scriptures record family living. Even when the word *house* refers to the house of God, meaning the Temple, or to the house of Israel, meaning all the people of Israel, it has a family connotation. Whether the dwelling was a cave or tent, a hut made of sun-baked mud brick, or a two-story stone house, Hebrew homes were places for rest, refreshment, and protection, places where children were born and cared for and where old people died, places, in short, where all the members of a family came together for mutual help and happiness.

## 1. ITS MATERIAL STRUCTURE

In biblical times the home might be constructed, like Abraham's and Sarah's, of woven goat's-hair material stretched between tent poles (Genesis 18:1), or of stone (Leviticus 14:42), or brick (Nahum 3:14). Some homes were merely caves (Obadiah 3). A house had a doorway with a threshold (Zephaniah 2:14). On the lintel and two side posts the blood of the Passover lamb was to be sprinkled (Exodus 12:22). The door turned on hinges (Proverbs 26:14) and was fastened with lock and bars (Nehemiah 3:15).

Some dwellings had windows which were screened with a lattice (Judges 5:28; II Kings 1:2). Frequently, houses were built with an outside staircase leading to the roof, on which a guest chamber was often built, like the one occupied by Elisha at Shunem (II Kings 4:10). The Law required that a parapet be built around the roof of a stone house (Deuteronomy 22:8) to prevent people from falling off.

A typical Palestinian home of the time of Jesus is described by Bernard R. Youngman in *The Lands and People of the Living Bible*, as follows:

Inside the house was only one room; this served as living and sleeping quarters for both family and animals. The front part at street level was occupied by the ox and ass, chickens and goats, kept for their work and food. Their presence gave warmth in winter. Two or three steps led to a kind of upper platform where the family lived. At this level there was a trough of crushed straw for the animals. On this raised part only the essentials for their simple lives were found. There was little furniture —well-made in Joseph's home, we may be sure—a chest for their belongings, stools, waterpots (porous to keep them cool), oil jars (glazed to prevent oozing), bins for meal; cavities in the walls were used for the sleeping mattresses and various utensils. In the floor was a covered hole where corn was kept; the millstone for grinding it was in another corner and not far away, on a carefully-made wooden tripod, was the precious olive oil lamp, always alight, for, it will be recalled, no one in Palestine slept in the dark and even by day the room was gloomy without it (p. 219).

## 2. FURNISHINGS AND DECORATIONS

Though ordinary houses were, as the above passage indicates, very simply furnished (II Kings 4:10), palaces had costly embroidered hangings and charcoal-burning braziers to combat the cold of winter (Jeremiah 36:22; Mark 14:54). Solomon's palace in Jerusalem was panelled with cedar cut from the great forests of Lebanon by Hiram's workmen (I Kings 7:7-8). People referred to Ahab's and Jezebel's palace in Samaria as "the ivory house" because it was decorated with carved ivory and furnished with handsome couches, tables, and chairs all inlaid with ivory (I Kings 22:39). Thousands of these beautifully carved ivory ornaments from the time of Ahab have been excavated by archaeologists at Samaria. The prophet Amos uttered dire warnings against unjust and evil rulers who lived in the "houses of ivory" (Amos 3:15) and slept "upon beds of ivory" (Amos 6:4).

A lamp to give "light unto all that are in the house" (Matthew 5:15) was usually placed either on a shelf or on a stand (candlestick) —not under a bowl or bushel, as Jesus reminded His listeners. The common lamp was a pottery vessel containing oil for burning and a wick. Cleaning the lamp and replenishing its oil must have been a daily household chore of the women. In the wilderness tabernacle this task was assigned to Aaron (Exodus 30:7).

Clay cookstoves frequently had a lower section for the charcoal or wood fire. A clay or metal cooking pot rested on the stove's rim above the fire. Flat, round, pancake-like loaves of bread were baked on hot stones (I Kings 19:6, RSV), in a clay oven, or perhaps sent to a public oven tended by a baker who had to watch his fire all night lest it burn away (Hosea 7:6). Other furnishings related to the preparation of food included: clay pots and bowls, spoons, forks, knives, ladles, and sieves. Bellows were used to keep the fire burning brightly in the stove. Grain was ground in a stone mill of the mortar and pestle type. Finally, there were water jars for fetching water from the village well and large pottery jars for storing grain, wine, and oil.

These material things, of such keen interest to archaeologists and sometimes to art students as well, are not the main concern of the Bible, for it deals with the spiritual life of a people. While these items help to create a vividly picturesque backdrop for the study of family living, the chief emphasis of the Bible is not how a house was built, but whether it was "the habitation of the just" (Proverbs 3:33), not how it was furnished, but whether it was "the house of the righteous" (Proverbs 12:7) and whether "the house be worthy" for the apostles' peace to come upon it (Matthew 10:13). No sentence sums up more eloquently the Bible's attitude toward the home than this one: "Except the Lord build the house, they labour in vain that build it" (Psalm 127:1).

## 3. "KEEPERS AT HOME"

A much-used phrase to describe homemakers is "keepers at home." It occurs in the letter to Titus, one of Paul's close associates traditionally believed to have been bishop of Crete. Among other matters, the letter discusses suitable behavior for older and younger women of the Church. Younger women were urged not to neglect family responsibilities, but to be "keepers at home" (Titus 2:5). The New English Bible translates the advice as follows:

The older women, similarly, should be reverent in their bearing, not scandal-mongers nor slaves to strong drink; must set a high standard, and school the younger women to be loving wives and mothers, temperate, chaste, and kind, *busy at home*, respecting the authority of their own husbands.

Titus 2:3-5, NEB

For "keepers at home" or "busy at home" the Revised Standard Version uses "domestic." The Douay Version uses "having a care of the house," which suggests unwelcome burdens. J. B. Phillips' translation, "home-lovers," is perhaps the most warmly descriptive of all the translations of this word.

Mothers of families performed many of the same chores as today's homemakers. They baked bread or cakes (Genesis 18:6), made savory stew (Genesis 27:17), ground meal (Matthew 24:41), swept the house (Luke 15:8), and sewed (Acts 9:39). They also drew water from the well and carried home heavy jars filled with water (Genesis 24:13). Their husbands, besides doing much of the farm work, threshed grain (Judges 6:11), killed animals for meat (Genesis 27:9), and probably brought in firewood.

## 4. HOME DEDICATION

It was common to dedicate a new house with ceremonies far more simple than those connected with Solomon's dedication of the new Temple in Jerusalem. In that case, after a lengthy and impressive prayer, Solomon offered sacrifices and held a seven-day feast for the people of Israel (I Kings 8:62-66). The occasion of the rededication of Jerusalem's wall was celebrated by Nehemiah with music and "with gladness, both with thanksgivings and with singing, with cymbals, psalteries, and with harps" (Nehemiah 12:27). When a new house was dedicated there were probably prayers and feasting and perhaps music and singing as well. The law allowed a man exemption from military service in order to dedicate a new and still unoccupied home, just as he was granted exemption to enjoy the fruit of a new vineyard, or to marry his betrothed wife (Deuteronomy 20:5-7).

The land on which a house stood really belonged, they believed, to God. As the pharaoh owned all land in Egypt (Genesis 47:20), so the Lord, Israel's true King, was the rightful owner of the Holy Land which His people were allowed to occupy.

> O God, our fathers have told us,
> What work thou didst in their days,
>     in the times of old. . . .
> For they got not the land in possession by their own sword,
>     neither did their own arm save them;
> but thy right hand, and thine arm,
>     and the light of thy countenance. . . .
>
> Psalm 44:1, 3

Because God, not man, owned the land, it could not be sold in perpetuity, for every fifty years, in the year of Jubilee, it reverted to its previous owner and could be redeemed by him (Leviticus 25:23-24). This law recognized God's ownership of all good things and His graciousness in lending them to men. A Hebrew family's tenure of its home and land was always subordinate to the Lord's possession.

## 5. LOVE OF HOME

The love of an aged man for his own home is expressed with great pathos in the story of Barzillai, who felt himself too old to enjoy the pleasures of Jerusalem as David's guest. Barzillai was a wealthy man of Gilead who, during Absalom's rebellion, aided David and his army by bringing to the weary, hungry men many needed supplies, including, "beds, and basins, and earthen vessels, and wheat, and barley, and flour, and parched corn, and beans, and lentiles, and parched pulse, and honey, and butter, and sheep, and cheese of kine . . ." (II Samuel 17:28-29).

As an added gesture of friendliness, Barzillai escorted David safely across the Jordan River. In gratitude for this aid and these courtesies, David invited his benefactor to the palace in Jerusalem. The aged Barzillai refused this invitation, saying, "I am now eighty

years old. Have I a taste for pleasure? Can your servant taste what
he eats and drinks? Can I still hear the voice of singing men and
women? Why, then, should your servant be a burden to my lord the
king?" (II Samuel 19:35, Moffatt).

But there was a deeper reason for Barzillai's refusal. The old
man was too much attached to his home to leave it. He said to
David, "Let thy servant, I pray thee, turn back again, that I may
die in mine own city, and be buried by the grave of my father and
of my mother" (II Samuel 19:37). So "the king kissed Barzillai and
blessed him, and he returned unto his own place" (II Samuel 19:39),
happy, as so many old people are, to spend his remaining years
among familiar scenes, surrounded by friendly faces, and to look
forward to a final resting place beside his parents.

The privilege of remaining in their own homes was denied to the
unhappy captives from Jerusalem whom King Nebuchadnezzar deported to Babylon beginning in 598 B.C. Mourning their sad lot in an
alien land, the homesick exiles sang their plaintive song:

> By the rivers of Babylon there we sat down,
>     yea, we wept when we remembered Zion.
> We hanged our harps upon the willows,
>     in the midst thereof.
> For there they that carried us away captive
>     required of us a song,
> and they that wasted us required of us mirth, saying,
>     "Sing us one of the songs of Zion."
> How shall we sing the Lord's song,
>     in a strange land?

> Psalm 137:1-4

## 6. GOD-CENTERED HOMES

The influence of a God-centered home spreads out in all directions,
bringing incalculable strength to the entire community. Homes that
serve the Lord are the strongest bulwark of a free society. This truth
is clearly seen in a story concerning Joshua, Moses' successor, and the
Israelite hero who led the tribes out of the wilderness and into the
Promised Land.

Near the end of Joshua's life, when the people were encamped at
Shechem, he summoned all the heads of families and clans, the

officials and judges to present themselves before the Lord. The Israelites were always in danger of worshiping other gods and betraying the covenant made with the Lord in the wonderful days of Moses at Mount Sinai. When they entered the Promised Land after their years of privation and hardship in the desert, they began to settle down among the pagan Canaanites. The moment was fraught with danger of apostasy. It was time for them to renew their sacred bond with the Lord.

Before the assembled leaders of the people Joshua stood up and in ringing words recited all the mighty acts of God, Who had delivered them and brought them into the good land. Joshua's account of their recent history must have stirred them profoundly. But a fateful choice now faced Israel. Joshua flung down his challenge to the responsible representatives of Israel gathered at Shechem. "Choose you this day whom ye will serve" (Joshua 24:15), he demanded of them. If they were unwilling to serve God, they must then serve either the gods of their remote ancestors living beyond the Euphrates, or the gods of the neighboring Amorites.

One can well imagine the buzz of excited conversation as men with differing viewpoints argued with one another. "Let us return to the old deities of Terah," said some of them. "The gods of the Amorites give them good harvests," observed another, while others spoke for the Lord.

Above the din of voices Joshua shouted his courageous decision, "But as for me and my house, we will serve the Lord!" (Joshua 24:15). A powerful leader supported by his loyal family ended the contagion of cowardice. The people's irresolution vanished. The issue now seemed perfectly clear to them and they cried, "God forbid that we should forsake the Lord, to serve other gods. . . . The Lord our God will we serve, and his voice will we obey" (Joshua 24:16, 24).

To engrave the decisive moment in their memories, Joshua wrote the words of their solemn pledge in the book of the law of God. Moreover, he placed a great witness stone under the huge oak growing beside the sanctuary so that Israel would always remember the renewal of her covenant with God.

The real test of a God-centered family's influence comes in the second generation. To his abiding credit and to that of his family also, it is recorded of Joshua: "And the people served the Lord all the days of Joshua, and all the days of the elders that outlived Joshua . . ." (Judges 2:7).


## 7. HOUSES DESCRIBED BY JESUS

Jesus described various kinds of homes that were not God centered. The first, an Empty House swept and put in good order, represents a man who has been emptied of his demon (Matthew 12:43-45). Unfortunately the man in Jesus' story failed to fill his empty house with prayer, good deeds, and the love of God. As George A. Buttrick says in his book *The Parables of Jesus,* "An empty house never remains empty. Spiders spin their webs, vermin claim the forsaken rooms, rat run behind the wainscoting. So our house of life left empty invites undesirable tenants" (p. 75).

In Jesus' parable the homeless demon returned to its former house, and finding it empty, "taketh with himself seven other spirits more wicked than himself, and they enter in and dwell there" (Matthew 12:45), so that the man's plight is worse at the end than at the beginning. Only when the love of God fills a house so that it is no longer empty, do the demons depart for good.

In a well-known parable Jesus dramatically contrasted a house built on rock with another built on sand. The wise man built his house upon a rock, "and the rain descended and the floods came and the winds blew and beat upon the house and it fell not, for it was founded upon a rock" (Matthew 7:25). The meaning of the rock is explained in the previous verse. In the words of George A. Buttrick in *The Interpreter's Bible,* ". . . Christ is the foundation. Beneath all the surface wisdom of the world he is rock. The thoughtful man digs into his truth until on that foundation life rests" (Vol.7, p. 335).

Jesus said of the mud brick house built on the deceptively dry sands of a Palestinian valley which the spring rains can turn into a raging river: "And the rain descended, and the floods came, and the winds blew, and beat upon that house, and it fell, and great was the fall of it" (Matthew 7:27). In George A. Buttrick's words, "This is Christ's comment on people who 'live any old way' or build on surface values. But the wise folk provide for themselves and for other men a refuge in the time of storm. Their house stands" (Vol.7, p. 335).

In another illuminating statement about life, Jesus made the statement quoted at the beginning of this chapter. When discord creeps into a family and finally usurps the place of love and harmony, the home disintegrates and falls apart.

This truth applies not only to families, but to individuals and to nations. Abraham Lincoln, during his debates with Stephen A. Douglas in 1856, in his famous "House Divided" speech made effective use of this saying of Jesus:

A house divided against itself cannot stand. I believe this government cannot endure permanently half slave and half free. I do not expect the Union to be dissolved—I do not expect the house to fall—but I do expect it will cease to be divided. It will become all one thing, or all the other.

## 8. OUR FATHER'S HOME

It is but a brief step from love-filled family homes in which Christ is no stranger to our heavenly abode in our Father's home. So our discussion of homes in the Bible may be brought to a fitting close by quoting some of the biblical insights which pierce the mystery of life now and hereafter.

To a few people in ancient times it was given to see beyond the earthly realm. Jacob at Bethel, after his vision of angels ascending and descending, exclaimed in awe, "This is none other but the house of God, and this is the gate of heaven!" (Genesis 28:17).

In possibly the most glorious and sublime of all the psalms, a nameless Hebrew poet gave immortal utterance to his faith that in the everlasting God man finds his true and eternal home:

> Lord, thou hast been our dwelling place
>     in all generations.
> Before the mountains were brought forth,
>     or ever thou hadst formed the earth and the world,
>     from everlasting to everlasting thou art God.
>                                         Psalm 90:1-2

Centuries later Augustine, the great Christian saint, voiced a conviction similar to that of the unnamed psalmist's when he exclaimed, "O God, thou hast made us for thyself, and our hearts are restless until they find rest in thee."

The two masterpieces among the one hundred and fifty psalms are unquestionably the ninetieth and the ninety-first. The latter gives profound assurance to all people suffering from every kind of trouble and adversity that no evil shall befall those who dwell in God. When the devil quoted to Jesus the last two lines below, Jesus refused to interpret them as a promise of physical security, for He knew that the whole psalm moves in the spiritual realm of God in which men's souls dwell secure.

> He that dwelleth in the secret place of the most High,
>     shall abide under the shadow of the Almighty.
> I will say of the Lord, He is my refuge and my fortress,
>     my God, in him will I trust. . . .
> Because thou hast made the Lord, which is my refuge,
>     even the most High, thy habitation,
> there shall no evil befall thee,
>     neither shall any plague come nigh thy dwelling.
> For he shall give his angels charge over thee,
>     to keep thee in all thy ways.
>
> Psalm 91:1-2, 9-11

Jesus' words to His disciples at the Last Supper bring ultimate assurance of the home to which He will bring us when we leave our earthly habitations:

Let not your hearts be troubled; ye believe in God, believe also in me. In my Father's house are many mansions; if it were not so, I would have told you. I go to prepare a place for you. And . . . I will come again and receive you unto myself, that where I am, there ye may be also.

John 14:1-3

Sure of Christ's promise, Paul, in the midst of his many earthly burdens, wrote to the Christians of Corinth, saying, "For we know that if our earthly house of this tabernacle were dissolved, we have a building of God, an house not made with hands, eternal in the heavens" (II Corinthians 5:1).

In the Bible's final vision of blessedness, hereafter, when the first heaven and earth passed away and the Lord made all things new, a voice was heard to cry from heaven saying, "Behold, the tabernacle of God is with men, and he will dwell with them, and they shall be his people, and God himself shall be with them, and be their God" (Revelation 21:3).

# CHAPTER 23

# Discipline in the Home

My son, do your father's bidding,
and reject not your mother's directions . . .
for their bidding will throw light upon your life,
their directions will enlighten you,
and to be trained thus is the way to live.
Proverbs 6:20, 23, Moffatt

Wise parents guide their children in the various aspects of daily living. It is true that, given a certain amount of freedom, a child develops initiative, but to turn him loose to do everything as he pleases is extremely unfair to the child. He lacks sufficient knowledge and experience to use complete freedom either wisely or safely. Home training helps him learn how to deal with his own whims and desires, find his own place in the family, respect other people, and discipline himself so that the difficulties of adult life may not later overwhelm him. As the Bible says, "The rod and reproof give wisdom, but a child left to himself bringeth his mother to shame" (Proverbs 29:15).

## 1. RESULTS OF THE LACK OF DISCIPLINE

We have seen the terrible results of parental indulgence and lack of proper control in the case of Eli's sons, Hophni and Phinehas, and David's sons, Amnon and Absalom.

The rowdy, undisciplined gang whom the prophet Elisha encountered on his way to Bethel also reflected lack of proper training at home. The boys had not been taught to respect older people or to reverence men of God. Possibly, in the hearing of their children, their parents had ridiculed Elisha. Then, too, the boys belonged to a gang in which one egged on the other until they became an uncontrolled, vicious mob. "Even a child is known by his doings, whether his work be pure and whether it be right" (Proverbs 20:11). Little did they heed the law that said, "Thou shalt not follow a multitude to do evil" (Exodus 23:2).

As Elisha came walking up the road toward Bethel with his staff in his hand, anyone could see that he was a prophet, for around his shoulders he wore the distinctive mantle of his great master, the fiery prophet Elijah. In the ninth century B.C., prophets of the Lord were entitled to respect and even kings honored them. But the rowdy gang of more than forty-two boys watching Elisha approach had no respect for him or for his prophetic office. All they saw was his bald head, which in those times was considered a disgrace. One after another of them began to laugh at him and mock him. For all their boldness, there must have been something about Elisha that awed them, for they waited until he had passed by and had proceeded on up the road before they screamed after him shouted derisively, "Go up, thou bald head; go up, thou bald head!" (II Kings 2:23).

At this unaccustomed derision Elisha stopped, turned around, and looked at the undisciplined gang. As their behavior was an insult to the Lord, Whom Elisha served, he cursed them in the name of the Lord.

The incredible consequences were like those in a tale told to frighten children in order to make them behave properly, for it is written that "there came forth two she bears out of the wood and tare forty and two children of them" (II Kings 2:24).

## 2. PUNISHMENT OF THE CHILD

From frequent references to rods in Proverbs and other biblical books, it appears that Hebrew parents often used corporal punishment. Reliance upon very severe measures in training children runs counter to most modern ideas on the subject. It has been humorously remarked that "everything in the modern home is controlled with a switch, except the children." Hebrew parents, however, believed that they had true love for their children when they brought them up strictly.

He who spares the rod hates his son,
>but he who loves him is diligent to discipline him.
>>Proverbs 13:24, RSV

Then, as now, children found innumerable ways to get into mischief. They were so prone to act foolishly that it was written, "Foolishness is bound in the heart of a child, but the rod of correction shall drive it far from him" (Proverbs 22:15).

## 3. CHASTENING, BOTH HUMAN AND DIVINE

The purpose of corporal punishment was not only to inflict upon the child the penalty for his wrongdoing, but to bring about his reform. This latter purpose is expressed by the word *chasten,* which appears many times in the King James Version of the Bible and means to correct and improve by means of punishment, as the following quotations make clear:

. . . as a man chasteneth his son, so the Lord thy God chasteneth thee.
>Deuteronomy 8:5

My son, despise not the chastening of the Lord,
>neither be weary of his correction,
>>for whom the Lord loveth he correcteth,
>>>even as a father the son in whom he delighteth.
>>>>Proverbs 3:11-12

Hebrew parents knew the importance of correcting, chastening, disciplining a child while he was young in order to spare him from more drastic punishment administered by civil or religious authorities later on.

Chastening, the wise parent realized, should not be destructive but corrective. Throughout their long history God had punished His people and by this they knew themselves to be His sons. Affliction has been called the hand and rod of God, the proof of His fatherly love. To make His children more like Himself He disciplines them. Chastening is inherent in sonship, both human and divine.

The most illuminating biblical passage on this subject compares human and divine chastening and indicates the spiritual fruits of God's discipline. After quoting the lines from Proverbs given above, the author of Hebrews declares:

If ye endure chastening, God dealeth with you as with sons; for what son is he whom the father chasteneth not? . . . Furthermore, we have had fathers of our flesh which corrected us, and we gave them reverence, shall we not much rather be in subjection unto the Father of spirits, and live? For they verily for a few days chastened us after their own pleasure, but he for our profit, that we might be partakers of his holiness.

Now no chastening for the present seemeth to be joyous, but grievous; nevertheless afterward it yieldeth the peaceable fruit of righteousness unto them which are exercised thereby.

Hebrews 12:7, 9-11

## 4. ADULT RESPONSIBILITY FOR THE CHILD

In passage after passage, the Bible reminds parents of their responsibility to pass on to their children the great heritage of Israel: God's Law, which contained the revelation of His nature and purpose, and man's obligations to God. At a time when few if any schools existed, it was essential for fathers to teach their children the Lord's commandments so "that the generation to come might know them, even the children which should be born, who should arise and declare them to their children" (Psalm 78:6).

By the first century A.D., though synagogue schools for teaching boys the Law were common, home training remained an important factor in religious education, as is evident from the following quotation:

And ye fathers, provoke not your children to wrath, but bring them up in the nurture and admonition of the Lord.

Ephesians 6:4

It is noteworthy that the statement above opens with a characteristically Christian note of kindness, in contrast to statements about a "rod" so frequent in Proverbs.

Jesus, whose tender love and concern for children as persons exceeded that of other teachers of the ancient world, warned adults of their responsibility toward those younger and weaker than themselves. Because children are easily led and influenced by their elders, Jesus taught that it was wrong for adults to hinder or put spiritual stumbling blocks in the paths of the young. His abhorrence of the sin of causing others to sin was so great that He declared, "But whoso shall offend one of these little ones which believe in me, it were better for him that a millstone were hanged about his neck, and that he were drowned in the depth of the sea" (Matthew 18:6).

## 5. THE DISCIPLINED ADULT

Discipline, though an unpopular word, accompanies all learning, all wisdom. Derived from the Latin *discere,* meaning "to learn," discipline involves training, instruction, education. Without discipline in childhood and youth one does not advance toward excellence in any field. Happy are those who, having been trained in childhood by loving parents, have learned to discipline themselves and are thus able to cope successfully with the strenuous demands of adulthood.

In His boyhood Jesus submitted to the discipline of His parents, "and was obedient to them" (Luke 2:51, RSV). His young followers were counselled by Paul, "Children, obey your parents in all things, for this is well pleasing unto the Lord" (Colossians 3:20).

When, as an adult, Jesus was tempted for forty days in the wilderness, He emerged victorious from the spiritual test. As Job remarked of his own trial, "When he hath tried me, I shall come forth as gold" (Job 23:10). By virtue of His self-discipline Jesus overcame every temptation to misuse His wonderful powers selfishly and thus He was enabled to become the great Teacher of mankind.

Inspired by the example of his Master, Paul wrote to his excited Greek converts in Thessalonica urging upon them a greater degree of self-discipline than they were practicing. He exhorted them "to aspire to live quietly, to mind your own affairs, and to work with your hands, as we charged you; so that you may command the respect of outsiders, and be dependent on nobody" (I Thessalonians 4:11-12, RSV).

While Paul's advice to Timothy, a young minister of the gospel, was addressed to one who aspired to be an effective teacher in the early Church, it described an adult whose self-discipline entitled him to exercise discipline.

. . . but set the believers an example in speech and conduct, in love, in faith, in purity. Till I come, attend to the public reading of scripture, to preaching, to teaching.                I Timothy 4:12-13, RSV

And the Lord's servant must not be quarrelsome but kindly to every one, an apt teacher, forbearing, correcting his opponents with gentleness.
                II Timothy 2:24-25, RSV

# CHAPTER 24

# Compassion for Those
# in Adversity

---

Defend the poor and fatherless;
do justice to the afflicted and needy.

Psalm 82:3

---

✳

Compassion for people in every kind of adversity was one of the chief glories of Israel. The Law, the prophets, and the wise men spoke with one voice enjoining generosity toward the poor, justice and help for the widow and orphan, kindliness for the stranger, and tender thoughtfulness for the aged and the afflicted. All were to be given not only sympathy but very real aid. Jesus, true to the traditions of His people, announced the beginning of His compassionate ministry by reading from the sixty-first chapter of Isaiah:

" 'The Spirit of the Lord is upon me, because he hath anointed me to preach the gospel to the poor; he hath set me to heal the brokenhearted, to preach deliverance to the captives, and recovering of sight to the blind, to set at liberty them that are bruised'. . . . This day is this scripture fulfilled in your ears."

Luke 4:18, 21

His followers continued His ministry of loving help for those in need, so that from beginning to end the Bible contains records and indications that biblical families both gave and received generous assistance.

## 1. AID TO THE POOR AND NEEDY

The Law stated that the Israelites must help any poor fellow countryman living in their midst, and freely and ungrudgingly give him what he needed.

If there be among you a poor man of one of thy brethren within any of thy gates in thy land . . . thou shalt not harden thine heart, nor shut thine hand from thy poor brother. But thou shalt open thine hand wide unto him, and shalt surely lend him sufficient for his need, in that which he wanteth.

Deuteronomy 15:7-8

Some Israelites were inclined to withhold help from the poor when the seventh, or sabbatical, year was near, for in that year produce of the land was given to the destitute (Exodus 23:11) and all debts were cancelled (Deuteronomy 15:1). But even when the seventh year was at hand, the Law stated that the needs of the poor were to be satisfied.

You shall give to him freely, and your heart shall not be grudging when you give to him; because for this the Lord your God will bless you in all your work and in all that you undertake. For the poor will never cease out of the land; therefore I command you, You shall open wide your hand to your brother, to the needy and to the poor, in the land.

Deuteronomy 15:10-11, RSV

Among her many virtues the good wife of Proverbs practiced charity. Out of the abundance of her well-run, prosperous household she "stretched out her hand to the poor; yea, she reacheth forth her hand to the needy" (Proverbs 31:20), as was mentioned earlier in the chapter on the mother's role.

A man might be reduced to borrowing when his crops failed, or his flocks sickened and died, or robbers stole his little hoard of money, or the landlord foreclosed his mortgage. Then it was that "a good man showeth favour, and lendeth" (Psalm 112:5). Such loans were made without interest, for the Law stated, "If thou lend money to any of my people that is poor by thee, thou shalt not be to him as an usurer [creditor], neither shalt thou lay upon him usury [interest]" (Exodus 22:25).

Because he paid no interest in his loan, a poor man was often required to give personal property, such as his cloak, as security for repayment. This security was called a pledge. But the Law humanely declared, "If ever you take your neighbor's garment in pledge, you shall restore it to him before the sun goes down; for that is his only covering, it is his mantle for his body; in what else shall he sleep?" (Exodus 22:26-27, RSV).

Moreover, a poor man who hired himself out to work for another was to be paid at the end of each day's labor: "You shall not oppress a hired servant who is poor and needy . . . you shall give him his hire on the day he earns it, before the sun goes down (for he is poor, and sets his heart upon it) . . ." (Deuteronomy 24:14:15, RSV). It was probably true that unless the man brought his wages home, his family would go to bed hungry. Poorly paid workers felt that "he that earneth wages earneth wages to put it into a bag with holes" (Haggai 1:6).

For infringements of these humane laws the Lord rebuked His people, saying, " 'What mean ye that ye beat my people to pieces, and grind the faces of the poor?' saith the Lord God of Hosts" (Isaiah 3:15).

## 2. HELP FOR THE FATHERLESS AND THE WIDOW

As we have already noted, widows and orphans in Hebrew society were protected by kindly provisions of the Law from exploitation and injustice. Their lot would have been more wretched than it was had not the Law explicitly stated, "Ye shall not afflict any widow or fatherless child" (Exodus 22:22). Dire warnings were issued for disobeying this command.

In treating widows and orphans, as well as all unprotected, helpless members of society, with consideration and justice, the Hebrews believed they were carrying out the divine will: "For the Lord your God . . . doth execute the judgment of the fatherless and widow, and loveth the stranger, in giving him food and raiment" (Deuteronomy 10:17-18).

The prophet Elisha, living in the middle of the ninth century B.C., was well known for his kindness. We have already seen how he restored the Shunammite woman's son to life. He also aided a nameless, impoverished widow whose prophet husband had died leaving the family in debt. She had no food and the creditors were

COMPASSION FOR THOSE IN ADVERSITY    [ 199 ]

coming to enslave her two sons when she appealed to Elisha for help. In his kindly sympathy for this afflicted widow and her orphaned sons, he performed a miracle for her by causing the oil in her jar to overflow, not only into all the vessels in her house, but into all the vessels she had borrowed from her neighbors. Elisha commanded her, "Go, sell the oil and pay thy debt, and live thou and thy children of the rest" (II Kings 4:7).

All of the prophets endorsed the humane commandments. "Learn to do well; seek judgment [justice], relieve the oppressed, judge [defend] the fatherless, plead for the widow" (Isaiah 1:17).

Deeply compassionate toward those who suffered from misery, wretchedness, or injustice, the prophets lashed out against powerful oppressors who manipulated laws to their own advantage at the expense of the poor, the weak, the innocent.

> Woe to those who issue harsh decrees,
>     penning orders that oppress,
> robbing the weak of their rights,
>     and defrauding the poor of their dues,
> till widows fall to them as spoil,
>     and orphans as their prey.
>                     Isaiah 10:1-2, Moffatt

A more poignant phrase regarding the widow occurs later in Isaiah. "There is none to guide her among all the sons, whom she hath brought forth; neither is there any that taketh her by the hand of all sons she has brought up" (51:18). The plight of the abject, captured Jerusalem, who had no comforters among the sons of Israel, here likened to the unfortunate widow, forsaken by her sons, is meaningful family symbolism.

One of the legal rights of the poor, the widow, the orphan, or any hungry person was that of plucking grain from his neighbor's field or gathering enough grapes from a vineyard to satisfy immediate hunger.

> When you go into your neighbor's vineyard, you may eat your fill of grapes, as many as you wish, but you shall not put any in your vessel. When you go into your neighbor's standing grain, you may pluck the ears with your hand, but you shall not put a sickle to your neighbor's standing grain.
>                     Deuteronomy 23:24-25, RSV

At harvest time the reapers usually left some grain standing in the field "for the stranger, for the fatherless, and for the widow" (Deuteronomy 24:19), as Boaz instructed his men to do for Ruth. While every three years a tithe of all the produce of the land, "of thy corn, of thy wine, and of thine oil, and the firstlings of thy herds and of thy flocks" was set aside for "the Levite (because he hath no part nor inheritance with thee), and the stranger, and the fatherless, and the widow," all of whom "shall come, and shall eat and be satisfied" (Deuteronomy 14:23,29). The tithing banquet, like today's Thanksgiving feast, was celebrated with rejoicings to the Lord.

Inspired by a profound sense of the value of human life and deep commitment to the will of God, Job was one of the most upright men of the Old Testament. He was righteous, just, and compassionate. "I was eyes to the blind, and feet was I to the lame. I was a father to the poor" (Job 29:15-16), he declared. In another passage he said:

> "If I have withheld the poor from their desire,
>     or have caused the eyes of the widow to fail,
> Or have eaten my morsel myself alone,
>     and the fatherless hath not eaten thereof . . .
> If I have seen any perish for want of clothing,
>     or any poor without covering, . . .
>     and if he were not warmed with the fleece of my sheep,
> If I have lifted up my hand against the fatherless, . . .
> Then let my arm fall from my shoulder blade,
>     and mine arm be broken from the bone."
>
> Job 31:16-22

## 3. KINDNESS TO THE STRANGER

Who were the strangers mentioned so frequently in the compassionate laws of Israel? They were foreigners, not those merely travelling through the land in a caravan or come for a brief trading visit, but resident aliens permanently living among the Hebrews. Hospitality was extended to transient foreigners, but the resident stranger was protected and aided by the Law. Though he was a free man, the stranger possessed no political rights nor could he own property. He was consequently forced to work for wages and was usually poor. Frequently he and his family needed the same consideration and help as that given to widows, orphans, and the destitute.

Abraham was a stranger in the Promised Land; as was Moses, a fugitive from the pharaoh, in Midian (Exodus 2:22); Ruth in Bethlehem; and all the Jewish exiles in Babylon. Because the Lord loved the stranger, the Israelites were commanded, "Love ye therefore the stranger, for ye were strangers in the land of Egypt" (Deuteronomy 10:19).

In the New Testament the word *stranger* has a different meaning. It denotes the casual visitor or a Christian brother far from home to whom courtesy, kindness, and helpfulness were to be shown.

## 4. THE BLIND AND THE DEAF

A special law protected the blind and the deaf. No one was allowed to curse the deaf or cause a blind man to stumble. "Thou shalt not curse the deaf, nor put a stumblingblock before the blind" (Leviticus 19:14). Of those who wantonly set a blind man on the wrong path it was said, "Cursed be he that maketh the blind to wander out of the way" (Deuteronomy 27:18). In his kindly concern for the afflicted, Isaiah proclaimed that when God came to save His people, "Then the eyes of the blind shall be opened, and the ears of the deaf shall be unstopped" (Isaiah 35:5).

Though these sorely afflicted people were treated with some consideration and given a measure of hope in Old Testament times, it was not until Jesus began His ministry of healing that the Bible records successful attempts to cure blindness and deafness. Jesus' cures were numerous and so well known that His disciples reported of Him to John the Baptist, "The blind receive their sight, and the lame walk, the lepers are cleansed, and the deaf hear, the dead are raised up, and the poor have the gospel preached to them" (Matthew 11:5). In his tenderness for the misery and distress of others, Jesus exceeded the requirements of the ancient Law.

## 5. RESPECT AND CARE FOR THE AGED

When long life was granted to men and women in Bible times, it was often accompanied with handicaps. Moses was unusual among aged men, for at one hundred and twenty years, when he viewed the Promised Land from afar, "his eye was not dim, nor his natural force abated" (Deuteronomy 34:7). But Isaac, Jacob, Eli, the prophet Ahijah (I Kings 14:4), and others were blind or partially so in old age. A staff was usually necessary to steady the uncertain steps of the elderly as they walked along rough paths. "The days of our years are threescore years and ten, and if by reason of strength they be fourscore years, yet is their strength labour and sorrow" (Psalm 90:10).

Old people often became a care to their families, but there are no words of complaint for the extra burden which was considered a natural phase of family life. Old age was venerated: "Thou shalt rise up before the hoary head and honour the face of the old man" (Leviticus 19:32). The younger members of a family, believing that "the hoary head is a crown of glory, if it be found in the way of righteousness" (Proverbs 16:31), respected the wisdom and goodness of the aged.

Men and women of great age had accomplished much in Israel's history. No one could forget the stories of Abraham, Sarah, Jacob, and Moses in old age. If King Rehoboam at his coronation had followed the temperate advice of his aged counselors, "the old men that stood before Solomon his father" (I Kings 12:6), he would not have lost half his kingdom. It was a sign of social anarchy when "the youth will be insolent to the elder" (Isaiah 3:5, RSV).

Old age could be a productive time, for as a psalmist sang, the righteous "shall still bring forth fruit in old age" (Psalm 92:14). When the Lord pours His spirit upon all people, so that your sons and daughters are inspired, then "your old men shall dream dreams, your young men shall see visions" (Joel 2:28). Old age was highly regarded, for "With the ancient is wisdom, and in length of days understanding" (Job 12:12).

Dreaming of a happy day when ruined and depopulated Jerusalem would once more be filled with happy families, Zechariah prophesied that both the very young and the very old would fill the city squares. "There shall yet old men and old women dwell in the streets of Jerusalem, and every man with his staff in his hand for very age. And the streets of the city shall be full of boys and girls playing in the streets thereof" (Zechariah 8:4-5).

## 6. THE COMPASSION OF JESUS

Jesus' ministry, as we have seen, opened with an announcement of compassionate concern for all in trouble and His days were filled with merciful acts of healing and ministering to all kinds of human need. Though He and His disciples were not wealthy men, they had a fund out of which they gave money to relieve the misery of the poor (John 13:29).

In His parable of the Good Samaritan, Jesus taught His followers to care for those in pain and trouble. He counselled the rich young ruler to give his wealth to the poor, but He rebuked ostentatious giving of alms (Matthew 6:1-4). He taught that those whose hospitality embraced "the poor, the maimed, the lame, the blind" (Luke 14:13) were blessed, for these weak and destitute people could make no return to their host. Possibly this teaching of Jesus' reflected a saying of the rabbis: "Let thy house be opened wide and let the needy be thy household."

In the early Church, Jesus' followers zealously carried on His works of healing and mercy, contributing their wealth to those in need (Acts 4:34-37), and organizing a fair distribution of charity (Acts 6:1-3). Among those remembered for their "good works and almsdeeds" (Acts 9:36) was Dorcas of Joppa, who was one of the first women engaged in social service in the Church.

Though much of today's burden of helping the unfortunate is borne by welfare agencies, the individual family can still open its heart to those in distress, remembering the words of Jesus:

"For I was an hungered and ye gave me meat. I was thirsty and ye gave me drink. I was a stranger and ye took me in, naked and ye clothed me. I was sick and ye visited me. I was in prison and ye came unto me. . . ."

"Lord, when saw we thee a stranger and took thee in?" . . .

"Verily I say unto you, Inasmuch as ye have done it unto one of the least of these my brethren, ye have done it unto me."

Matthew 25:35-40

# Illness in the Family

And Jesus went about all Galilee, teaching in their synagogues, and preaching the gospel of the kingdom, and healing all manner of sickness and all manner of disease among the people. And his fame went throughout all Syria. And they brought unto him all sick people that were taken with divers diseases . . . and he healed them.

Matthew 4:23-24

✳

## 1. GOD, THE HEALER

In illness, Bible families felt God to be very near and an ever-present source of strength. The Psalmist cried out to God, Who "healeth all thy diseases" (103:3). Luke, the physician, writing of the Pharisees and doctors of law from every town of Galilee, and Judah, and Jerusalem, who came to listen to his teaching, makes the positive affirmation "the power of the Lord was present to heal them" (Luke 5:17).

After the Resurrection, new spiritual power came to the followers of Jesus, enabling them to heal many and to fulfill their Master's command, "Heal the sick, cleanse the lepers, raise the dead, cast out devils. Freely ye have received, freely give" (Matthew 10:8).

Later, Paul effected similar cures (Acts 19:11-12). He healed, among others, a man at Lystra, crippled from his mother's womb (Acts 14:8-10); a mentally disturbed girl at Thyatira (Acts 16:16-18); and the father of Publius, the governor of the island of Melita on which Paul was shipwrecked (Acts 28:8).

Healing was a recognized part of the ministry of the early Church in which many a family must have known the blessedness of having a loved member restored to health. The "gifts of healing" (I Corinthians 12:9) given by the Spirit seem to have been exercised by a regular order of healers (I Corinthians 12:28-29). In addition, forgiveness of sins and anointing with oil in the name of the Lord had a place in the treatment of the sick, as the following passage indicates:

> Is any sick among you? Let him call for the elders of the church. And let them pray over him, anointing him with oil in the name of the Lord. And the prayer of faith shall save the sick, and the Lord shall raise him up. And if he have committed sins, they shall be forgiven him.
>
> James 5:14-15

## 2. THE WEAKNESS OF OLD AGE

The Bible mentions most of the illnesses common among families today, such as alcoholism, blindness, dumbness, lameness, neuroses, palsy, the weakness of old age. There is one difference. Science has found vaccines and antibiotics that have partially wiped out some of the diseases of Bible times. For example, science has conquered the Bubonic plague, the probable disease that destroyed seventy thousand people (II Samuel 24:15), after David took the census. Today's families accept the conquest of disease somewhat complacently, but the biblical world never ceased to give thanks to God for overcoming disease, whatever the means.

A touching picture of the extreme weakness of old age is given in the Genesis account of the last days of Jacob. As he lay ill, his beloved son Joseph, and his sons, Manasseh and Ephraim, went to his bedside. When Jacob was told that Joseph had arrived, he "strengthened himself, and sat upon the bed" (Genesis 48:2).

Although his eyes were dim with age, Jacob "kissed his grandsons and embraced them" (48:10). And he told Joseph that he had not expected to see his face again. Jacob assured Joseph that God would be with him when he was gone and would bring him back to the land of his fathers. Jacob then called all of his sons together and directed them concerning his burial.

The final word is that Jacob "was gathered unto his people" (49:33), his parents, Isaac and Rebekah, and his grandparents,

Abraham and Sarah. Jacob, it seems, died from the normal weaknesses that may come at the end of a very long life.

## 3. STERILITY IN A FAMILY

The first instance of illness and healing mentioned in the Bible is that of the wife and maidservants of Abimelech, King of Gerar, a country into which Abraham wandered with his beautiful wife Sarah. This people, it seemed, had not learned of God and his power to heal. They believed on the other hand in demons, which might be described as guilt complexes.

Although King Abimelech took Sarah into his court, a king's privilege in antiquity, especially after Abraham had passed her off as his sister, he suffered a guilt complex when he learned he had taken a man's wife. As a result, an act that was never consummated made him fearful that his wife and maidservants would be stricken with sterility. And they were, for it is reported "the Lord had fast closed up all the wombs of the house of Abimelech, because of Sarah Abraham's wife" (Genesis 20:18).

But Abimelech soon learned of Abraham's God, to whom Abraham prayed, "and God healed Abimelech, and his wife, and his maidservants; and they bare children" (Genesis 20:17).

## 4. DAVID'S SICK AND DYING SON

In David's palace the little prince was very sick. Everything was done for the child that his mother, his attendants, and the court physicians knew how to do, yet he grew worse. He was David's eldest son by Bath-sheba, the beautiful wife of Uriah whom David had unlawfully taken. People whispered that the Lord had afflicted the child in order to punish David for his sin—an idea that Jesus was later to repudiate (Luke 13:2-3).

For all his sins and shortcomings David loved the Lord. He believed in the power of prayer and he "therefore besought God for the child. And David fasted and went in and lay all night upon the earth. And the elders of his house arose and went to him to raise him up from the earth, but he would not, neither did he eat bread with them" (II Samuel 12:16-17).

After seven days David's son died, but the courtiers were afraid to tell the king lest in his acute sorrow he do something desperate to himself. David, however, noticed them whispering together and realized that his son's sickness must have taken a turn for the worse, so he asked, " 'Is the child dead?' And they said, 'He is dead' " (II Samuel 12:19).

To everyone's surprise David arose, "washed and anointed himself, and changed his apparel, and came into the house of the Lord and worshipped. Then he came to his own house and when he required, they set bread before him, and he did eat" (II Samuel 12:20).

No one could understand why David had fasted and wept while the child was still alive, yet ceased when he died. Prayer was the reason, as David explained to them:

"While the child was yet alive, I fasted and wept, for I said, Who can tell whether God will be gracious to me, that the child may live? But now he is dead, wherefore should I fast? Can I bring him back again? I shall go to him, but he shall not return to me."

II Samuel 12:22-23

Thus David bravely accepted the finality of death and worshiped the Lord in His house and went to comfort his wife Bath-sheba, the mother of the little dead prince.

## 5. THE HEALING OF TWO SONS

Both Elijah and Elisha seemed to understand how to contact God in famine and in battle, in sickness and in death. And like Jesus, both restored joy and order in a home by raising an only, beloved son from the dead.

Elisha's raising of the son of the woman who lived at Shunem, a town on the edge of the well-watered Valley of Jezreel, is so much like Elijah's earlier raising of the son of the widow of Zarephath, a town eight miles south of Sidon on the road to Tyre, that one seems to be almost a repetition of the other. In both there is the same strong certainty of God's power to raise the dead. There is also the same setting, an upper room set apart from the rest of the house, where each prophet went in alone to pray as well as to breathe new life into the child's mouth. Each prophet stretched himself upon the child, Elijah three times and Elisha seven times. Elijah cried out to God as he raised the Zarephath child:

O Lord, my God, I pray thee, let this child's soul come into him again. And the Lord heard the voice of Elijah; and the soul of the child came into him again, and he revived. And Elijah took the child, and brought him down out of the chamber into the house, and delivered him unto his mother: and Elijah said, See, thy son liveth. And the woman said to Elijah, Now by this I know that thou art a man of God, and that the word of the Lord in thy mouth is truth.

I Kings 17:21-24

Elijah, who like Enoch was translated in to heaven, transferred his spiritual leadership to Elisha, and also his knowledge of how to heal the sick and how to resuscitate the dead. Elisha often passed through Shunem as he went about his ministry. There the "great woman," as she is called (II Kings 4:8), and her husband set up a special room for him. Elisha's presence in the Shunem house first led to the miraculous birth of the son. The husband was "old" (II Kings 4:14), and when Elisha announced to the Shunamite that she would have a child, she was so surprised that she answered, "Nay, my lord, thou man of God, do not lie unto thine handmaid" (II Kings 4:16). But the woman conceived and gave birth to a son.

When he was grown the son went with his aged father during the harvest season into the fields, where he was stricken with a sudden illness. The father ordered a lad standing by to carry the child to his mother. "And when he had taken him, and brought him to his mother, he sat on her knee till noon, and then died" (II Kings 4:20). The husband's explicit confidence in his wife during their son's illness, and the spiritual strength she demonstrated when her child stopped breathing, depict the wise handling of a family crisis. After laying the child in the prophet's upper room, the mother rushed to Elisha, for she seemed to realize that wherever the prophet went there was power.

And when Elisha was come into the house, behold, the child was dead, and laid upon his bed. He went in therefore, and shut the door upon them twain, and prayed unto the Lord. And he went up, and lay upon the child, and put his mouth upon his mouth, and his eyes upon his eyes, and his hands upon his hands: and he stretched himself upon the child; and the flesh of the child waxed warm. Then he returned, and walked in the house to and fro; and went up, and stretched himself upon him: and the child sneezed seven times, and the child opened his eyes. And he called Gehazi, and said, Call this Shunamite. So he called her.

And when she was come in unto him, he said, Take up thy son. Then she went in, and fell at his feet, and bowed herself to the ground, and took up her son, and went out.                    II Kings 4:32-37

This method of resuscitation used by Elijah and Elisha has recently been reflected in new artificial respiration techniques. Mouth-to-mouth resuscitation, sponsored by the Red Cross and the Army Surgeon General's office at leading medical centers, was officially begun in 1959. The Biblical wisdom evident in II Kings 4:34, is now confirmed by modern medicine and is being used in various resuscitation emergencies—near-drowning, electric shock, smoke or gas inhalation, and other similar incapacitating occurrences.

Although this method has its own validity, it must not be forgotten that when these prophets went alone into an upper room with a child who had stopped breathing, they called upon the Lord for help. Neither prophet placed explicit confidence in either himself or the resuscitation method, but upon God, Who he knew would bring the spirit of life back into the child.

Each mother, it also must be remembered, approached the prophet with the same sublime faith, acknowledging that the prophet was in close contact with a God who heals.

## 6. JESUS, THE GREAT PHYSICIAN

Jesus, often called the great physician, showed special concern for the wholeness of the family. Many of His healings took place in homes, or in response to an urgent appeal from a member of the family. As He labored to raise the sick and the dying, a certain power seemed to go forth from Him, enabling the person healed to be raised up in mind, body, and soul. And those who were healed and others who witnessed their healing seemed to sense that illness, suffering, and an untimely death were neither right nor natural.

Of His many healing miracles, at least nine of the ones most often cited centered around the family. These were the raising from the dead of the son of the widow of Nain, the healing of the son of the nobleman, the healing of the man born blind, the raising of Lazarus (and the restoration of order to the Bethany home of his sisters, Martha and Mary), the healings of the Syro-Phoenician's demoniac daughter, the centurion's servant, Peter's mother-in-law, Jairus' daughter, and the lunatic child.

In three of these cases, namely that of the demoniac daughter of the Syro-Phoenician woman, the sick son of the nobleman, and the lunatic child of another man, Jesus sought the co-operation of the parent, demonstrating that the vital and mysterious life bond between parent and child can bring forth a life-giving power from the Almighty. These deep-lying sympathies binding parents to their children are akin to the divine power, and Jesus desired that this power be vitally tied to a living faith, so as to produce a living union with God. He, who had a perfect alliance with the divine source of all life and health, seemed to realize that parents who were filled with faith could achieve such an alliance too.

## 7. A NOBLEMAN'S SICK CHILD

"Sir, come down ere my child die" (John 4:49), mournfully spoke the nobleman of Capernaum to Jesus. He tested the father's faith by saying, " 'Go thy way. Thy son liveth.' And the man believed the word that Jesus had spoken unto him, and he went his way" (John 4:50).

Believing and hoping with his whole heart, the father returned to his home in Capernaum where he was greeted with the joyful news that his son's fever had gone down at the exact hour when Jesus had pronounced him cured. Then the father truly "believed and his whole house" also (John 4:53).

## 8. A WIDOW'S SON

"The only son of his mother, and she was a widow" (Luke 7:12) is the poignant manner in which Luke, the physician, writes of the death of the young man in Nain whom Jesus raised from the dead. A whole sermon could be based on those ten words in Luke, for the prototoypes of this widow and son may be found everywhere.

Jesus arrived in the town of Nain, on the extreme south of the slopes of the Hill of Moreh, as the widow's son was being carried away for burial. And Jesus had compassion on her and told her to weep not, and then he touched the bier, and spoke, "Young man, I say unto thee, Arise" (Luke 7:14). The young man could not arise of his own free will, but Jesus gave him the power. And he sat up, ready to walk forth again.

One of the most inspiring phrases is that Jesus "delivered him to his mother" (Luke 7:15). All of this occurred in the sight of a crowd of disciples and others attending Jesus, as well as funeral-bound neighbors and relatives, who came to comfort the widow.

The widow of Nain probably depended upon this only son and now looked to him for further comfort in her old age. Widows who lose only sons can comfort themselves with the thought that Christ has compassion on them too. He would say to every widow grieving for an only son, "weep not." Christ's spirit lives on, bringing compassion and comfort to all members of the family who grieve.

## 9. A BLIND SON

"Master, Who did sin, this man, or his parents, that he was born blind?" (John 9:2), asked Jesus' disciples at the Feast of Tabernacles in Jerusalem. Jesus answered, "Neither hath this man sinned, nor his parents: but that the works of God should be made manifest in him" (John 9:3). The question of the disciples indicated that the sins of the parents might have caused their son's blindness, for a false superstition existed that sin and suffering were related. The Apocrypha state that "children unlawfully begotten are witnesses of wickedness, against parents when God searched them out" (Wisdom of Solomon 4:6).

But Jesus promptly dismissed any idea that the blindness of the son was caused by the sins of the parents. He saw in the son's blindness an opportunity for God's miraculous healing to be displayed.

"I must work the works of him that sent me, while it is day. . . . As long as I am in the world, I am the light of the world" (John 9:4-5), He said. And then Jesus spat on the ground and made a clay spittle, anointed the blind man's eyes with clay and saliva, and sent him to the pool of Siloam to wash. And the man was blind no more.

Jesus' opponents, disputing the cure, called the man's parents forth. They testified that this was their son who had been born blind, but they did not acknowledge that it was Jesus who had healed him. "He is of age; ask him: he shall speak for himself" (John 9:21), they answered timorously, for they feared persecution, if they publicly professed Christ.

The son, called forth later by sanctimonious onlookers, declared, "one thing I know, that, whereas I was blind, now I see" (9:25).

## 10. A BROTHER WHO WAS DEAD

"Therefore his sisters sent unto him, saying, Lord, behold, he whom thou lovest is sick" (John 11:3). The sisters were Martha and Mary and the brother was Lazarus.

"This sickness is not unto death, but for the glory of God, that the Son of God might be glorified thereby" (John 11:4), spoke Jesus to these sisters whom He loved.

Jesus proceeded on into Judea, but in his absence Lazarus died and was buried. When He returned Martha hastened to meet him to say, "Lord, if thou hadst been here, my brother had not died. But I know, that even now, whatsoever thou wilt ask of God, God will give it thee. Jesus saith unto her, Thy brother shall rise again" (John 11:21-23). Later Mary repeated to Jesus the same words that her sister Martha had spoken: "Lord, if thou hadst been here, my brother had not died" (John 11:32).

Ever sympathetic to the sorrows of others, especially friends as close as Martha and Mary and their brother Lazarus, "Jesus wept" (John 11:35). He then walked with the sisters and other onlookers to the tomb, where Lazarus was laid four days earlier. After requesting that the stone over the grave be removed, Jesus said:

"Father, I thank thee that thou hast heard me. And I knew that thou hearest me always: but because of the people which stand by I said it, that they may believe that thou hast sent me." And when he thus had spoken, he cried with a loud voice, "Lazarus, come forth." And he that was dead came forth, bound hand and foot with graveclothes: and his face was bound about with a napkin, Jesus, saith unto them, "Loose him, and let him go." Then many of the Jews which came to Mary, and had seen the things which Jesus did, believed on Him.

John 11:41-45

## 11. AN AFFLICTED DAUGHTER

"Have mercy on me, O Lord . . . my daughter is grievously vexed with a devil" (Matthew 15:22), cried the Syrophoenician woman, also described as the Canaanite because she lived in the region of Tyre and Sidon.

The mother whose daughter was afflicted with a mental disease, "vexed with a devil" as the record states, was not a Jewess, but a Gentile. While Jesus was in her town, she followed Him, begging Him to have pity on her grievously afflicted daughter. The disciples were annoyed at her importunity and wanted to send her away. But she came and knelt at Jesus' feet and said, "Lord, help me" (Matthew 15:25).

To test her faith, He made a strange remark about the unfairness of throwing the children's bread to the dogs. Undaunted by this rebuff, she replied quickly and with wit, "Truth, Lord. Yet the dogs eat of the crumbs which fall from their masters' table" (Matthew 15:27).

Jesus, appreciating her courage, her energy, her humor, but above all her faith, answered, "O woman, great is thy faith. Be it unto thee even as thou wilt" (Matthew 15:28).

Mark ended the story dramatically:

And he said unto her, "For this saying go thy way. The devil is gone out of thy daughter." And when she was come to her house, she found the devil gone out, and her daughter laid upon the bed.

Mark 7:29-30

In his exposition of this Syro-Phoenician mother in *The Interpreter's Bible,* Halford E. Luccock makes this inspiring comment:

Suppose that all Christian parents and all churches had the same persistence and ingenuity in bringing to their children the saving influence of Christ! If parents had something of this woman's relentless determination to bring into their homes Jesus' power, his power to heal life, to preserve it, to enrich it, to cast evil spirits from it, how much smaller the number of children who would drift away! . . . It would be an awkward name for a church—"The Church of the Syrophoenician Woman"! But a church marked by her spirit would be a joy to God and a saving power in the world (Vol. 7, pp. 755-756).

## 12. A SICK SERVANT

"And they that were sent [friends of the centurion], returning to the house found the servant whole that had been sick" (Luke 7:10). The centurion, a man of influence and spiritual insight, hearing that Jesus was near his house in Capernaum, sent this courteous message, "Lord, trouble not thy self: for I am not worthy that thou shouldest enter under my roof: Wherefore neither thought I myself worthy to come unto thee: but say in a word, and my servant shall be healed" (Luke 7:6-7).

Declaring that He had not found such great faith in all Israel as that possessed by this centurion, Jesus accomplished the healing of the servant without entering the man's house.

## 13. A LITTLE DAUGHTER AT DEATH'S DOOR

"My little daughter lieth at the point of death: I pray thee, come and lay thy hands on her, that she may be healed; and she shall live" (Mark 5:23), spoke Jairus, ruler of the synagogue at Galilee, as he hastened to Capernaum, where Jesus was. And there Jairus fell at Jesus' feet, and earnestly sought His help.

While Jesus paused to heal a woman with an issue of blood, people hurried from Jairus' house to report to him that his daughter was dead. Jesus confidently assured Jairus that he must not be afraid but must have the faith that his daughter would live again. Followed by Peter, James, and John, Jesus went into Jairus' house, and asked the mourners there, "Why make ye this ado, and weep? The damsel is not dead, but sleepeth" (Mark 5:39).

The mourners laughed Him to scorn and when He put them out of the house, He took the mother and father into the house and said to their daughter, "Arise." Her parents were so astonished that they forgot to bring food for their daughter, but when Jesus reminded them that they must, they knew she was restored not only to life but also to a good state of health.

In the healing of Jairus' daughter every parent with a sick child, can find comfort and hope, for Jesus declared, "He that believeth on me, the works that I do shall he do also: and greater works than these shall he do; because I go unto my Father" (John 14:12).

## 14. A SON WITH "A DUMB SPIRIT"

"Master, I have brought unto thee my son which hath a dumb spirit" (Mark 9:17), declared an anxious father to Jesus. Mark further described how this child "foameth, and gnasheth with his teeth" (9:18). Matthew called the child a lunatic (17:15), and the Revised Standard Version describes the child as an epileptic. The father told Jesus that he first appealed to his disciples but they had not been able to heal the child. Then Jesus asked the father how long his son had suffered. The father answered that the child had been afflicted from infancy. Much troubled because of his son's illness, he begged of Jesus to "have compassion on us and help us" (Mark 9:22).

When Jesus told the father that blessings often are granted according to faith, he cried out tearfully, "Lord, I believe: help thou mine unbelief" (Mark 9:24). Jesus charged the son's deaf and dumb spirit to come out and enter no more. As it disappeared, the child acted as one dead, but Jesus took him by the hand and lifted him up, and he arose again.

After restoring wholeness to this family, Jesus went back to his own disciples, who asked why they had been unable to heal the child; and He told them that this kind of healing could come forth by nothing but "prayer and fasting" (Mark 9:29).

## 15. AN ILL MOTHER-IN-LAW

". . . Simon's wife's mother lay sick of a fever" (Mark 1:30). Luke calls her disease "a great fever" (4:38). But when Jesus took the hand of Simon's mother-in-law, the fever left her.

A circle of love, embracing both Simon Peter and his mother-in-law, seems to have surrounded this home, the kind of love that has a healing quality in itself. This love soon radiated over a larger circle, for it is reported that Simon's mother-in-law went forth and ministered to others.

All nine of these families, to whom Jesus came with His healing ministry, are prototypes of families today. The knowledge of this healing power that Jesus brought was used effectively by the Christian Church of the first few centuries, but is too little used in the Church today because of a lack of faith and wholehearted discipleship.

# The Family in Its More Spiritual Aspects

*

# CHAPTER 26

# The Holy Family

And they came with haste, and found Mary, and Joseph, and the babe lying in a manger.

Luke 2:16

✳

The story of the Holy Family is told in the Gospels of Matthew and Luke with exquisite restraint and haunting beauty. Artists have painted the mother, her new-born Child, and Joseph in scenes glowing with the bright colors of faith. Poets have enshrined the story in verse. Some of the world's most treasured music celebrates the Holy Family. But with our mind's ear we listen to the far more glorious music that echoed over the dark fields of Bethlehem nearly two thousand years ago as the heavenly host praised God and sang, "Glory to God in the highest, and on earth peace, good will toward men" (Luke 2:14).

We can imagine the shepherds hurrying toward the lowly stable in David's royal city and we see on their faces a look of amazement and joy. Above, the Star which guided the Wise Men from the east shines again, glistening on the rich treasures presented to the Child —gold, frankincense, and myrrh.

Amid such scenes as these, filled with the very "poetry of faith," the Holy Family comes to us, bringing continuing inspiration to families today.

## 1. ANCESTORS OF JESUS

The New Testament gives two different genealogies for Jesus, one in Matthew (1:1-16), and the other in Luke (3:23-38). Both trace Joseph's lineage rather than Mary's. Matthew's list of the fathers of forty-two successive generations begins with Abraham. Luke's genealogy begins with Joseph and works backward through seventy-five generations to Adam.

The purposes of these lists is explained by Walter Russell Bowie in *The Interpreter's Bible*: "Matthew's concern is that the lineage of Jesus shall be led unmistakably through David, the great king, back to Abraham himself, the father of the Jewish race. Luke's purpose is a still wider one. He wants to identify the life of Jesus not only with one nation but with all mankind" (Vol. 8, p. 82).

The eagerly awaited Messiah of the Jews was expected to be a "son of David," empowered by God to rule David's restored kingdom. In reference to this belief Paul declared that Jesus was "made of the seed of David according to the flesh, and declared to be the Son of God with power, according to the spirit of holiness, by the resurrection from the dead" (Romans 1:3-4).

## 2. HIS MOTHER

Mary, a virgin of Nazareth, was espoused to Joseph when the angel Gabriel appeared to her and announced:

"Hail, thou that art highly favoured, the Lord is with thee. Blessed art thou among women. . . . And, behold thou shalt conceive in thy womb, and bring forth a son, and shalt call his name JESUS. He shall be great, and shall be called the Son of the Highest, and the Lord God shall give unto him the throne of his father David. And he shall reign over the house of Jacob for ever. And of his kingdom there shall be no end."

Luke 1:28, 31-33

At this sublime revelation Mary was at first frightened and awestruck. Then she began to be perplexed, wondering how this could be, since she had no husband. But the angel said to her, "The Holy Ghost shall come upon thee, and the power of the Highest shall overshadow thee, therefore also that holy thing which shall be born of thee shall be called the Son of God. . . . with God nothing shall be impossible" (Luke 1:35,37).

In lowly obedience Mary accepted the divine will. "Behold the handmaid of the Lord. Be it unto me according to thy word" (Luke 1:38).

Soon after the Annunciation, Mary went into the hill country north of Jerusalem to visit her cousin Elisabeth, wife of a priest named Zacharias. On Mary's arrival at her cousin's house she found that, as the angel had said, Elisabeth also was with child. A tender scene took place between Mary and the older woman, who asked from a sense of her own unworthiness, "And whence is this to me, that the mother of my Lord should come to me? For lo, as soon as the voice of thy salutation sounded in mine ears, the babe leaped in my womb for joy. And blessed is she that believed, for there shall be a performance of those things which were told her from the Lord" (Luke 1:43-45).

Into the sympathetic ears of her cousin Elisabeth, Mary poured the wonderful song of her rejoicing, a song that has come to be known as the Magnificat, because Mary magnified God, more than any mother in history. The Magnificat takes its theme from the hymn of Hannah (I Samuel 2:1-10), mother of Samuel. Mary, finding rapturous joy in her approaching motherhood, burst forth in this song of praise:

> My soul doth magnify the Lord,
> and my spirit hath rejoiced in God my
>     Saviour.
> For he hath regarded the low estate of his handmaiden:
> for behold, from henceforth all generations
>     shall call me blessed.
>
> For he that is mighty hath done to me great things;
>     and holy is His name.
> And his mercy is on them that fear him
>     from generation to generation.
>
> He hath shewed strength with his arm;
> he hath scattered the proud in the
>     imagination of their hearts.
> He hath put down the mighty from their seats,
>     and exalted them of low degree.

He hath filled the hungry with good
   things;
    and the rich he hath sent empty away.

He hath holpen [helped] his servant Israel,
   in remembrance of his mercy;
As he spake to our fathers,
   to Abraham and to his seed for ever.

Luke 1:46-55

Mary's Magnificat, divided here into four strophes, as it sometimes is when sung by a choir first on one side and then on the other, is one of the most triumphant songs in the Bible. With all the strength and resources of her spiritual being, in the first strophe Mary praised God for regarding the low estate of His handmaiden.

In the second strophe she dwelt on the distinguished honor that was to be hers as the mother of the coming Messiah. She no doubt. was familiar with the Old Testament prophecies, that of Isaiah (7:14; 9:6), where he foretold of the miraculous birth of the "Immanuel," and predicted that "His name shall be called Wonderful, Counsellor, The Mighty God, The everlasting Father, The Prince of Peace." She probably knew too that Daniel (9:24-26) had told of the coming Messianic kingdom, that Micah (5:2) had proclaimed that the Messiah would be born at Bethlehem, and that Malachi (3:1) had announced His coming to His temple and the triumph of His name.

In the third strophe Mary set forth some relations of the birth of her son to the action of God's Providence in the history of human nations and human lives. This is all miraculous in light of the fact that Mary had only the angel's promise to fall back upon. No miracles had yet been performed. No one had heard that her son would preach the Sermon on the Mount, that He would rise from the grave and go forth and teach again, or that His apostles would begin a ministry that would become world-wide. Far in advance of all of these, Mary spoke with gratitude of what God had done. "He hath shewed strength," she said. Also He "hath scattered; he hath put down; he hath exalted; he hath filled; he hath sent away."

In the fourth and concluding strophe Mary leaves us with the conviction that God's promises may for long remain unfulfilled, but that they will be fulfilled at last. The promise had come long ago to Abraham. At Haran God had said to him, "In thee shall all families of the earth be blessed" (Genesis 12:3). At Hebron God had said to Abraham, "I will establish my covenant with Isaac for an everlasting covenant, and with his seed after him" (Genesis 17:19). On the plain at Mamre the Lord had said, "Abraham shall surely become a great and mighty nation, and all the nations of the earth shall be blessed in him" (Genesis 18:18). To Isaac in Gerar (Genesis 26:3-4) and to Jacob in Bethel (Genesis 28:14), God had made the same promises, and Mary probably was familiar with all of them.

In Mary's Magnificat, which gives her son Jesus the most exalted position of any figure in history, we sense her consciousness of her nearness to God, the wonder of His promises, and her understanding of the fulfillment of those promises. Truly, Mary gave to her divine son the most wondrous prenatal influence of any child in history.

And her cousin Elisabeth, spiritually sensitive woman that she was, seemed to understand the miraculous role that Mary would fill as the greatest mother in the world's history. After a visit in Elisabeth's home lasting about three months, and shortly before the birth of John the Baptist to Elisabeth and Zacharias, Mary returned to Nazareth. Some months later she accompanied Joseph to Bethlehem, the city of their royal ancestor David, to be enrolled according to a decree of the Roman emperor, Caesar Augustus.


## 3. JESUS' INFANCY

While they were in Bethlehem, lodging in a stable because there was no room for them in the inn, the time came for Mary to be delivered. "And she brought forth her firstborn son, and wrapped him in swaddling clothes, and laid him in a manger . . ." (Luke 2:7).

Jesus' first bed was a hollowed-out stone placed on the ground and half-filled with straw and soft chaff. Before being placed in this, He, like other babies of the time, was washed, rubbed with salt, and placed diagonally on a square cloth which Mary probably brought along with her for the purpose. The corners of the cloth were folded over His sides and up over His feet, making a bundle which Mary tied with swaddling bands. Every day she loosened the bands and rubbed her Baby with olive oil.

Angels sang in the night, shepherds arrived with wonder transfiguring their weathered faces, splendidly appareled Wise Men knelt at the manger of the newborn Child. "But Mary kept all these things, and pondered them in her heart" (Luke 2:19).

As Joseph and Mary were devout parents, obedient to all the requirements of the Law, they waited for eight days before naming their Baby, Jesus, as the angel had said, and circumcising Him. He was forty days old when they took Him to Jerusalem for the ancient rite of presentation in the Temple. In another ritual Mary offered the sacrifice of a poor mother for purification after childbirth, according to the Law (Leviticus 12:6, 8).

All was accomplished and Joseph and Mary were hurrying away when an aged man named Simeon stopped them. Recognizing their Son as the coming glory of Israel, Simeon took the infant Jesus in his arms and gave thanks to God, saying:

> Lord, now lettest thou thy servant depart in peace,
>     according to thy word;
> for mine eyes have seen thy salvation,
>     which thou hast prepared before the face of all people,
> a light to lighten the Gentiles,
>     and the glory of thy people Israel.
>
> Luke 2:29-32

Joseph and Mary marvelled at the old prophet's words, yet Mary must have felt a stab of pain when Simeon said, "Yea, a sword shall pierce through thy own soul, also . . ." (Luke 2:35).

Before they left the Temple, Anna, a devout widow of eighty-four, "coming in that instant gave thanks likewise unto the Lord, and spake of him to all them that looked for redemption in Jerusalem" (Luke 2:38).

After the Presentation in the Temple Joseph was warned by an angel to flee to Egypt with Mary and Jesus in order to escape from Herod. Obedient to the angel's command, Joseph departed by night and journeyed with his little family down to Egypt where they remained until Herod died. Once more Joseph set out on a journey with his wife and Son. Arriving in Judea, Joseph was warned in a dream not to remain there, so "he turned aside into the parts of Galilee. And he came and dwelt in a city called Nazareth . . ." (Matthew 2:22-23).

## 4. JOSEPH

In the background of the lovely stories of Jesus' birth and childhood stands Joseph, a person to whom too little attention is paid. He was a strong, capable man on a journey, protecting Mary and the Child on their frequent wayfarings over the rough, dangerous roads of first-century Palestine. But Joseph was much more than an able traveller. The stories show him to have been kind, understanding, dependable, pious. He was spiritually sensitive, too, for three times he heard the angel's message and obeyed it. It can be assumed that he was devoted to his family and acted always in their behalf.

Jesus learned very practical lessons from Joseph, not least of which were probably the skills of the carpenter's trade. Joseph undoubtedly taught Him that a good craftsman is exact and careful, handling his tools with respect and observing the characteristics of the different kinds of wood.

Some of Joseph's tools are mentioned in the following passage, together with the wood available to him:

> The carpenter stretcheth out his rule; he marketh it out with a line; he fitteth it with planes, and he marketh it out with the compass. . . . He heweth him down cedars, and taketh the cypress and the oak. . . .
>
> Isaiah 44:13-14

In addition, Joseph employed such other tools as saws, hammers, chisels, awls, and he doubtless used fir and pine from the hills, woods from which ceilings, doors, and floors of Solomon's Temple had been made.

Among his fellow townsmen in Nazareth Joseph surely found ready buyers for his tables, benches, and stools. Those building a home needed door- and window-frames. Perhaps the synagogue ordered a new ark for the scrolls of the Law. A young couple setting up housekeeping required a threshing board, a broom handle, a lamp stand, and a cradle. Farmers from the countryside bought his yokes for their oxen. Jesus learned to make these smooth and well-fitting so that they did not gall the beasts. In later years, remembering His easy yokes, He invited all those bearing heavy burdens:

> "Come unto me, all ye that labour and are heavy laden, and I will give you rest. Take my yoke upon you, and learn of me, for I am meek and

lowly in heart, and ye shall find rest unto your souls. For my yoke is easy, and my burden is light."

Matthew 11:28-30

Hard-working, patient, God-fearing Joseph must have been a family man and a good neighbor with a warm heart and broad sympathies. Such was the man from whom Jesus first learned the meaning of the word "father."

## 5. THE HOME AT NAZARETH

Not until they settled at Nazareth did Joseph, Mary, and their Son enjoy secure home life. But there they apparently lived peacefully and uneventfully together during Jesus' childhood and perhaps longer.

Secluded in its cup of Galilean hills, Nazareth provided a picturesque setting for the Holy Family. Its little white houses nestled on the slopes, its gnarled olive trees and dusty threshing floors, its narrow streets all leading to the town well—these were familiar to Jesus. Above Nazareth, from "the brow of the hill whereon their city was built" (Luke 4:29) could be seen the fertile valley below. On a clear day Mount Carmel was visible only twenty miles to the west, while beyond it sparkled the blue waters of the Mediterranean. To the east lay the Jordan Valley and the mountains of Gilead beyond. Far to the north rose Mount Hermon, snow-capped and majestic, while to the south stretched the fertile Plain of Esdraelon with its grain fields, vineyards, olive groves, and its important highways linking all parts of the country. Jesus must have been sensitive to the sights and sounds of His environment, for in His preaching He mentioned much of the natural beauty with which His childhood was surrounded at Nazareth, where it is recorded that "the child grew and waxed strong in spirit, filled with wisdom, and the grace of God was upon him" (Luke 2:40).

## 6. MARY'S HOME DUTIES

In His teachings Jesus painted vivid word pictures of household tasks He must have seen His mother perform in their Nazareth home.

Two women shall be grinding together; the one shall be taken, and the other left.

Luke 17:35

The kingdom of heaven is like unto leaven, which a woman took and hid in three measures of meal, till the whole was leavened.

Matthew 13:33

They toil not, neither do they spin.

Matthew 6:28

No man also seweth a piece of new cloth on an old garment: else the new piece that filled it up taketh away from the old, and the rent is made worse.

Mark 2:21

... what woman having ten pieces of silver, if she lose one piece, doth not light a candle, and sweep the house, and seek diligently till she find it?

Luke 15:8

When she ground corn Mary was perhaps helped by a member of her family or a neighbor who sat opposite her with the heavy household mill between them. Each woman gave the upper millstone a half-turn with one hand while pouring in grain with the other.

Mary made dough from the meal. She added yeast to leaven it and make it rise before baking her loaves of bread. She toiled at her spinning and wove cloth from the spun thread. She stitched new garments and patched old ones. Sweeping was toil also, for the floor of the house was earthen. In summer she may have cooked outdoors over a charcoal pan, but in winter she used an indoor stove and oven.

Though some vegetables were eaten raw, she boiled lentils and greens in water and oil. The corn porridge was made with corn meal, water, salt, and butter. Cakes were baked from a variety of crushed or ground grain such as barley, corn, rye, wheat, or millet. When meat was available it was boiled, though lamb was frequently roasted on a spit at an open fire.

## 7. THE CHILDHOOD DAYS OF JESUS

Mary and Joseph, like good parents everywhere, were their Son's first teachers. From them He unconsciously absorbed the basic wisdom of Israel. By joining His family in their religious observances—their daily prayers and recitation of the Shema, and their annual festivals and fasts—He was introduced to the faith of His people. When He asked Joseph the age-old question, "What mean ye by this service?" (Exodus 12:26), He was taught Israel's glorious history under God.

At the age of six or seven He was sent to the elementary school attached to the syngogue. Here, with scribes for teachers, He received instruction in the Law written in Deuteronomy and Leviticus, thus gaining a firm basis for the instruction He received at home. Though the curriculum of the synagogue school centered around religious education, reading and writing were also taught.

A few girls attended these schools, but attendance was not compulsory for them as it was for boys. The pupils sat cross-legged on mats placed upon the ground, while their teachers sat before them upon benches. As people spoke Aramaic in Palestine in Jesus' day, children needed help in understanding the Scriptures written in classic Hebrew. Instruction, which was given orally, seemed to have been aimed, not at encouraging students to think for themselves, but at storing their memories with the Law. Recitation consisted in droning out the memorized lesson.

But Jesus made good use of His education, for, as His teachings show, His mind was not only furnished with knowledge of the Law, but He had thought deeply about it. He had also studied the prophets and other Old Testament books and had made the Psalms His own.

Though Jesus' childhood centered around His home, the synagogue, and Joseph's workshop, He must have enjoyed typically boyish activities. As the canonical Gospels give no details of these and the apocryphal gospels weave only tales that are obviously fanciful, clues as to His youthful interests and pleasures must be sought in His later teachings. We can picture Him walking among the "lilies of the field" (Matthew 6:28), gazing at eagles soaring and circling overhead (Luke 17:37), finding a fox's hole or a bird's nest (Matthew 8:20), watching a farmer sow his seed (Mark 4:3), bringing home a strayed sheep upon His shoulders (Luke 15:5), playing with other children in the market place (Luke 7:32), netting fish in the Sea of Galilee (Matthew 13:47), and going on pilgrimages to Jerusalem (Luke 2:42-50).

## 8. JESUS AT HIS FIRST PASSOVER

The beautiful story of the boy Jesus going up to Jerusalem with His parents to celebrate His first Passover illuminates one of the meaningful aspects of their family life together. When Jesus was twelve years old, His devout parents decided that their Son was old enough to accompany them on their annual pilgrimage to the Holy City. What a marvellous opportunity for a boy to participate in the great commemoration of God's deliverance of Israel! They remained in Jerusalem for the eight days of the celebration, which also included the Feast of Unleavened Bread, so called in memory of the bread hastily baked by the Hebrews on the eve of their departure from Egypt.

Jesus found the Temple and all the life that went on within it so absorbing that He failed to notice His family's departure for home. For their part, His parents, "supposing him to have been in the company, went a day's journey. And they sought him among their kinsfolk and acquaintance. And when they found him not, they turned back again to Jerusalem, seeking him" (Luke 2:44-45).

After three days of anguished searching, Mary and Joseph "found him in the temple, sitting in the midst of the doctors, both hearing them, and asking them questions. And all that heard him were astonished at his understanding and answers. And when they [his parents] saw him, they were amazed . . ." (Luke 2:46-48).

## 9. THE LAST DAYS TOGETHER

After His parents found Him in Jerusalem talking with the teachers, they brought Him home to Nazareth. The closeness of Jesus to his parents becomes clear in the conclusion of the story.

And he went down with them and came to Nazareth, and was obedient to them; and his mother kept all these things in her heart. And Jesus increased in wisdom and in stature, and in favor with God and man.

Luke 2:51, 52, RSV

The verse above contains the last mention of Joseph, for about twenty years later at the marriage at Cana when Mary reappeared, Joseph was not with her. He is thought to have died in the intervening time.

Mary was in Jerusalem at the time of her Son's crucifixion. During all His agony on the Cross she remained with Him. His love and care for her endured to the very end, for in the Bible's most poignant scene Jesus committed His mother to the care of the beloved disciple.

Now there stood by the cross of Jesus his mother, and his mother's sister, Mary, the wife of Cleophas, and Mary Magdalene. When Jesus therefore saw his mother and the disciple standing by, whom he loved, he saith unto his mother, "Woman behold thy son! Then saith he to the disciple, Behold thy mother!" And from that hour that disciple took her unto his own home.

John 19:25-27

After His Resurrection, faith in Jesus evidently began to stir the hearts of His followers, for we read that the eleven disciples "continued with one accord in prayer and supplication with the women, and Mary the mother of Jesus, and *with his brethren*" (Acts 1:14). Paul recorded the fact that the risen Christ "was seen of James, then of all the apostles" (I Corinthians 15:7).

The last scriptural mention of Mary is in the sentence from Acts 1 quoted above, where it is recorded that she waited with the disciples, His brethren, and some of the women in the upper room in Jerusalem on the eve of Pentecost. The last family ties were now ended. But the influence of the Holy Family had just begun. No family in the world's history has been so honored and loved and such an influence *for good*. No family better typified in their own daily lives a more holy pattern in family living. It is no wonder that the word "holy" is associated with this family from the time of their son's conception when the angel said to Mary "that which is conceived in her is of the Holy Ghost" (Matthew 1:20). During His ministry, both Mark and Luke said of Him, "I know thee who thou art, the Holy One of God" (Mark 1:24; Luke 4:34). And Peter, after Christ's earthly ministry had ended, referred to Him as "the Holy One and the Just" (Acts 3:14), God's son, whom he "hath glorified" (Acts 3:13).

CHAPTER 27

# Jesus and the Family

He that loveth father or mother more than me is not worthy of me: and he that loveth son or daughter more than me is not worthy of me.

Matthew 10:37

❋

Jesus' life was an acted parable of family love and loyalty. During the thirty years He lived with His family in Nazareth, as we have seen in the preceding chapter, He shared their anxieties and joys, their mourning and festivities, their labor and hard-earned repose.

These years were His real preparation for His ministry. Though He knew the value of periodic retreats into solitude for prayer and meditation, and spent forty days alone in the wilderness after His baptism, His training took place, not among such semimonastic groups as the Qumran community or the pious Essenes, but in the everyday round of family living, both in His own home and the homes of friends.

The word *family* never occurs in His teachings, but His emphasis on the family is everywhere evident—in His love of God the Father, in His reverence for motherhood, in His tenderness toward little children, in His many references to sonship and brotherhood, and in His love of home. In using the imagery of the family in these and other instances, Jesus struck chords of hope and understanding with the ordinary people to whom He ministered, people among whom He lived all of His life.

[ 231 ]

## 1. HIS CONTACTS WITH OTHER FAMILIES

During His earthly life He was often to be found in His own Nazareth home or workshop or in the various homes of His friends. Not for Him were the remote writing rooms and quiet library of the withdrawn community at Qumran, recently excavated, among the Judean cliffs overlooking the Dead Sea. He celebrated a wedding with the family at Cana. Peter's mother-in-law helped serve Him dinner at Peter's house in Capernaum. He dined at the home of His disciple Matthew (Matthew 9:10) and accepted an invitation from a Pharisee (Luke 7:36).

He visited homes like that of Zacchaeus at Jericho. Zacchaeus, a tax collector for the Roman government, had amassed his fortune dishonestly by exacting from people more than they owed and pocketing the difference. When Jesus came to Jericho, Zacchaeus was curious to see Him, but being a small man, he had to climb a sycamore tree to see over the heads of the crowd. Sure that a good man like Jesus would not speak to a despised tax collector like himself, he could hardly believe his ears when Jesus, looking up at him in the tree, said, "Zacchaeus, make haste and come down, for to-day I must abide at thy house" (Luke 19:5).

The Master's presence in his home not only filled Zacchaeus with amazement and joy, but gave him a change of heart. Generously he declared that he would give half his wealth to the poor and restore fourfold his ill-gotten wealth to its rightful owners. His entire household must have rejoiced at Jesus' words to them, "This day is salvation come to this house. . . . For the Son of man is come to seek and to save that which was lost" (Luke 19:9-10).

Jesus "sat at meat" (Mark 14:3; Luke 7:36-50) in the Bethany home of Simon "the leper," also called the Pharisee. While here the "sinful woman" with the alabaster box of precious ointment came and washed Jesus' feet with her tears and then poured precious ointment on them.

Another home He visited was that of Martha, Mary, and their brother Lazarus in Bethany. Evidently it was a comfortable home, large enough to provide rest and refreshment for the Master and His disciples, for the Gospels record two occasions when Jesus was entertained there (Luke 10:38-42; John 12:1-3). The friendship of these two sisters and their brother must have been congenial to Jesus, while their home provided the relaxation and comfort He needed to ease the fatigue of His arduous ministry.

Jesus felt close to this family, for the record states, "Now Jesus loved Martha, and her sister, and Lazarus" (John 11:5). His ties with the Bethany family and their faith in His healing power prompted the sisters to send Him a message that their brother was ill, but before Jesus reached Bethany, Lazarus died.

Jesus' grief at His friend's death is adequately conveyed in the shortest verse in the Bible, "Jesus wept" (John 11:35), a verse that seems to express, not merely His own sorrow on this particular occasion, but His overwhelming sadness for all family partings which death brings.

The outcome of the story is well known. Jesus raised Lazarus from the dead in the presence of many witnesses, some of whom believed in Him because of the miracle. Other witnesses reported it to the chief priests and Pharisees, who became convinced that Jesus was dangerous to them and must die.

Later, in the upper room of a home in Jerusalem, Jesus and His disciples ate their last meal together. The name of the householder whose home was honored by being the scene of the Last Supper is unknown, but from the following passage, describing the preparations for it, the "goodman of the house" seems to have been a friend of Jesus.

And he sendeth forth two of his disciples, and saith unto them, "Go ye into the city, and there shall meet you a man bearing a pitcher of water: follow him. And wheresoever he shall go in, say ye to the goodman of the house, 'The Master saith, "Where is the guestchamber where I shall eat the passover with my disciples?' "

"And he will shew you a large upper room furnished and prepared. There make ready for us."

Mark 14:13-15

## 2. FATHER AND FATHERHOOD

Though Jesus taught that spiritual loyalty to Him transcends that accorded to the family, He continued to show profound understanding of the common human ties with father, mother, son, and brother. Indeed, these family terms gave Him words with which to explain spiritual relationships centering in God the Father.

Throughout His ministry Jesus not only preached the Fatherhood of God, but He embodied this fundamental spiritual truth in His actions, so that Father became the distinctively Christian name for God in the New Testament. Even as a twelve-year-old boy, He explained to Mary and Joseph, "Wist ye not that I must be about my Father's business?" (Luke 2:49). He lived in the Father's presence and taught that God is very near, nearer than one's earthly father. To the multitude and to His disciples He said, "And call no man your father upon the earth, for one is your Father, which is in heaven" (Matthew 23:9).

Never separating Himself from His followers by claiming a unique relationship to the Father, Jesus helped them to understand that He and they had one and the same Father.

He stressed the universality of Fatherhood when he said to the Samaritan woman, "the hour cometh and now is when the true worshippers shall worship the Father in spirit and in truth: for the Father seeketh such to worship him" (John 4:23). Further communicating His own experience of God to man, he declared to the Samaritan woman that "he that hath seen me hath seen the Father" (John 14:9).

Since God is the Father, and man is His child, from the Father to the child Jesus further conveyed a message of paternal love:

"If ye keep my commandments, ye shall abide in my love; even as I have kept my Father's commandments, and abide in his love. . . . This is my commandment, that ye love one another, as I have loved you."

John 15:10, 12

His prayers show Jesus living close to His Heavenly Father. He taught His disciples to pray, "Our Father, which art in heaven . . ." (Luke 11:2). In the Garden of Gethsemane on the eve of His crucifixion He addressed God in agonized prayer, using the intimate word for father, "Abba, Father, all things are possible unto thee. Take away this cup from me; nevertheless not what I will, but what thou wilt" (Mark 14:36). When He was nailed to the Cross, He interceded for His tormentors, "Father, forgive them, for they know not what they do" (Luke 23:34). As He was dying, His last words were spoken to God, "Father, into thy hands I commend my spirit" (Luke 23:46).

## 3. MOTHER AND MOTHERHOOD

Jesus lifted motherhood to its highest plane in history and idealized it for eternity. Love—the kind of love nurtured by His mother Mary in their home—is the basis for his greatest commandment: "And thou shalt love the Lord thy God with all thy heart, and with all thy soul, and with all thy mind, and with all thy strength" (Mark 12:30).

His mother was the only woman really close to Him during His ministry, in the sense that Peter and John were, and she spent far more years in His presence than did any other person. Neither His disciples nor His own father Joseph had the close contact with her divine son that she did. When He was a child, she fed and clothed Him and led Him gently by the hand. She was with Him at the marriage at Cana, and she was with Him all the way to the Cross. Her gentleness, patience, sympathy, and tenderness are reflected in Him. Her humility shines forth in her Magnificat, in which she rejoiced in God her Savior, for "He hath regarded the low estate of his handmaiden" (Luke 1:48). Jesus later declared, "He that shall humble himself shall be exalted" (Matthew 23:12).

Of the pains and joys of motherhood, He spoke with understanding. As mentioned earlier in the chapter on children, He said of the mother in travail that she experiences sorrow when her hour to give birth has come, but that her sorrow turns to joy when her child is born into the world (John 16:21).

Jesus exhibited love and compassion for all mothers who crossed His path. Even on the way to Calvary as He bore His Cross, followed by the multitudes, many of them mourning mothers, He turned to the latter and said, "Daughters of Jerusalem, weep not for me, but weep for yourselves and your children. For, behold, the days are coming, in the which they shall say, Blessed are the barren . . ." (Luke 23:28-29).

## 4. FATHERS AND MOTHERS

As a true son of Israel, Jesus inherited from the divinely inspired leaders of His people a body of wise laws and precepts governing family living. He put the whole weight of His authority behind these laws, freeing them from the legalism in which they had become entangled, and revealing their divine sanction. Family living received fresh guiding principles in His teachings.

To the eager young man who desired to win eternal life, Jesus prescribed the Fifth Commandment, "Honour thy father and thy mother" (Mark 10:19). Deep respect, affection, and care for one's parents are never out-of-date nor old-fashioned, for God Himself enjoins them. Hence they were fundamental to personal fulfillment. Jesus denounced the scribes and Pharisees for cancelling God's commandment with their own laws. Scribal tradition permitted a man to inform his parents that the money he might have contributed to their needs was vowed to the Temple. Moral obligations cannot be repudiated in this way. Jesus said:

"You drop what God commands and hold to human tradition. . . . Thus, Moses said, *Honour your father and mother.* . . . But you say that if a man tells his father or mother, 'This money might have been at your service, but it is Korban' (that is, dedicated to God), he is exempt, so you hold, from doing anything for his father or mother. That is repealing the word of God in the interests of the tradition which you keep up."

Mark 7:9-13, Moffatt

## 5. CHILDREN AND CHILDHOOD

Jesus, who had an ideal childhood Himself, lifted our whole concept of childhood to a new plane, giving it a beauty never known in the ancient world. While He was still in Perea, a number of mothers brought their children to Him to have Him touch them, and pray for them, even as He had the halt, the lame, and the blind. But the disciples, feeling that Jesus was too busy with larger matters, rebuked these mothers for their presumption. Mark tells us that Jesus was "much displeased" (10:14) with His disciples for their failure to understand the depth of His love for children, so He said unto them "Suffer the little children to come unto me, and forbid them not: for of such is the kingdom of God" (Mark 10:14).

The children's rights were vindicated and the worth of the little ones stated, but Jesus went even further, in effect counselling His disciples not to think He was too busy for little children, for they possessed a spiritual secret. "Whosoever shall not receive the kingdom of God as a little child, he shall not enter therein. And He took them up in His arms, put his hands upon them, and blessed them" (Mark 10:15-16).

As he closed His period of instruction to His apostles and sent them forth on their first evangelistic tour, He told of giving drink to the "little ones." Many scholars believe that in these and other examples where Jesus uses "little ones" He was referring to His disciples. In using this family term, in connection with His own family of disciples, He combined the greatness of His love for them and their own worth as the seed of the Kingdom of Heaven.

## 6. SON AND SONSHIP

As God is the Heavenly Father, so Christ is His Son. When Jesus went to the Jordan to be baptized by John, "there came a voice from heaven, saying, 'Thou art my beloved Son, in whom I am well pleased'" (Mark 1:11).

The sentence which of all those in the New Testament best expresses the heart of the gospel is put in family terms: "For God so loved the world, that He gave His only begotten Son, that whosoever believeth in Him should not perish, but have everlasting life" (John 3:16).

Again the voice was heard, this time on a high mountain where Peter, James, and John beheld Jesus transfigured before them and clothed in shining white raiment. "And there was a cloud that overshadowed them. And a voice came out of the cloud saying, 'This is my beloved Son; hear him'" (Mark 9:7).

Christ's followers declared the meaning of His divine Sonship in the following two quotations:

No man hath seen God at any time. The only begotten Son, which is in the bosom of the Father, he hath declared him.

John 1:18

But when the time had fully come, God sent forth his Son, born of woman, born under the law, to redeem those who were under the law, so that we might receive adoption as sons. And because you are sons, God has sent the Spirit of his Son into our hearts, crying, "Abba! Father!" So through God you are no longer a slave but a son, and if a son then an heir.

Galatians 4:4-7, RSV

## 7. BROTHER AND BROTHERHOOD

Jesus had little to say about relationships between real brothers. His emphasis was on a new brotherhood of all men. To achieve this, however, He said "men must be born again." His own practical application of brotherhood was mirrored in His relationship to His apostles. They called all Christians "brother" and all the world "neighbor."

Love of the brethren was important to the followers of Christ, for they believed that it was evidence of a person's love of God. "If a man say, 'I love God' and hateth his brother, he is a liar, for he that loveth not his brother whom he hath seen, how can he love God whom he hath not seen?" (I John 4:20).

Brotherly love became an outstanding virtue in the Church. Paul wrote to the Roman Christians advice he had given in every church he founded, "Be kindly affectioned one to another with brotherly love" (Romans 12:10). The same exhortation is echoed in the First Epistle of Peter, "Finally, all of you, have unity of spirit, sympathy, love of the brethren, a tender heart and a humble mind" (I Peter 3:8, RSV).

Moreover, brotherly love in the Church was not mere sentiment but an active force binding together in a powerful unity all those who were in Christ. "But if any one has the world's goods and sees his brother in need, yet closes his heart against him, how does God's love abide in him? Little children, let us not love in word or speech but in deed and in truth." (I John 3:17-18, RSV).

## 8. BEYOND THE FAMILY

There were times when Jesus preached a higher loyalty even than that of the family, for He knew that truth is more important than domestic harmony and that only God's kingdom has ultimate value. In words quoted in part from Micah, Jesus foretold of divisions within families over the question of loyalty to Him:

"Think not that I am come to send peace on earth. I came not to send peace, but a sword. For I am come to set a man at variance against his father, and the daughter against her mother. . . . And a man's foes shall be they of his own household. He that loveth father or mother more

than me is not worthy of me; and he that loveth son or daughter more
than me is not worthy of me."                    Matthew 10:34-37

His dramatic words reveal that His peace cannot be achieved by
compromise or evasion, but may have to be won at the price of family
tranquillity. In another saying He expressed a different aspect of
loyalty to Him:

"If any man come to me, and hate not his father, and mother, and
wife, and children, and brethren, and sisters, yea, and his own life also,
he cannot be my disciple."                    Luke 14:26

Hate is a paradoxical word in connection with these close relationships. Jesus may have used it to shock the complacent multitudes
basking in His presence, yet refusing to give Him unqualified loyalty.
Both of His sayings indicate that following Him is not a soft, easy
way of life, but one in which the claims of self, or home, or loved
ones must be set aside when they conflict with the requirements of
discipleship.

James and his brother John were in their boat mending their fishing
nets when Jesus came by. "And straightway he called them, and they
left their father Zebedee in the ship with the hired servants and went
after him" (Mark 1:20). Here was an instance of Jesus' demands
eagerly accepted.

The rewards of acceptance are very great, now and hereafter.
"Verily I say unto you, There is no man that hath left house, or parents, or brethren, or wife, or children for the kingdom of God's sake,
who shall not receive manifold more in this present time, and in the
world to come life everlasting" (Luke 18:29-30). In the early
Church, according to the New Testament, the rewards of following
Him proved to be very great. There was sharing of possessions with
those in need, warm hospitality, and brotherly love. Above all, there
was the inexpressible joy of belonging to the family of Christ both
now and hereafter.

On the memorable occasion when "his brethren and his mother"
(Mark 3:31) came for him, the multitude that sat about "said unto him,
'Behold, thy mother and thy brethren without seek for thee.' " (Mark
3:32). Jesus indicated that He had a larger family. "And He looked
round about on them which sat about Him, and said, 'Behold my
mother and my brethren! For whosoever shall do the will of God, the
same is my brother, and my sister, and my mother' " (Mark 3:34-35).

# CHAPTER 28

# Paul's Guide to Family Conduct

The night is far spent, the day is at hand: let us therefore cast off the works of darkness, and let us put on the armour of light. Let us walk honestly, as in the day; not in rioting and drunkenness, not in chambering and wantonness, not in strife and envying. But put ye on the Lord Jesus Christ, and make not provision for the flesh, to fulfill the lusts thereof.

Romans 13:12-14

In his letters to the young churches at Rome, Corinth, Ephesus, Colossae, Thessalonica, and other centers of the emerging Christian fellowship, Paul set up modes of family conduct, characterized by righteousness, purity, justice, holiness, and other qualities reflecting the nature of God and His son Jesus Christ. Although these letters are directed to the church and not to the family, this chapter will focus on those passages where Paul deals specifically with family problems inside the churches.

## 1. HIS LEGACY TO CHRISTIAN FAMILIES

Speaking as a "servant of God, and an apostle of Jesus Christ," Paul exhorted his followers to be "blameless and harmless, the sons of God, without rebuke, in the midst of a crooked and perverse nation; among whom ye shine as lights in the world" (Philippians 2:15).

These early churches, founded in cities where the godless had reigned for many centuries, faced immorality in its most flagrant forms. A constant "cold war" raged between those who worshiped the goddess of earthly love, Venus, and those who worshiped Christ, the Son of God. Paul realized that these new Christians must set up very high standards in their own personal conduct, first in order to attract other followers and second in order to lay a sound foundation for a Christian civilization.

Rules of Christian conduct to guide the family occur again and again in the letters to young churches, most of which are either the writing or the thought of Paul. Since some of these epistles repeat the same principles of ethical conduct, recent biblical scholarship contends that a common catechetical system was in general use, presumably for candidates for baptism.

References to the family appear in most of the epistles, but the messages most pertinent to the family are in Romans, Corinthians, Ephesians, Colossians and Thessalonians. Paul's words are so applicable to problems in today's families that he seems to be writing for our own century.

## 2. RIGHTEOUSNESS IN THE FAMILY (Romans 1:21-32; 2:22; 13:13-14)

In his Epistle to the Romans, Paul struck out against omnipresent evils which he was convinced were the results of idolatry. He saw divine retribution falling upon ungodly people who denied the truth of God and failed to honor Him. "Because that, when they knew God, they glorified him not as God, neither were thankful; but became vain in their imaginations, and their foolish heart was darkened. Professing themselves to be wise, they became fools, and changed the glory of the uncorruptible God into an image made like to corruptible man, and to birds, and fourfooted beasts, and creeping things" (Romans 1:21-23).

Idolatry, which is the fundamental error of worshiping "the creature more than the Creator" (Romans 1:25), resulted in "vile affections," and every kind of uncleanness. Paul listed truly appalling examples of social corruption in the following passage:

Thus, because they have not seen fit to acknowledge God, he has given them up to their own depraved reason. This leads them to break all rules of conduct. They are filled with every kind of injustice, mischief, rapacity, and malice; they are one mass of envy, murder, rivalry, treachery, and malevolence; whispers and scandal-mongers, hateful to God, insolent, arrogant, and boastful; they invent new kinds of mischief, they show no loyalty to parents, no conscience, no fidelity to their plighted word; they are without natural affection and without pity. They know well enough the just decree of God, that those who behave like this deserve to die, and yet they do it; not only so, they actually applaud such practices.                                    Romans 1:28-32, NEB

Paul was not content merely to catalogue the evils surrounding his readers in ancient Rome. "Be not overcome of evil," he urged them, "but overcome evil with good" (Romans 12:21). In the four beautiful chapters (Romans 12-15:13) which have been likened to the Sermon on the Mount, he described Christian behavior which does indeed defeat evil.

Paul boldly denounced adultery, revelry, bouts of drinking, and other evils listed in the verses at the head of this chapter. Such evils have their origin inside the family, Paul seemed to say, and they may spread from there like a disease into the larger church family.

His ardent call for righteousness has had a vital influence on Christians down the centuries, including the fourth-century philosopher and Church Father, Augustine, who explained in his *Confessions* that he had had a long struggle with the flesh. The turning point came in his thirty-second year when he was in a garden and opened the Bible at Romans 13:12-14, the verses cited at the head of this chapter.

Augustine was transformed from the moment that he read Paul's words. Hurrying to his saintly mother Monica, who had prayed for him for eighteen long years as he wallowed in debauchery and sensuality, he acknowledged to her his own wickedness, and praised God, "the author of safety, and Jesus Christ, the Redeemer." Augustine further disclosed that when he had read Paul's words he closed the Bible. His companion told him that had he read one verse farther he would have come upon this: "Him that is weak in the faith receive ye" (Romans 14:1).

After this mystical experience Augustine prayed:

O Lord, truly I am Thy servant; I am thy servant, and the son of Thine handmaid: Thou hast loosed my bonds. I will offer to thee the sacrifice of thanksgiving. Let my heart and my tongue praise Thee, and let all my bones say Lord, who is like unto Thee? . . . How evil have not my deeds been; or if not my deeds, my words; or if not my words, my will? But Thou, O Lord, art good and merciful, and Thy right hand . . . removed from the bottom of my heart that abyss of corruption.

## 3. PURITY IN THE FAMILY (I Corinthians 5; 6:9-20; 7:1-16; 25-40)

Paul's teachings on purity echoed one of Christ's Beatitudes, "Blessed are the pure in heart, for they shall see God" (Matthew 5:8). Later writers upheld Paul's insistence on purity (Jude 4-19).

The great apostle knew that those who lead impure lives and think impure thoughts "shall not inherit the kingdom of God" (Galatians 5:21). If families were to be happy and churches strong, Christians must lead upright lives. To that end he wrote the church at Philippi:

> Finally, brethren, whatsoever things are true, whatsoever things are honest, whatsoever things are just, whatsoever things are pure, whatsoever things are lovely, whatsoever things are of good report . . . think on these things.
>
> Philippians 4:8

In the wealthy and notoriously dissolute Greek seaport of Corinth, Christian brothers were not only thinking but acting impurely. While Paul was in Ephesus disturbing news of the troubles in Corinth reached him. This church, which he had founded on his second missionary journey, included in its membership many former pagans. Perhaps it is not surprising that some of these recent converts had relapsed into their pagan ways. Some of the church members were disturbed by conflicts with the pagan society surrounding them. One case of flagrant immorality was reported to Paul.

Because Paul could not go to the Corinthians, he wrote them offering wise advice on their problems and inspiring his readers to new reaches of Christian living. His memorable chapter on love is part of this correspondence.

One can well imagine the sense of joyful expectancy in the church as the leader opened Paul's letter preparatory to reading it. Listening to its phrases, the Corinthians were reminded of the way their revered apostle preached. But their mood changed when the leader read a certain portion. Consternation, excited whispering, frowns, muttering swept like wildfire over the assembly. Why should Paul be so harsh about what they considered a little matter of sexual irregularity? But there was no mistaking the apostle's words.

> I actually hear reports of sexual immorality among you . . . the union of a man with his father's wife. And you can still be proud of yourselves!

You ought to have gone into mourning; a man who has done such a deed should have been rooted out of your company. . . . Your self-satisfaction ill becomes you. Have you never heard the saying, "A little leaven leavens all the dough"?

I Corinthians 5:1-3, 6, NEB

At this point the man in question may have stamped out of the assembly followed by his tearful and confused wife-stepmother. Soon others probably followed him, for Paul included many in his condemnations. "I now write that you must have nothing to do with any so-called Christian, who leads a loose life, or is grasping, or idolatrous, a slanderer, a drunkard, or a swindler" (I Corinthians 5:11, NEB).

With such forthright language as this echoing in their ears, the evildoers probably left the church. Few would have lingered among the brethren to hear Paul's warning:

Know ye not that the unrighteous shall not inherit the kingdom of God? Be not deceived: neither fornicators, nor idolaters, nor adulterers, nor effeminate, nor abusers of themselves with mankind, nor thieves, nor covetous, nor drunkards, nor revilers, nor extortioners, shall inherit the kingdom of God.

I Corinthians 6:9-10

Paul found prostitution such an evil practice that he frequently warned his readers about it. He explained his bitter opposition to it, as follows: "Know ye not that your bodies are the members of Christ? shall I then take the members of Christ, and make them members of an harlot? God forbid. What? know ye not that he which is joined to an harlot is one body? for two, saith he, shall be one flesh. But he that is joined unto the Lord is one spirit. Flee fornication. Every sin that a man doeth is without the body; but he that committeth fornication sinneth against his own body. What? know ye not that your body is the temple of the Holy Ghost which is in you, which ye have of God, and ye are not your own? For ye are bought with a price: therefore glorify God in your body, and in your spirit, which are God's" (I Corinthians 6:15-20).

## 4. JUSTICE IN THE FAMILY (Ephesians 5:22-33; 6:1-5)

If justice is to prevail in the church and nation, and around world council tables, it must begin with the family in the home. In no place does fair play mean more. This letter to the church at Ephesus, a metropolis of the Roman province of Asia Minor, sharing with the Syrian Antioch and the Egyptian Alexandria the honor of being one of the three great cities of the eastern Mediterranean, seems to have been written by Paul while he was in prison in Rome. In none of Paul's other letters is there such specific counsel for every member of the family: husbands, wives, children, parents, masters, servants.

Paul exhorted his followers as "dear children" to "walk in love." He told them to live in such purity and love that they did not even jest about immoralities. Instead of engaging in foolish talk about filthy things, give thanks, said the steadfast Paul. "For this ye know that no whoremonger, nor unclean person, nor covetous man who is an idolator, hath any inheritance in the kingdom of Christ and of God" (Ephesians 5:5).

In his outline of duties for the Christian family (Ephesians 5:22-33), Paul opened with counsel for husbands and wives. Speaking again as a marriage counsellor, Paul's subject this time was mutual subordination in the Christian household. He exhorted Christians in general, out of reverence to Christ, to be subject to one another. The primary submission, according to Paul's concept, must devolve upon the wife. Never did Paul intimate that the woman is naturally or spiritually inferior to the man, or the wife to her husband; but he held to the divine order of marriage established at the Creation, and in this order the wife comes after her husband.

Paul recognized the husband to be the head of the household, just as Christ is recognized as the head of the Church. But Paul reminded the church at Ephesus that a husband cannot afford to be a domestic tyrant. A husband must bestow upon his wife the same selfless love that Christ bestows upon the Church. "For the husband is the head of the wife, as Christ is the head of the church,: and he is the Saviour of the body" (Ephesians 5:23). With Christ the real head of the Church, nothing is implied that is inconsistent with the dignity and personal freedom of the wife. Such an analogy of Christ and His Church suggests complete harmony. The subjection required implies nothing servile. The ideal is that the wife spontaneously yields to her husband whom she honors and loves.

Paul added another revealing, important point to his thoughts on the husband as the head of the family, when he proclaimed to the church at Ephesus that "So ought men to love their wives as their

own bodies. He that loveth his wife loveth himself" (5:28). Paul
proceeded to exhort the wife to "reverence her husband" (5:33).
With reverence comes love, esteem, and a desire to please. If both
husband and wife follow Paul's advice, there can be no friction.

In his outline of conjugal duties, Paul sought to overcome the bit-
terness that existed between so many husbands and wives in the
church at Ephesus. This marriage counsellor went one step further in
his spiritual advice. He declared marriage to be "a great mystery"
(5:32), pointing to a transcendental, eternal reality, a theme more
fully developed in the first chapter of this book.

Paul further outlined domestic duties in his letter to church members in Ephesus. In Ephesians 6:2-4 he presented the duties of children which were mentioned in an earlier chapter. The child who
obeys the Fifth Commandment is promised the good things of life,
and a long span of years to enjoy them. The child's obedience to the
parent, according to Paul, must include an inward reverence as well
as an outward expression of obedience.

The Christian family must govern itself by the law of love for God.
Parents who emphasize worldly success, both in example and in teaching, may learn too late that they have cheated their children of their
spiritual birthright. In the church at Ephesus, a city of much wealth
but vast corruption, the emphasis no doubt was in the wrong direction, or Paul would not have had to admonish parents to bring their
children up "in the nurture and admonition of the Lord."

## 5. A TABLE ON OBLIGATIONS TO ONE'S OWN HOUSEHOLD
(Colossians 3:18-22)

Family problems in the church at Colossae appear to have been
similar to those in the church at Ephesus, about one hundred miles
from Colossae. Epistles to the churches in both of these cities bear
remarkable parallelisms in language and in ruling, as may be noted:

*Wives,* submit yourselves unto your own husbands, as it is fit in the
Lord.

*Husbands,* love your wives, and be not bitter against them.

*Children,* obey your parents in all things; for this is well pleasing
unto the Lord.

*Fathers,* provoke not your children to anger, lest they be discouraged.

*Servants,* obey in all things your masters according to the flesh; not with eyeservice, as menpleasers; but in singleness of heart, fearing God.

Colossians 3:18-22

The beginning words of each of these five verses are all-inclusive. Strong is the household whose members observe these rules in their daily lives. Too often friction in a household is caused because one's greatest enemies walk beside one in the home.

In this Colossian epistle there is not quite the liberality toward wives that there is in the earlier Galatian epistle, which says, "There is neither male nor female: for ye are all one in Christ Jesus" (3:28).

## 6. HOLINESS IN THE FAMILY (I Thessalonians 4:3-5, 7)

Thessalonica (now Salonika), the chief city of Macedonia, was the site of another Christian church founded by Paul. It appears from the text of Thessalonians, one of the earliest Pauline letters on record, that there were many in this gulf town who opposed his Christian message on righteousness, purity, and justice. Therefore Paul again made a stirring plea:

For this is the will of God, your sanctification: that you abstain from immorality; that each one of you know how to take a wife for himself in holiness and honor, not in the passion of lust like heathen who do not know God; that no man transgress, and wrong his brother in this matter, because the Lord is an avenger in all these things, as we solemnly forewarned you. For God has not called us for uncleanness, but in holiness. Therefore whoever disregards this, disregards not man but God, who gives His Holy Spirit to you.

I Thessalonians 4:3-8, RSV

An impure life leaves its most lasting damage on the family, the oldest human social unit, and such damage spreads to every area of a nation's life. The moral breakdown and fall of nations throughout the history of mankind are a testimony to the soundness of Paul's call to holiness. In this one thesis lies another basic principle for family strength.

Just as the evils Paul listed were those he encountered in his travels far and wide in the Roman Empire, so the fruits of the Spirit he enumerated must have been observed by him in many Christian households where he was welcomed. Paul described a new spiritual fellowship ruled by love, with Christ the head of this new brotherhood, which was indeed "the household of God" (Ephesians 2:19).

# CHAPTER 29

# Households of Faith

---

Let us do good unto all men, especially unto them who are of the household of faith.

Galatians 6:10

---

✳

Family living in the Bible reached its richest sense of purpose in the New Testament Church, which had its birth in homes and among families. The biblical experience of the family, which in Old Testament times had become so meaningful that it was first applied to Hebrew tribes, nations of Israel and Judah, was in New Testament times applied to the Church. And so, for the first time, we come upon such phrases as Household of God (Ephesians 2:19) or Household of Faith (Galatians 6:10). And finally there evolved the Church (Acts 2:47).

The family today is still a living unit of the Church itself, a miniature church as it were, provided it has the same sense of mission in the world as does the Church. Through the centuries the family and the home have provided for the Church an inspiration that may be traced back to those first families, as will be shown in this chapter.

## 1. CHRISTIAN FAMILIES

It is amazing that after nearly nineteen centuries we still know the names of many important households of the early Church. Among these were the households of: Chloe of Corinth (I Corinthians 1:11);

Stephanas, Paul's first convert in Achaia (I Corinthians 16:15);
Jason, whose home in Thessalonica was assaulted because he gave
Paul and Silas hospitality (Acts 17:5, 7); Justus, with whom Paul
stayed at Corinth (Acts 18:7); Crispus, a ruler of the synagogue who
"believed on the Lord with all his house" (Acts 18:8); and Onesi-
phorus, who visited Paul in prison (II Timothy 4:19).

The sixteenth chapter of Romans contains greetings to other families in addition to that of Aquila and Priscilla: Aristobulus and his
household, the family of Narcissus, Rufus and his mother, Nereus
and his sister, Andronicus and Junia, who was probably his wife, also
Tryphena and Tryphosa, who may have been twin sisters, and Philo-
logus with his wife Julia.

How we wish we knew more about the little family groups appear-
ing in the New Testament! Those at Tyre that accompanied Paul and
his fellow apostles are vividly portrayed, for they "brought us on our
way, with wives and children, till we were out of the city. And we
kneeled down on the shore and prayed. And when we had taken our
leave one of another, we took ship, and they returned home again"
(Acts 21:5-6).

Without some fortunate discovery, we shall know only what can
be inferred from the New Testament and other early sources concerning these families, but they remain households beloved of Paul
and shining examples among Christian families.

## 2. THE BELIEVING HOUSEHOLD OF CORNELIUS
   (Acts 10:1-48)

The Book of Acts records that the first Gentile family to become
Christian through the preaching of Peter was that of Cornelius. He
was a centurion commanding a hundred men in the Italian cohort
garrisoned at Caesarea, the seat of the Roman government of Judea.
Though a Roman, Cornelius was one of those Gentile adherents of
the synagogue called "God-fearers." In the first century A.D. many
men and women of heathen backgrounds were so much attracted by
the high ideals and ethical living of Judaism that they joined local
synagogues. Through his association with pious Jews, Cornelius became "a devout man and one that feared God with all his house,
which gave alms to the people, and prayed to God alway" (10:2).

When tidings of the new gospel preached by the apostles came to

Cornelius, he sent messengers to Peter, at Joppa, to invite him to his house in Caesarea. Arriving there, Peter was surprised to see his host prostrate himself. "Stand up," said Peter to the Roman officer, "I myself also am a man" (10:26).

Inside the house a greater surprise was in store for Peter. Instead of one or two haughty, supercilious and merely idly curious Romans, he "found many that were come together" (10:27), eagerly and earnestly awaiting his message, for Cornelius "had called together his kinsmen and near friends" (10:24), and also his whole family.

Inspired by their interest and enthusiasm, Peter expounded the Christian gospel to them. The keenest surprise of the day still awaited him, for "While Peter yet spake these words, the Holy Ghost fell on all them which heard the word" (10:44) The Jewish Christians who had come to Cornelius' home with Peter were astonished "because that on the Gentiles also was poured out the gift of the Holy Ghost. For they heard them speak with tongues and magnify God" (10:45-46).

It was like Pentecost—a Gentile Pentecost—so Peter decided that Cornelius' household and all the assembled company should be baptized in the name of Jesus Christ. After their overwhelming experience, Cornelius and his family and friends begged Peter to remain with them a few days longer to teach them further about the Lord Jesus Christ.

## 3. HOUSEHOLD BAPTISMS (Acts 16:12-15; 19-40)

Paul also preached to entire family groups who became converts of the Christian way. When Paul arrived in Philippi, the capital of Macedonia, and the first European city to be evangelized he converted two families. The first was the household of Lydia, an important business woman who sold purple dye in the city. Lydia, like Cornelius, was a "God-fearer" who worshiped God and "whose heart the Lord opened, that she attended unto the things which were spoken of Paul" (16:14).

The baptism of all members of Lydia's household indicates that there was real love, faith, and family solidarity under the roof. Lydia invited Paul and Silas to "come into my house and abide there" (16: 15). Here was Christian hospitality at its best, a visible expression of love in the growing Church. As in the case of Cornelius, she also felt the need of learning from the apostles more of the faith into which she had just been baptized.

The second household to which Paul preached in Philippi was the jailer's. Paul and Silas were beaten and thrown into prison because they had healed a slave girl of an abnormal mental condition which made her a profitable fortuneteller for her owners. At midnight, while the two imprisoned apostles were singing hymns and praying, an earthquake shook the building, its doors flew open, and the fetters fell from the feet of Paul and Silas. Seeing the doors open, and believing his prisoners had escaped because of his neglect of duty, the jailer drew his sword and prepared to kill himself. But Paul cried out, "Do thyself no harm, for we are all here" (16:28).

Calling for a light, the jailer fell down trembling before Paul and Silas and asked, " 'Sirs, what must I do to be saved?' And they said, 'Believe on the Lord Jesus Christ, and thou shalt be saved, and thy house' " (16:30-31).

Then the apostles preached not only to the jailer but "to all that were in his house," children, young people, and grownups, all who had been awakened by the earthquake. Paul and Silas, still bruised and bleeding from their beating, were washed by the jailer. Then he "was baptized, he and all his, straightway. And when he had brought them into his house, he set meat before them and rejoiced, believing in God with all his house" (16:33-34).

The next day, freed by the magistrates of Philippi, Paul and Silas "went out of the prison, and entered into the house of Lydia. And when they had seen the brethren, they comforted them and departed" (16:40).

## 4. CHURCHES OF THE HOUSEHOLD

Not having any buildings for their activities (church buildings were not erected until long after the apostolic age), the members met in each other's homes for fellowship, worship, and a common meal, sometimes called the "breaking of bread," which commemorated the Last Supper. The life and relationships of the first Christians within these early house churches is set forth in Acts 2:42-47.

One of the most significant lines in this account tells us that they broke bread "from house to house" (Acts 2:46). Paul used this same theme of teaching from "house to house" when he addressed the presbyters at Ephesus, saying "I kept back nothing that was profitable unto you, but have shewed you, and have taught you publicly, from house to house" (Acts 20:20).

The Church itself came into being on the day of Pentecost, as we have already noted, in the upper room of a home in Jerusalem that possibly belonged to John Mark's mother. Here several family groups and others intimately associated with them were waiting when they heard the rush of a mighty wind and saw tongues of fire and they were filled with the Holy Spirit.

Prominent among the house churches mentioned in the Bible is that of Paul's tent-making friends, Aquila and his wife Priscilla, whom Paul first met in Corinth. They sailed with him to Ephesus, from which city Paul wrote this greeting to the Corinthians, "Aquila and Priscilla salute you much in the Lord, with the church that is in their house" (I Corinthians 16:19). Another passage (Romans 16:5) greets the house church believed to have been established later by Aquila and Priscilla in Rome.

Other house churches include that of Philemon, master of the escaped slave Onesimus. Paul, in his letter asking Philemon to forgive Onesimus, greeted the master and "the church in thy house" (Philemon 2). In another letter Paul greeted a certain man named Nymphas living in Asia Minor at Laodicea and included in the salutation "the church which is in his house" (Colossians 4:15).

One of the early house churches was actually discovered, not long ago, by the Yale University expedition which carried on excavations at Dura-Europos on the Euphrates River. There archaeologists unearthed a house, one room of which had been used as a Christian church. The walls are decorated with faded frescoes of Christian stories, and at one end of the small room there is a baptistry. The entire room was brought to America and reconstructed in the Yale Art Gallery.

## 5. HOSPITALITY

A golden thread running through all these stories of the households of faith is the theme of hospitality. In New Testament times this virtue was practiced, partly because it was an ancient custom, but more significantly because it was an expression of love for Jesus, the apostles, and other Christian brothers traveling through lands where public lodging places were few.

". . . I was a stranger and ye took me in. . . ." Lord . . . when saw we thee a stranger and took thee in?

"Verily I say unto you, Inasmuch as ye have done it unto one of the least of these my brethren, ye have done it unto me."

Matthew 25:35, 38, 40

Paul, well aware from his own experience of the enormous role hospitality played in extending the Christian gospel, urged the Roman Christians to practice this friendly virtue (Romans 12:13). Some who evidently practiced it grudgingly were admonished, according to J. B. Phillips' translation, "Be hospitable to each other without secretly wishing you hadn't got to be!" (I Peter 4:9).

To be enrolled among the respected Christian widows a woman was required to be "well reported of for good works," such as having "brought up children . . . lodged strangers . . . and relieved the afflicted" (I Timothy 5:10). Among the qualifications of a bishop were that he "must be blameless, the husband of one wife, vigilant, sober, of good behavior, given to hospitality . . ." (I Timothy 3:2).

## 6. THE HOUSEHOLD OF GOD

When entire households, such as those we have been describing, were caught up into the life of the Church, they intensified a family atmosphere pervading the whole Christian community. Examples of a warm family relationship abound in the New Testament. Phebe, a deaconess of the church at Cenchrea, Paul described as "our sister," while a few sentences later he saluted a certain "Rufus chosen in the Lord, and his mother and mine" (Romans 16:1, 13). John affectionately wrote to "my little children," and called them "beloved" (I John 2:1; 3:2).

From the very earliest days of the Church the Christian brethren showed by their acts that they were indeed members of a boundless family who acknowledged their responsibility for weaker or unfortunate members not only in their immediate community (Acts 4:34-37), but throughout the Church (Acts 11:29).

The unity of the household of God is memorably proclaimed in the following passage:

Now therefore ye are no more strangers and foreigners, but fellow-citizens with the saints, and of the household of God; and are built upon the foundation of the apostles and prophets, Jesus Christ himself being the chief corner stone. In whom all the building fitly framed together groweth unto an holy temple in the Lord, in whom ye also are builded together for an habitation of God through the Spirit.

Ephesians 2:19-22

The household of God of which the apostles wrote transcended racial barriers, for in New Testament times, as the above quotation states, "foreigners" and "strangers" were welcomed into the Church. No longer did the Church comprise Abraham's family and the people descended from them, for in Christ salvation was offered to the wider family of humanity, and the idea of a world-wide spiritual family was born.

One of the great prayers of the Bible, in fervently summing up the wonderful destiny and purpose of the Church, reflects family living in all its glory:

For this cause I bow my knees unto the Father of our Lord Jesus Christ, of whom the whole family in heaven and earth is named, that he would grant you, according to the riches of his glory, to be strengthened with might by his Spirit in the inner man; that Christ may dwell in your hearts by faith; that ye, being rooted and grounded in love, may be able to comprehend with all saints what is the breadth, and length, and depth, and height; and to know the love of Christ, which passeth knowledge, that ye might be filled with all the fulness of God.

Ephesians 3:14-19

The writer of Ephesians, no doubt expressing the thought of Paul, seems to be saying to the church at Ephesus that all people of all ages and climes belong to the family of God, because their life has come from the same Father, "of whom every family in heaven and earth is named." These earthly families are the nations of the world, who ascribe their unity to descent from a common ancestor, a theme to be further developed in the next chapter. "One Family Under God." In this prayer the term is extended to families in heaven, probably with the thought that a social order of some kind exists among them.

# CHAPTER 30

# One Family Under God

---

God that made the world and all things therein . . . hath made of one blood all nations of men for to dwell on all the face of the earth, and hath determined the times before appointed, and the bounds of their habitation.

Acts 17:24, 26

---

✻

## 1. FAMILY SYMBOLISM

The Bible story of family life is incomplete unless it is seen in its world-wide significance. Before we finish our study, a more searching analysis is needed of the common values that cement the nations of the world together. The family, the very bulwark of civilization, provides the necessary symbolism for such a study. All of the nations of the world, according to Paul's interpretation above, are of "one blood," and God is the Father.

Thomas Carlyle has stated it well: "The Bible is our first, oldest statement of the never-ending problem—man's destiny, and God's way with him here on earth." Let us probe more deeply into what the Bible has to say on the destiny of one family under God.

A family symbolism related to the world of nations contributes a useful framework for a better understanding of the ongoing process of the nations of the world: their survival, their peaceful co-existence, their fullness of life. Jesus, always glorious and large in His concept, referred not to one family but to one fold:

And other sheep I have, which are not of this fold: them also I must bring, and they shall hear my voice; and there shall be one fold and one shepherd.

John 10:16

Jesus also gave us one of the main clues to world survival when He spoke of a ministry that must be world-wide. "Unto the eleven as they sat at meat," He said, " 'Go ye into all the world, and preach the gospel to every creature' " (Mark 16:14, 15).

## 2. GENESIS DOCUMENT ON FAMILY OF NATIONS

Now let us go back to the beginning of recorded time for a better understanding of the races and nations which, according to the Bible, sprang from one parent stem, Noah and his wife. In Genesis 10 we find a family register, one of the Bible's most important documents and one of the most remarkable in any literature, for it actually sets forth the idea that God made of one family all nations to dwell on the earth.

Listed as if they were branches of one family are the principal races and peoples known to the Israelites. This Genesis genealogy describes in detail the settlement of families, as they went forth over the face of the earth. According to this record of the generations of Noah's sons, Shem, Ham and Japheth, and their sons, and their settlement in various parts of the world after the Flood, all nations of the world actually sprang from the same family beginnings. After the naming of the progeny of each of the sons of Noah, it is written:

These are the families of the sons of Noah, after their generations, in their nations: and by these were the nations divided in the earth after the flood.

Genesis 10:32

## 3. FIRST CONFUSION IN FAMILY OF NATIONS

The moral and spiritual confusion of tongues, so far removed from what God conceived for effective communication between nations, had its beginning in the Tower of Babel. This tower arose, scholars now believe, about one hundred years after the Flood, when the human race, all descending from Noah's sons, had grown to about thirty thousand persons.

Men had the great ambition to build a city and in it a man-made tower that would reach to heaven.

And the Lord came down to see the city and the tower, which the children of men builded. And the Lord said, "Behold the people is one, and they have all one language; and this they begin to do: and now nothing will be restrained from them, which they have imagined to do. Go to, let us go down, and there confound their language, that they may not understand one another's speech." So the Lord scattered them abroad from thence upon the face of all the earth: and they left off to build the city. Therefore is the name of it called Babel; because the Lord did there confound the language of all the earth: and from thence did the Lord scatter them abroad upon the face of all the earth.

Genesis 11:5-9

God's punishment for the attempted building of this tower of materiality, according to Genesis, was the destruction of family solidarity. In the words of Dr. Walter Russell Bowie in *The Interpreter's Bible:*

. . . our world can be brought from its confusion into closer and more confident life only by a spiritual humility which will stop men from trusting in their towers of Babel. God's trust and God's judgment are still on high, and no human pride or power can climb above them or bring them down. There are eternal moral principles which cannot be defied. That is what all nations alike must learn if there is to be a human family instead of a planetary failure (Vol. 1, p. 565).

Immediately following the Genesis 11 account of the confusion of the nations, God calls Abraham in whom "shall all the families of the earth be blessed" (Genesis 12:3), as mentioned earlier. Then follows the long biblical account of how the family of Abraham became the family of Israel and of God, because he had chosen the Israelites to be "a peculiar people unto himself, above all the nations that are upon the earth" (Deuteronomy 14:2).

## 4. ISAIAH—THE WORLD AND ITS NATIONS

In his prophecy of the coming of Christ's kingdom, Isaiah dreamed of the universal reign of the Lord when

he shall judge among the nations, and shall rebuke many people: and they shall beat their swords into plowshares, and their spears into pruning hooks: nation shall not lift up sword against nation, neither shall they learn war any more.

Isaiah 2:4

In his incomparable Chapter 40, Isaiah seemed to sense better than any other Old Testament prophet the majesty of God and the littleness of nations:

> Who has measured the waters in
>     the hollow of his hand
> And marked off the heavens with
>     a span,
> Enclosed the dust of the earth in a
>     measure
> And weighed the mountains in the scales
>     and the hills in a balance? . . .
> Whom did he consult for his enlightenment,
> And who taught him the path of
>     justice,
> And taught him knowledge,
>     and showed him the way of understanding?
> Behold, the nations are like a drop
>     from a bucket,
> And are accounted as the dust on the scales . . .
> All nations are as nothing before him;
> They are counted by him as less than nothing,
>     and emptiness.
>
> Isaiah 40:12, 14-15; 17 RSV

We see in succeeding chapters, Isaiah 41 and 42, that it is God Who causes events to occur, God Who determines their course and sequence, God Who makes them known and brings them to fulfillment. In a further prophecy, Isaiah declared:

> For the nation and kingdom that will not serve thee [God] shall perish; yea, those nations shall be utterly wasted. . . . A little one shall become a thousand, and a small one a strong nation: I the Lord will hasten it in his time.                Isaiah 60:12, 22

## 5. A WORLD IN WAITING

Arnold Toynbee, one of the eminent historians of the twentieth century, like the prophets of old, envisions a world that must learn to live as one family. He writes in his *Study of History*:

> I believe that, if mankind cannot now bring itself at last to live as one family, the penalty, in our new situation, must be genocide sooner or later. And I wish, with all my heart, that the human race may survive,

because I believe that man has been given the capacity to see God, and I believe that this is the summum bonum toward which all creation groans and travails (Vol. 12, p. 620).

In an optimistic note, Toynbee explains that the advance of modern humanitarianism is a step toward bringing about the unity of man with man and man with God. He enthusiastically reports a progressive advance in the practice of Christianity's moral precepts, such as the abolition of the slave trade and of slavery itself, the abolition of barbarous forms of punishment, the humanization of the treatment of prisoners and lunatics, the establishment of old-age pensions and national health services, and in general, the narrowing of the gulf between a poor majority and a rich minority's condition of life. Toynbee further observes that this conscious and deliberate advance toward brotherhood, that of being our "brother's keeper instead of our brother's murderer," is a step in the direction of achieving the long-realized dream of the world as One Family under God, a dream that is given birth in Genesis and finds its fulfillment in the ministry of Jesus Christ.

It is important to note that Luke, in his lineage of Jesus, identifies Him not just with one nation but with all mankind (Luke 3). It may be further pointed out that when the aged Simeon took the child Jesus in his arms, he saw in Him the Messiah and declared, "This day, Master . . . I have seen with my own eyes the deliverance which thou hast made in full view of all the nations" (Luke 2:31-32, NEB).

Christ's great commission was "Go ye therefore, and teach all nations, baptizing them in the name of the Father, and of the Son, and of the Holy Ghost" (Matthew 28:19). The family, as mentioned in the preceding chapter, actually became the first center of instruction for the application of the teachings of God's own son, Christ.

The Bible utilizes this theme to its last pages. After the powers of darkness have been conquered, John, in his "Visions of the End," reveals that a time shall come when all nations shall recognize God as the Father over all. "Who shall not fear thee, O Lord, and glorify thy name?" he asks, "for thou only art holy: for all nations shall come and worship before thee: for thy judgments are made manifest" (Revelation 15:4).

According to this, all nations finally become *one family living under God the Father.*

# Selected Bibliography

Buttrick, George Arthur, ed., *The Interpreter's Bible,* 12 vols. New York and Nashville: Abingdon Press, 1952-57.

Davies, G. Henton, Richardson, Alan, and Wallis, Charles L., eds., *The Twentieth Century Bible Commentary,* New York, Harper & Brothers, 1956.

Geike, John Cunningham, *Hours with the Bible,* 6 vols. New York: James Pott and Co., 1897.

Hastings, James, ed., *The Greater Men and Women of the Bible,* 6 vols. Edinburgh: T. & T Clark, 1913.

Henry, Matthew, *Commentary on the Whole Bible.* London and Edinburgh: Fleming H. Revell Co., 1935.

Landman, Isaac, ed., *The Universal Jewish Encyclopedia,* 10 vols. New York: Universal Jewish Encyclopedia Co., 1939-43.

Leupold, H. C., *Exposition of Genesis.* Columbus, Ohio: The Wartburg Press, 1942.

Moffatt, James, ed., *The Moffatt New Testament Commentary,* 16 vols. New York: Harper & Brothers, 1927-50.

Orr, James, ed., *The International Standard Bible Encyclopaedia.* Grand Rapids, Mich.: Wm. B. Eerdmans Publishing Co., 1949.

Robinson, H. Wheeler, ed., *The Bible in Its Ancient and English Versions.* Oxford: Clarendon Press, 1940.

Simpson, E. K., and Bruce, F. F., eds., *Epistles to the Ephesians and the Colossians, The New International Commentary on the N. T.* Grand Rapids, Mich.: Wm. B. Eerdmans Publishing Co., 1957.

Singer, Isidore, *The Jewish Encyclopedia,* 12 vols. New York: Funk & Wagnalls Co., 1903-6.

## DICTIONARIES

Corswant, W., *A Dictionary of Life in Bible Times.* New York: Oxford University Press, 1960.

Davis, John D., and Gehman, Henry Snyder, *The Westminster Dictionary of the Bible.* Philadelphia: The Westminster Press, 1944.

Hastings, James, ed., *A Dictionary of the Bible.* New York: Charles Scribner's Sons, 1948.

————, ed., *A Dictionary of Christ and the Gospels*. Edinburgh: T & T Clark, 1906-8.

Miller, Madeleine S. and J. Lane, *Harper's Bible Dictionary*. New York: Harper & Brothers, 1952.

Richardson, Alan, ed., *A Theological Word Book of the Bible*. New York: The Macmillan Company, 1960.

Vaux, Roland de, *Ancient Israel, Its Life and Institutions*. New York: McGraw-Hill, 1961.

## CONCORDANCES

Joy, Charles R., *Harper's Topical Concordance*. New York: Harper & Brothers, 1940.

Stevenson, Burton, compiler, *The Home Book of Bible Quotations*. New York: Harper & Brothers, 1949.

Strong, James, *Exhaustive Concordance of the Bible*. New York and Nashville: Abingdon Press, 1955.

Young, Robert, *Analytical Concordance to the Bible*. Grand Rapids: Wm. B. Eerdmans Publishing Co., 1936.

## TOPICAL BIBLES

Hitchcock, Roswell D., ed., *Topical Bible*. Grand Rapids: Baker Book House, 1952.

Nave, Orville J., ed., *Topical Bible*. Chicago: Moody Press, 1921.

## INTERPRETIVE BIBLES

Harper *Annotated Bible Series*. New York: Harper & Brothers, 1949 ff.

Masonic. *Holy Bible*. Chicago: John A. Hertel Company, 1949.

*Westminster Study Edition of the Holy Bible*. Philadelphia: The Westminster Press, 1948.

## OTHER BIBLE SOURCE BOOKS

Baly, Denis, *The Geography of the Bible*. New York: Harper & Brothers, 1957.

Barclay, William, *The Mind of Jesus*. New York: Harper & Brothers, 1961.

Beek, M. A., *A Journey through the Old Testament*. New York: Harper & Brothers, 1960.

Bouquet, A. C., *Everyday Life in New Testament Times*. New York: Charles Scribner's Sons, 1955.

Buttrick, George A., *The Parables of Jesus*. New York: Harper & Brothers, 1928.

Deen, Edith, *All of the Women of the Bible*. New York: Harper & Brothers, 1955.

Free, Joseph P., *Archaeology and Bible History*. Wheaton, Ill.: Scripture Press Book Division, 1956.

Grollenberg, L. H., ed., *Nelson's Atlas of the Bible.* London and New York: Thomas Nelson & Sons, Ltd., 1957.

Harkness, Georgia, *Christian Ethics.* Nashville and New York: Abingdon Press, 1957.

Heaton, E. W., *Everyday Life in Old Testament Times.* New York: Charles Scribner's Sons, 1955.

Heinisch, Paul, *Theology of the Old Testament.* St. Paul: The Liturgical Press, 1955.

James, Fleming, *Personalities of the Old Testament.* New York: Charles Scribner's Sons, 1939.

Miller, Madeleine S. and J. Lane, *Encyclopedia of Bible Life.* New York: Harper & Brothers, 1944.

Marshall, L. H., *The Challenge of New Testament Ethics.* New York: The Macmillan Company, and London: St. Martin's Press, 1960.

Murray, John, *Divorce.* Grand Rapids, Mich.: Baker Book House, 1953.

Parmelee, Alice, *A Guidebook to the Bible.* New York: Harper & Brothers, 1948.

Thielicke, Helmut, *Our Heavenly Father.* New York: Harper & Brothers, 1960.

Tournier, Paul, *A Doctor's Casebook in the Light of the Bible.* New York: Harper & Brothers, 1960.

Trever, John C., *Cradle of Our Faith.* San Angelo, Texas: Newsfoto Publishing Co., 1954.

Wright, George Ernest, and Filson, Floyd Vivian, eds., *The Westminster Historical Atlas to the Bible.* Philadelphia: The Westminster Press, 1945.

## OTHER RELIGIOUS SOURCE BOOKS

Bailey, Derrick Sherwin, *The Man-Woman Relation in Christian Thought.* London: Longmans, Green and Co., 1959.

Chavasse, Claude, *The Bride of Christ.* London: Faber and Faber Ltd., 1940.

Kohler, Ludwig, *Hebrew Man.* New York and Nashville: Abingdon Press, 1957.

Youngman, Bernard R., *The Lands and Peoples of the Living Bible,* Walter Russell Bowie, ed. New York: Hawthorne Books, Inc., 1959.

## GENERAL SOURCE BOOKS ON FAMILY LIFE

Bowman, Henry A., *A Christian Interpretation of Marriage.* Philadelphia: The Westminster Press, 1959.

Bunch, Josephine and Christopher, *Prayers for the Family.* Westwood, N. J.: Fleming H. Revell Co., 1961.

Church of England, Moral Welfare Council, *The Family in Contemporary Society:* The report of a group convened at the behest of the Archbishop of Canterbury with appended reports from the USA, Canada,

India and London. London Society for Promotion of Christian Culture, 1958.

Duvall, Evelyn Millis, *Family Development*. Philadelphia: J. B. Lippincott Co., 1957.

Goodsell, Willystine, *A History of Marriage and the Family*. New York: The Macmillan Company, 1934.

Kirkpatrick, Clifford, *The Family*. New York: The Ronald Press Co., 1955.

Leavell, Martha Boone, *Christian Marriage*. Nashville: Convention Press, 1956.

Lofthouse, W. F., *Ethics and the Family*. London, New York, Toronto: Hodder and Stoughton, 1912.

Mace, David R., *Hebrew Marriage*. New York: Philosophical Library, 1953.

Moore, Bernice Milburn, and Leahy, Dorothy M., *You and Your Family*. Boston: D. C. Heath Co., 1948.

Neufeld, E., *Ancient Hebrew Marriage Laws*. London: Longmans, Green and Co., 1944.

Trueblood, Elton and Pauline, *The Recovery of Family Life*. New York: Harper & Brothers, 1953.

Werner, Hazen G., *Christian Family Living*. Nashville: The Graded Press, 1958.

Wynn, John Charles, *Sermons on Marriage and Family Life*. Nashville: Abingdon Press, 1956.

————, *Pastoral Ministry to Families*. Philadelphia: The Westminster Press, 1957.

# Index of Names and Subjects